Embracing CHRISTIAN SEX
IN A PAGAN WORLD

Rev. Joseph A. Sirba

Scripture quotations, unless otherwise indicated, are from the Revised Standard Version of the Bible, copyright © 1946, 1952, and 1971, Apocrypha, copyright © 1957; The Third and Fourth Books of the Maccabees and Psalm 151, copyright © 1977, the Division of Christian Education of the National Council of the Churches of Christ in the United States of America. Used by permission. All rights reserved.

Quotation from Grace Notes on page 256 used with author's permission.

In accord with canon 830 §3 of the *Code of Canon Law*, I hereby grant my permission (*licentiae*) to publish <u>Embracing Christian Sex in a Pagan World</u> by Rev. Fr. Joseph A. Sirba.

Given by ✝Bishop Paul D. Sirba, Diocese of Duluth at the Chancery on May 31, 2014.

Censor deputatus
Rev. Fr. Eric F. Hastings, STB, JCL

In no manner is this permission to be understood as an endorsement or agreement with the author's statements. Ecclesiastical permission presupposes that the censor found nothing objectionable; it guarantees that the writing in question contains nothing contrary to the Church's authentic Magisterium on faith or morals, and it attests that all the pertinent prescriptions of canon law have been fulfilled.

ISBN: 978-0-9915341-0-4

Distributed by:

Leaflet Missal Company
976 Minnehaha Ave.
Saint Paul, MN 55104
Phone 651-487-2818
www.leafletonline.com

Table of Contents

PREFACE

Our pagan world is just plain wrong about sex. Quite wrong in fact. It tells us that sex is a form of entertainment, a kind of recreational sport. It tells us that sex is just for fun and games. But is it really? Is that what it is all about? Sure, sex can be very enjoyable, but pleasure is not really what sex is all about.

In fact, if sex was just about fun and games, then why is it whenever we treat sex that way, we are left feeling so empty and so unfulfilled? Even more to the point, why are so many people left hurting when sex is only used for fun?

Our pagan world tells us that sex is just another form of entertainment, but if that were true, it is certainly a messy and risky form of entertainment. For example, there are all the unintended pregnancies followed by a very limited option of painful choices. Then there are the sexually transmitted diseases (STDs), many of them incurable, lifetime "gifts" from forgettable partners. A woman can look forward to all of the pills and shots which not only disrupt her body's natural function but also have numerous side effects, many of them quite serious.

Then there is all the superficiality, and what is so fun about that? Last but not least, there is the tragedy of divorce and the broken families it leaves behind. How is it that so many couples who once loved each other so tenderly can grow so far apart they end up divorcing? Clearly, something is wrong with this picture. But what?

In this book you will find answers to these questions that make sense. Furthermore, these answers will help you experience sexual intimacy in the way it was intended, a way that will make it truly enjoyable and fulfilling. Finally, these answers may come as a surprise to you because they will come from a Christian perspective.

In point of fact, Jesus Christ taught that sex is for something far more profound and significant than simply pleasure, or fun or entertainment. Quite the contrary, God designed sex to be a sign of something very personal and very good. He intended that it be a gift from one lover to another, and in that context, it is far more than just a pleasurable activity.

1

When God's plan for intimacy is respected, sex is not just good, it becomes holy and the sign of a sacramental union between a man and a woman. Even if you are a Christian or have come from a Christian background, you have probably never heard of sex described in this way. Nevertheless, it is the right way to think about sex and the only way that will lead to true happiness.

So, if you are tired of uncommitted relationships and one night stands, if you feel something is missing from the whole cohabiting thing or if you are uneasy with the things you have to do or take to keep from getting pregnant (or getting someone pregnant), then read on. In this book, you will find the answers to your questions.

Introduction

If you turn on the TV and surf through the channels, one program after another will be about sex. Boot up the computer and popup ads appear with "Misty" inviting you to call and chat. She along with pornography of every sort is just a click away on the Internet. Stop in the store to buy grandma a birthday card and there it is again, all those cards with sexual references. Go grocery shopping and while in the checkout line, you can read about the 40 newest sex techniques to try out on your partner. Stop at the mall and there is Victoria with nearly all her secrets revealed. Drive home and turn on the radio and your ears are filled with more of the same. Go to a ball game, the park or even a church wedding and you can see young women and girls (and not a few older women) "showing their stuff" while other couples make out in public.

Now if you are early middle-aged or younger, someone born after 1975, it might not occur to you that there is a problem with any of this. Because you grew up immersed in the values of our pagan world, what I have just described is perfectly normal to you. It is all you have ever experienced. It is just the way things are.

On the other hand, if you are someone who was born before 1960, you grew up in a time where pornography was confined to some sleazy district downtown, where there were absolutely no nude scenes on TV or at the movies, where women wore dresses that went below their knees, and where cleavage and cracks were never seen in public. For those who remember what it was like before the 60s, the before and after, the then and now are amazingly different. In fact, the contrast between what was then and what is now is almost incomprehensible. So how did we get to where we are today? How did the morals of our grandparents' day change so radically and so rapidly into what we have now?

To answer these questions, we need a short history lesson. Because the pagan view of sex is the only view most people now know, it has never occurred to them that there once was another way to look at sex, a different way that did not have all the problems associated with today's pagan sexual morality. So then, how did we get to where we are today?

It was not by accident. Rather, there was a movement led by people who wanted to change the culture and how it dealt with human sexuality. These folks did not like the morals and customs of the times. They rejected Christian customs such as monogamy and modesty and the idea that children were a good thing in marriage and that marriage should be a life-long relationship that ended only when death parted the couple. Instead, they wanted a different kind of morality, one not based on Christian (or even natural) principles. Above all, they had one goal in particular, and that was to free sexually active women from the fear of pregnancy. They wanted women to be just as free as men to have sexual relations without any ensuing responsibilities.

Now this next point is going to be hard for most people to understand because it is so far beyond our present experience, but if you go back around a hundred years (back to the early 1900s), there were no sure-fire birth control methods (and even today there is still no birth control method that prevents pregnancy all of the time). When people had sex in those days, they naturally expected babies would be coming. In other words, the connection between sex and babies was very clear.

For that reason and also for religious reasons, there was a common understanding that couples would consummate their union on their wedding night and not before. However, if pre-marital sex did occur, it was just that, pre-marital, and both parties knew that marriage would be following shortly.

When there were unintended pregnancies (and there were), most of the burden fell on the woman, especially if the man walked away from his responsibilities and refused to marry her. Obviously, men had more freedom than women when it came to sex outside of marriage. They could more easily walk away from their responsibilities, leaving the woman alone to bear the consequences, namely a baby. However, as was noted, this state of affairs did not sit well with everyone.

One person who sought to change this was Margaret Sanger. She was born in New York in 1879, the sixth of eleven children. Sanger believed that men and women should be on equal terms when engaging in sex, and for her that meant separating sex from babies. Doing so would free women from the fear of unwanted pregnancies and allow them to enjoy sex as much as men. In the early 1900s, Sanger began promoting birth control, and in 1921, she founded the American Birth Control League to help find ways to separate sex from babies. In 1942, her organization was renamed Planned Parenthood Federation of America.[1]

Here it should be noted that not only was birth control illegal in many states, but until 1930, it was frowned upon and rejected by every Christian denomination of significance from Catholic to Orthodox to Protestant. It was only in 1930 at the Seventh Lambeth Conference of Anglican Bishops that the Anglicans became the first Protestant denomination to approve the use of birth control (but only in very limited circumstances). However, their approval of even limited birth control was a turning point and opened the way to wider approval and acceptance.

About this time, another development unintentionally linked to Sanger's movement also helped change attitudes and promote a greater acceptance of birth control. In an effort to prevent venereal disease, condoms were widely distributed to male U.S. military personnel during World War II, and they were also heavily promoted with films, posters, and lectures. When our servicemen returned home after the war, they brought with them this new knowledge and experience which could not only be used to prevent venereal disease but also babies.

After World War II, Planned Parenthood continued to promote Sanger's ideas that pleasure and fun were the primary reasons for having sex. Planned Parenthood's philosophy might be paraphrased as "do what's right for you without limits as long as no one gets hurt."

Not long after World War II, others began to follow Sanger's lead.

---

[1] Today, Sanger's views on sexuality have become widely accepted. However, that is still not the case with her positions on eugenics and race (at least not openly). It should be noted that Sanger was an advocate of the selective breeding of humans. One of her slogans was "more [children] from the fit and less from the unfit." Among those she considered unfit were Black Americans. To deal with these "unfit," Sanger deliberately located her clinics in urban areas (where most Planned Parenthood clinics are still located). Since the advent of legalized abortion, these clinics have offered abortion in addition to their other services. It is also a fact that while only about one-eighth of the female population in America is Black, nearly one-third of all abortions are performed on Black women. Were this not the case, the percentage of Blacks in the United States would be considerably higher than it is. A similarly disproportionate number of abortions are performed on Hispanic women. An argument could be made that Sanger's advocacy for the selective breeding of humans lives on in the work of her clinics.

Sexologists such as Alfred Kinsey and later, Masters and Johnson claimed all sorts of things about sex and relationships, things that were not true and were based upon flawed methods and fraudulent research. Their dishonest conclusions and doctored results helped to further break down inhibitions and prepare the way for the sexual revolution.

In December of 1953, Hugh Hefner introduced the first widely distributed porn magazine, <u>Playboy</u>. Each issue featured a playmate of the month, some young woman Hefner claimed was just like "the girl next door."

Although Catholics, some conservative Protestants and Orthodox Jews continued to oppose it, by the mid-1950s, birth control had become widely accepted. With its acceptance, the natural connection between sex and babies was fast breaking apart. Furthermore, abortions, although illegal, were being done quietly but with greater frequency and acceptance.

Then came the birth control pill which became commercially available in 1960. The pill changed many things and helped to usher in the sexual revolution. All of these developments profoundly changed how people thought about sex, marriage and family life. From this point on, traditional Christian sexual morality was not simply being challenged, it was being rejected by many.

A series of further changes in sexual morality rapidly followed. No-fault divorce was first passed in California and became effective in that state on January 1, 1970. By 1983, no-fault divorce had spread to forty-eight states. Many argue it contributed to the skyrocketing divorce rate. Also about this time, movies with R and X ratings were introduced and with them, easy access to pornography. The homosexual rights movement began in the summer of 1969 with a protest at the Stonewall Inn in New York City. In early 1973, abortion was legalized nationwide. During the 70s and 80s, cohabitation (formerly known as "living in sin") increased dramatically. With the development of the Internet in the 80s and 90s, pornography became readily available to anyone with a computer and Internet access. Most recently, with the advent of so called "gay marriage" in the new millennium, one more piece of the old Christian sexual morality was left behind.

Today, things are pretty much as Margaret Sanger dreamed. Inhibitions, modesty and a natural reticence when talking about sex have been cast aside with the result that we now live in a culture saturated with sex, a culture where you can hardly go anywhere or do anything without encountering some explicit sexual references.

Women are now as free as men to engage in uncommitted sex (although the burden of unintended pregnancy still falls more heavily on them). The natural connection between sex and babies has been broken. Few still hold to the belief that sex is supposed to be between a man and a woman within marriage (or even between a man and a woman).

Despite this new sexual morality, society is not better off. Quite the contrary, statistics tell us that people are not having all the fun they were promised. Divorce, infidelity, promiscuity, unplanned pregnancies, STDs, and pornography have all taken their toll. All these things have led to profound changes in how people approach sexual relationships and of how men and women relate to each other in general.

One example is the general inability to keep (or even make) commitments. After experiencing the divorce of parents, siblings, other relatives and friends, many young men and women today have a fear of commitment. Younger men, who often grow up without fathers, do not seem to know what to do with their lives. Without families to care for and support, they waste time and energy on trivial pursuits. On the other hand, many younger women who also have no experiential knowledge of fathers who loved their mothers (or of fathers who were also married to their mothers) make bad choices about the men with whom they choose to live.

Clearly, our current approach to sexuality has not led to happiness. At this point, reason would suggest it is time to rethink things. Clearly, Sanger and her cohorts were wrong in their view of sex. Fortunately, there is another and better way to approach sexuality, and that way can be found in the teachings of Jesus Christ and His Church. While this may come as a surprise to those unfamiliar with Christianity, it may come as a surprise to many Christians as well.

Contrary to what many believe, the Church has much more to say about sex than just "No." For example, the Bible (which Christians revere as the inspired word of God) is full of references to sex and sexual morality. In addition, the Church has carefully considered these passages and has drawn many important conclusions from them about God's plan for sex.

This book will examine God's plan for sex and how it is revealed to us through His Church and through the Sacred Scriptures. Part one will explain what is meant by the term pagan and then take a look at how the first Christians responded to the ancient pagan world, especially in the area of sexual morality. It will also explain how we have entered into a new paganism, and then how modern Christians have responded to it. Part two will explain how to talk about sex and how sex is part of God's creation. Part three will examine the nature of love and the Christian understanding of sex and its purpose. Part four will offer some practical advice for married couples concerning love making, family size and teaching their children about sex. Part five will address chaste behavior and offer some pointers for single people. Finally, part six, will look at some ways in which sex is presently being misused in our culture.

In this book, you will also see how growing up with a pagan view of sexuality (as most of us have) has distorted our perspective about God's wonderful plan for sex. You will also learn how by living out God's plan for sex (which is not always easy and can sometimes be very hard), you can experience greater peace, happiness and joy in your life. As this book's title suggests, it really is about embracing Christian sex in a pagan world.

PART ONE

SORTING THINGS OUT

PART ONE: SORTING THINGS OUT

Each of us has his or her own way of looking at things, and each of us has his or her own way of doing things. This fact should come as no surprise since we are all individuals. We all have our favorite color or hairstyle or sport. We all like certain activities or hobbies. These are the things that make us unique.

On the other hand, we also have certain ways of looking at things and doing things that we share in common. For example, nearly all of us celebrate Thanksgiving Day. We all know we need to recharge our cell phone batteries. We know that green means go and red means stop.

Among the more important things we share in common, Americans have certain freedoms and rights such as the rights to life, liberty and the pursuit of happiness. These rights also include the right to free speech, to say what is on our minds and the right to own private property. These particular ideas and others make up the American experience. We have grown up with these ideas, and they have come to shape and form us as a people with common beliefs, goals and expectations.

These things we share in common allow us to function and work together as a people. In fact, it is essential that we have shared ideas and customs and ways of doing things if we are going to live and work together in harmony. Together, these things we share form the building blocks for what we call a culture or society (or more broadly a world).

The alternative to sharing certain ideas and customs is for everyone to do his or her own thing. However no society can prosper or, for that matter, even survive when the majority of its people are only concerned about what is good for them (the private or individual good), as opposed to what is good for everyone (the common good). A society in which everyone does his or her own thing is doomed and will soon cease to exist.

These common ideas and customs that bind a society or culture together, these common ways of doing things extend beyond traffic laws, national holidays or even a common language or a common understanding of fundamental rights. In nearly every society, they also include agreement

11

about who God is and about the moral and ethical norms which flow from that culture's understanding of God.

It was not that long ago when most Americans understood our nation to be a Christian nation. As proof of this, many Christians cite an 1892 Supreme Court decision where Justice David Brewer wrote in a unanimous decision, "No purpose of action against religion can be imputed to any legislation, state or national, because this is a religious people ... this is a Christian nation." [2]

However, a more explicit proof that America was indeed a Christian nation can be seen by simply examining its legal documents. Thus the last article of the United States Constitution, Article VII, concludes with these words, "Done in Convention by the Unanimous Consent of the States present the Seventeenth Day of September in the Year of our Lord one thousand seven hundred and Eighty seven and of the Independence of the United States of America the Twelfth. In Witness whereof We have hereunto subscribed our Names." By these words, Jesus Christ is proclaimed as Lord of the United States in the Constitution, the highest law of the land.

In addition, until recent times, all manner of legal documents from wills and deeds to contracts and proclamations have followed a customary formula of dating: "made this _____ day of _____ in the year of our Lord one thousand _____." Each legal document so formulated proclaims Jesus Christ is Lord. One final proof that America was once a Christian nation still survives in the custom whereby each newly elected president places his hand on the Holy Bible while taking the presidential oath of office. [3]

Indeed, that Christ was Lord was not just an American perspective but a European one as well. When speaking of the impending Battle of Britain, Winston Churchill said that the survival of "Christian civilization" would depend upon its outcome. [4] In fact, Christ and Christianity were once seen

---

[2] Church of the Holy Trinity v. United States, 143 U.S. 457 (1892). This case was argued on January 7, 1892 and decided on February 29, 1892.

[3] Only three presidents have not done so, John Quincy Adams, Theodore Roosevelt and Lyndon Johnson. However, in Johnson's case, he was aboard Air Force One after President Kennedy's assassination and a Bible was apparently not available but a Roman Catholic Missal was, and it was used instead.

[4] Churchill used the phrase in his "Finest Hour Speech," given on June 18, 1940,

as having special revelations not simply for the West but for the entire world.

While America's founders did not intend to establish any particular religion, it is a fact that the morals and ethics of Protestant Christianity shaped the laws and customs of the country (and most of these laws and customs were also supported by Catholics). The "Blue Laws" which required stores and businesses to close on Sunday, the Christian Sabbath are one example of this.

Christianity also shaped our culture's sexual morality. For example, marriage was restricted to one man and one woman. Thus, Utah's attempts at statehood were delayed for years over the issue of polygamy. Utah (with its predominantly Mormon population) was allowed entrance into the union in 1896, only after polygamy was explicitly outlawed in the Utah state constitution.[5]

"Gay marriage" was not even an idea. Rather, homosexual relations were referred to as sodomy and were illegal in every state. So too was adultery. The Federal "Comstock Law" (passed by a Protestant majority Congress in 1873) made it a crime to sell or distribute materials that could be used for contraception or abortion, to send such materials through the U.S. mail, or to import such materials from abroad. Divorce, while not illegal was frowned upon and much more difficult to obtain than at present. When Adlai Stevenson (who was divorced) ran for president in 1952, there were people who held his divorce against him.[6] They reasoned if he could not manage his own family, then neither could he manage the country.

These laws and others like them were inspired by and represented the Christian culture of our founders. However, in more recent times, a newer

---

to the House of Commons. There he said, "I expect the battle of Britain is about to begin. Upon this battle depends the survival of Christian civilization."

[5] ARTICLE III, First: – Perfect toleration of religious sentiment is guaranteed. No inhabitant of this State shall ever be molested in person or property on account of his or her mode of religious worship; but polygamous or plural marriages are forever prohibited. This prohibition of polygamy was declared unconstitutional on December 13, 2013 by Federal Judge Clark Waddoups.

[6] See for example, <u>Time Magazine</u>, August 4, 1952, pages 16 and 18.

pagan (or non-Christian) culture has replaced that Christian culture.[7] Because of this pagan culture's radically different views, especially with regard to sexual morality, nearly all of these laws have either been ruled unconstitutional or withdrawn. Consequently, we now live in a far different world than did the people prior to the mid-Twentieth Century.

In point of fact, it is this new pagan culture which now shapes most people's attitudes about sex and sexual morality. Indeed, this new pagan culture's influence is so powerful and so pervasive that in the area of sexual morality, many Christians have never even heard of the Church's teachings on this subject. Consequently, they have adopted many pagan attitudes towards sexual issues, often without even realizing they have done so, and these Christians now live and behave in ways no different from their pagan friends and neighbors.

In fact, this uniformity in sexual behavior and practice is evidence that most people, Christian or not, get their ideas about sex and sexual morality from the dominant pagan culture rather than from the teachings of Jesus Christ.

Furthermore, even those Christians who insist that their sexual morality does come from their Christian faith would do well to take a second look. That is because in recent years, more than a few "Christian" denominations have modified their teachings on sexual morality to reflect those of the new pagan culture which dominates modern society. In that sense, not only have these denominations failed in their mission to convert this new pagan world, but it is in fact they who have been "converted" by it and not the other way around.

Before we can say any more about what we mean by Christian sex, we need to know something about the world as it was before the coming of Christ. Only then will it become clear how profoundly different the Christian and the pagan worlds were (and are) from each other, especially in the area of sexual morality. In fact, it will also become obvious there could never be any room for

---

[7] Modern pagans who are behind this new pagan culture are not like the ancient pagans who never knew Christ. Modern pagans come from Christian backgrounds, or at the very least they have Christian ancestors. However, modern pagans have very consciously and deliberately rejected Christianity and its teachings. They have as their goal to build a new culture not based on Christian beliefs or morals. Pagans and their ideas will be examined in more detail in subsequent chapters.

compromise between the two because they have completely different views of God, of man and of what God expects of man.

Over the next four chapters, we will take a closer look at these two very different worlds. In them, we will see how the Christian world and the pagan world each had its own way of looking at things, each with its own customs, beliefs and ethics. Chapter One will take a closer look at the ancient pagan world into which Christ was born. Chapter Two will review how the first Christians separated themselves from the pagan world in which they lived. Chapter Three will examine why the first Christians responded as they did. Finally, Chapter Four will take a look at the new paganism now reshaping our nation and the western world. It will also note how this new pagan world bears a striking resemblance to its ancient counterpart.

Chapter One
THE WORLD BEFORE CHRIST

Historians tell us that Jesus the Christ was born around the year 4 B.C. in Bethlehem in what was then the Roman province of Judea. The Scriptures add that Christ's birth took place during the reign of Caesar Augustus when Quirinius was governor of Syria (Lk 2:2). At that time, except for God's chosen people (who while centered in Judea, were also represented by Jews living in cities throughout the Roman Empire[8]), all the rest of the world was pagan.

At this point, there were no Christians. The New Testament did not yet exist. There were no churches or monasteries; there were neither Christian writings nor music nor art. Consequently, there was no Christian culture. Even our familiar division of time (B.C. and A.D.) which is based upon the approximate birth of Christ had not yet been invented. Instead, the Romans numbered their years from the founding of the City of Rome which they regarded as the world's most important event.[9] Thus, Jesus was born into a pagan world, a world in which Christian customs, beliefs and ethics were unknown.

This ancient world was not monolithic. Rather, it was a world composed

---

[8] In these various cities, the cultural identity of the Israelites was maintained in the Jewish quarters in the midst of other dominant cultures. It is also interesting that there were more Jews living in these cities than in their ancestral homeland.

[9] The traditional date for the founding of the City of Rome has been 753 B.C. According to Roman reckoning, this would have been the year 1. Today when we refer to the Roman system for enumerating years, the abbreviation A.U.C. is placed after the year. These letters stand for the Latin words *ab urbe condita,* which mean "from the founding of the City." Thus, if Jesus was born in 4 B.C., it would have been the year 749 A.U.C. according to the Romans. It was not until 525 A.D. that a monk named Dionysius Exiguus (c. 470 to c. 544 A.D.) devised a new system for enumerating years based upon the birth of Christ. His system divided all of time into that which came before the birth of Christ (B.C.) and that which came after the birth of Christ (A.D.), the event he regarded as the most important and momentous in all of human history.

of many different peoples and nations; among these were the ancient Romans, Greeks, Egyptians, Persians and Chinese. While composed of many different peoples and nations, each with their own customs, all of these peoples and nations had one thing in common. They had not been influenced by Christianity. This was also the case with the Incan and Aztec Empires of the New World as well as the Mongols and other cultures in Asia and Africa which arose in later centuries.

In this ancient world, nearly all of the people were polytheists; they worshiped multiple gods. Throughout every city in ancient Rome or Greece or Egypt, pagan temples could be found dedicated to these gods. In some of these cultures, human sacrifice to the gods was practiced.

Slavery was widespread and in fact, most ancient economies were based upon it. Organized care for the poor, the sick or the dying did not exist. There were no hospitals, and only the rich could afford to be seen by physicians. Life was cheap and death swift and sudden.

In the ancient world, customs, beliefs and ethics were far different from those Christianity would later promote, and this was especially true in the area of sexual morality. In that area, nothing was based upon Christian teaching, and very little was even based upon natural law.[10] For example:

* Polygamy was widely practiced. Egyptian pharaohs were usually polygamous with a harem of queens. This was true even among Jewish kings of old such as David and Solomon and later King Herod the Great who had ten wives.

* Divorce was common. The Roman emperors, statesmen and generals provide many examples of this. In fact, even the Jews had lost sight of life-long marriage. Jesus directly challenged this practice when He said, "Whoever divorces his wife, except for unchastity, and marries another, commits adultery; and he who marries a divorced woman, commits adultery (Mt 19:9)." Upon hearing this, the Apostles reacted with shock

---

[10] Traditionally, Natural Law has been understood to be that law which can be derived from reflection and experience on the human condition. For example, it is understood that murder, the killing of innocent human life, is always wrong. It should be noted that Natural Law is not based upon Christian principles (or any other religious principles for that matter), and also that it applies to all human persons irrespective of religion, ethnicity, social status and so on.

and said, "If such is the case of a man with his wife, it is not expedient to marry (Mt 19:10)."

* Incestuous relationships were not unheard of among the Roman emperors. Caligula (37–41 A.D.) was a sexual pervert who, according to Suetonius, committed incest with his sisters and raped whomever he wished. Domitian (81–96 A.D.), after divorcing his wife, lived openly with his niece Julia. When she became pregnant, it was alleged that he forced her to have an abortion from which she died; Domitian then had her deified.

* Multiple sexual partners were common. In ancient Greece, wives were expected to remain chaste, manage the home and bring up the children. On the other hand, husbands could and did look elsewhere for sexual pleasure and companionship.[11] The Egyptian Queen Cleopatra was involved with Julius Caesar while he was married and had a son by him. She later became involved with the Roman general Mark Antony with whom she had more children. Mark Antony would later enter into a bigamous marriage with her.

* Prostitution was common in Greek and Roman societies, and prostitutes were licensed and taxed by the state. Masters often had sexual relations with their slaves and fathered children by them. Licentious orgies were a form of recreation and entertainment.

* Pornography was common. Examples of this can be seen in the many erotic paintings that survive on lamps and other household items. These artifacts depict very graphic heterosexual and homosexual acts and have been found throughout the Roman empire.[12] These kinds of images are also common in Greek vase paintings.[13] Phallic symbols were also common in Greek and Roman life, especially at certain festivals.

* Homosexuality was widespread among Roman men at the beginning

---

[11] Diseases in Antiquity by Don Brothwell and A. T. Sandison, 1967, p. 739.

[12] "Infanticide at Ashkelon," by Lawrence E. Stager, Biblical Archaeological Review, July/August 1991, pp. 41–43.

[13] Diseases in Antiquity by Don Brothwell and A. T. Sandison, 1967, p. 740.

of the Christian era. Men either preferred relations with other men rather than their wives or would have their wives "play the boy" (anal intercourse) when they did have relations with them.[14] The Roman emperors Caligula, Nero and Elagabalus were said to have engaged in homosexual practices. Upper class Greek men took older boys into their homes where they mentored and guided them but where they also used them for sex.[15] Writings survive which debate the relative merits of sex with a man as opposed to a woman.

* Contraception was also widely practiced. Ancient societies were aware of the contraceptive and abortifacient properties of various plants. Among these plants were Queen Anne's Lace, pennyroyal, artemisia and silphium. This latter plant was so effective that over harvesting led to its eventual extinction. Most physicians in later centuries discounted these ancient methods of birth control regarding them as ineffective. However, modern scientific tests have shown that these plants do in fact have the ability to block the production of progesterone and to act as spermicides.[16] These ancient contraceptive practices were effective enough that by the beginning of the Christian era the Roman population was in decline. Caesar Augustus even promulgated laws to induce Roman men and women to marry and have more children but to no avail.[17]

* Abortion was common. The Greek philosophers Plato and Aristotle both proposed abortion in certain circumstances.[18] Roman husbands who had the power of life and death over the members of their households would often order their wives to undergo abortions. Since the methods

---

[14] Ibid., p. 744.

[15] Ibid., p. 740.

[16] "Ever Since Eve...Birth Control in the Ancient World" by John M. Riddle, J. Worth Estes, and Josiah C. Russell, Archaeology, March/April 1994, pp. 29–33.

[17] The Rise of Christianity by Rodney Stark, 1996, pp. 115–122.

[18] Republic by Plato, Book V, 460e–461c; Politics by Aristotle, Book VII, Chapter 16, 20.

were crude and there were no disinfectants, many women died from the poisons they took or from either the surgery or the infections which set in after surgery. Their deaths helped to create a serious imbalance in the numerical equality between the sexes.[19]

* Infanticide was widely practiced by the Greeks and Romans, especially of baby girls which also added to the numerical imbalance between the sexes.[20] For example, in the city of Ashkelon, a seaport on the eastern Mediterranean, archaeologists excavated one of the city sewers. In it they found the skeletons of nearly 100 infants. The evidence suggests that these children were killed and then thrown into the drain immediately after birth.[21] This would have been consistent with the Roman practice of abandonment and exposure of unwanted infants to the elements. A letter written by a certain Hilarion to his pregnant wife illustrates this attitude. In it Hilarion wrote, "Know that I am still in Alexandria. And do not worry if they all come back and I remain in Alexandria. I ask and beg you to take good care of our baby son, and as soon as I receive payment I will send it up to you. If you are delivered of child [before I get home], if it is a boy keep it, if a girl discard it. You have sent me word, 'Don't forget me.' How can I forget you. I beg you not to worry."[22]

* Human sacrifice was also practiced. For example, the Phoenicians were infamous for their practice of child sacrifice. In their city of Carthage, there was a burial ground known as the Tophet. In it were found the bones of tens of thousands of infants and young children which had been placed in urns that were in turn buried. These children had been burned

---

[19] The Rise of Christianity by Rodney Stark, 1996, pp. 119–121.

[20] These practices have once again led to a serious numerical imbalance between the sexes in China, India and elsewhere. In her book, Unnatural Selection, 2011, Mara Hvistendahl estimates that the number of missing women in these and other Asian countries stands at 160 million (as of 2010) and is climbing.

[21] "Bones of a Hundred Infants Found in Ashkelon Sewer" by Patricia Smith and Gila Kahila, Biblical Archaeology Review, July/August 1991, p. 47.

[22] Life in Egypt Under Roman Rule, by Lewis Naphtali, Oxford: Clarendon, 1985, p. 54.

as sacrifices by their parents to the god Ba'al Hammon and the goddess Tanit. This grisly practice was outlawed when the Romans conquered the city in 146 B.C.[23] However, it seems that the Israelites themselves (probably influenced by their Phoenician neighbors) also fell into this practice. As the Bible attests, "They served their idols, which became a snare to them. They sacrificed their sons and their daughters to the demons; they poured out innocent blood, the blood of their sons and daughters, whom they sacrificed to the idols of Canaan; and the land was polluted with blood (Ps 106:37–38)." Also, "And they burned their sons and their daughters as offerings (2Kg 17:17)." [24]

To repeat, Christian teachings prohibited (and still do prohibit) all of the above mentioned practices.

It was into this world that Jesus the Christ was born. It was into this world that He grew up, taught, suffered, died and rose again on the third day and finally, ascended into heaven. It is also into this world that He established His Church to preserve and pass on His teachings of salvation until His second coming. Finally, it was into this world that He sent His Apostles to proclaim the good news of salvation to all who would listen.

---

[23] See "Child Sacrifice at Carthage — Religious Rite or Population Control" by Lawrence E. Stager and Samuel Wolff, Biblical Archaeology Review, January/February 1984, pp. 31–51.

[24] Other references to the practice of child sacrifice among the Israelites can be found in Jer 7:30–32, 32:35 and 2Kg 23:10.

Chapter Two

CHRISTIANS SEPARATE FROM THE PAGAN WORLD

After Christ's Ascension, His disciples began to live out the way of life He had taught them. One immediate issue was how this could be done in a world so completely at odds with Christian teachings. It soon became clear that Christians would have to separate themselves from the pagan world, but not in the sense of isolation or departure. Rather, Christians would have to separate themselves from the pagan world's morals, beliefs and culture. Christians would live in the pagan world but not be part of it.

An example of this stance with regard to the pagan world can be found in a letter written by an early Christian to a pagan named Diognetus.[25] While the name of this early Christian is unknown to us, his words are not. Below is a portion of his description regarding Christian life in the early Church.

"Christians are indistinguishable from other men either by nationality, language or customs. They do not inhabit separate cities of their own, or speak a strange dialect, or follow some outlandish way of life. Their teaching is not based upon reveries inspired by the curiosity of men. Unlike some other people, they champion no purely human doctrine. With regard to dress, food and manner of life in general, they follow the customs of whatever city they happen to be living in, whether it is Greek or foreign.

And yet there is something extraordinary about their lives. They live in their own countries as though they were only passing through. They play their full role as citizens, but labor under all the disabilities of aliens. Any country can be their homeland, but for them their homeland, wherever it may be, is a foreign country. Like others, they marry and have children, but they do not expose them. They share their meals, but not their wives.

They live in the flesh, but they are not governed by the desires

---

[25] Scholars place the date of this letter sometime in the late 200s or early 300s (with some dating it much earlier).

of the flesh. They pass their days upon earth, but they are citizens of heaven. Obedient to the laws, they yet live on a level that transcends the law. Christians love all men, but all men persecute them. Condemned because they are not understood, they are put to death, but raised to life again. They live in poverty, but enrich many; they are totally destitute, but possess an abundance of everything. They suffer dishonor, but that is their glory. They are defamed, but vindicated. A blessing is their answer to abuse, deference their response to insult. For the good they do they receive the punishment of malefactors, but even then they rejoice, as though receiving the gift of life. They are attacked by the Jews as aliens, they are persecuted by the Greeks, yet no one can explain the reason for this hatred.

To speak in general terms, we may say that the Christian is to the world what the soul is to the body. As the soul is present in every part of the body, while remaining distinct from it, so Christians are found in all the cities of the world, but cannot be identified with the world. As the visible body contains the invisible soul, so Christians are seen living in the world, but their religious life remains unseen. The body hates the soul and wars against it, not because of any injury the soul has done it, but because of the restriction the soul places on its pleasures. Similarly, the world hates the Christians, not because they have done it any wrong, but because they are opposed to its enjoyments.

Christians love those who hate them just as the soul loves the body and all its members despite the body's hatred. It is by the soul, enclosed within the body, that the body is held together, and similarly, it is by the Christians, detained in the world as in a prison, that the world is held together. The soul, though immortal, has a mortal dwelling place; and Christians also live for a time amidst perishable things, while awaiting the freedom from change and decay that will be theirs in heaven. As the soul benefits from the deprivation of food and drink, so Christians flourish under persecution. Such is the Christian's lofty and divinely appointed function, from which he is not permitted to excuse himself." [26]

---

[26] From a letter to Diognetus (Nn. 5–6; Funk, 397–401)

The attitude expressed by this early Christian writer can find antecedents in the Scriptures themselves. For example, Saint John refers to the fundamental opposition that exists between Christ and antichrist, and between Christianity and the world. He says, "Little children, you are of God, and have overcome [the spirits of antichrist]; for He who is in you is greater than he who is in the world. They are of the world, therefore what they say is of the world, and the world listens to them. We are of God. Whoever knows God listens to us, and he who is not of God does not listen to us. By this we know the spirit of truth and the spirit of error (1Jn 4:4–6)."

It is important to realize that this practice of separation to which Saint John refers is not only as old as Christianity but in a certain sense, even predates it. Just as Saint John divided the world's peoples into two groups, those who were Christians and those who were not, so too, the Jews who were God's chosen people divided all of the world's peoples into two groups, those who were Jews and those who were not. The Jews referred to those who were not as Gentiles.

For example, after having seen the Christ Child, Simeon, the priest, uttered this prayer, "Lord, now you let your servant go in peace; your word has been fulfilled: my own eyes have seen the salvation which you have prepared in the sight of every people: a light to reveal you to the nations and the glory of your people Israel (Lk 2:29–32)."

Quoting the Prophet Isaiah, Saint Matthew writes, "Behold, my servant whom I have chosen, my beloved with whom my soul is well pleased. I will put my Spirit upon Him, and He shall proclaim justice to the Gentiles. He will not wrangle or cry aloud, nor will any one hear His voice in the streets; He will not break a bruised reed or quench a smoldering wick, till He brings justice to victory; and in His name will the Gentiles hope (Mt 12:18–21)."

In separating themselves from the Gentiles, the first Christians were, in some sense, following a practice set by Jesus Himself. For example, on one occasion, a Syrophoenician woman came to Jesus and begged Him to heal her daughter which He did. However, before He did so, Jesus said that He had come first to the children of Israel (Mk 7:27).

In most versions of the Bible, the Greek word used in the New Testament for those who were non-Jews, "ἔθνη" (ethne), is generally translated as

"Gentiles" or "nations." [27] Later, this term would also come to describe those who were non-Christian.

Since most of the first Christians were Jews, it is not surprising that they continued to observe many of the religious practices to which they were accustomed. This is all the more understandable when one considers the spiritual connection between Christians and Jews. As Pope Pius XI once said, "Spiritually, we are all Semites." [28] In other words, Christians are the spiritual descendants of Israel and are sustained by Jewish roots (see Rm 11:13–24). However, because Christians saw themselves as the true Israel, it was now non-Christians who were the Gentiles rather than just those who were non-Jews.

For a short time after Christ's ascension, the Apostles continued this practice of separation from all who were not Jewish by birth (with some arguing one had to first accept Judaism before becoming a Christian). However, with further revelations to Saint Peter (Acts 10), the definition of Christian was soon expanded to include non-Jewish as well as Jewish believers.

This new understanding is clearly illustrated by Saint Paul's comments when he said, "Jews demand signs and Greeks seek wisdom, but we preach Christ crucified, a stumbling block to Jews and folly to Gentiles, but to those who are called, both Jews and Greeks, Christ the power of God and the wisdom of God (1Cor 1:22–24)." [29]

In the writings of the Church fathers, we see that this distinction between Christians and non-Christians continued beyond the apostolic age. For example, about the year 325, in his commentary on Isaiah, Bishop Eusebius of Caesarea wrote,

> "It was in the wilderness that God's saving presence was proclaimed
> by John the Baptist, and there that God's salvation was seen. The
> words of this prophecy were fulfilled when Christ and His glory

[27] The Greek phrase "τὰ ἔθνη" (ta ethne), similar in meaning to "γένος" (genos), is used 162 times in the NT. It is translated in the Latin Vulgate Bible as *gens, gentes.*

[28] Extemporaneous remarks of Pope Pius XI to a group of Belgian pilgrims on September 6, 1938. Cited in the Belgian Newspaper, *Cité Nouvelle,* September 14, 1938.

[29] Although Saint Paul sometimes refers to the non-Jewish population as Greeks, his usage in these cases would be interchangeable with Gentiles.

were made manifest to all: after His baptism the heavens opened, and the Holy Spirit in the form of a dove rested on Him, and the Father's voice was heard, bearing witness to the Son: 'This is my beloved Son, with whom I am well pleased (Mt 3:22).'"

"The prophecy meant that God was to come to a deserted place, inaccessible from the beginning. None of the pagans had any knowledge of God, since His holy servants and prophets were kept from approaching them." [30]

There are also many other examples. Saint Athanasius, another early bishop, wrote a work in defense of Christian doctrine which he entitled, Discourse Against the Pagans.[31] In his book, The City of God, Saint Augustine develops this distinction and also the inherent opposition which existed between Christianity and paganism.

Gradually, as the Church spread into the Latin speaking areas of the Roman empire, instead of being referred to as Gentiles, non-Christians came to be called pagans from the Latin word *paganus* which means rustic or country-dweller. Being outside the influence of city life where Christianity first spread, these country people were among the last to hear about and to accept the faith. Hence, pagan became synonymous with non-Christian. It is that word which has been used down through the centuries to refer to those who did not follow Christ.

A second Christian response to the ancient pagan world was a vigorous and sustained effort to convert it, and this was in direct response to a command from Christ Himself. No doubt the Apostles recalled Christ's explicit prayer that all would be one (Jn 17:20–23). They also remembered His command to them shortly before His ascension when He said, "Go into all the world and preach the gospel to the whole creation. He who believes and is baptized will be saved; but he who does not believe will be condemned (Mk 16:15–16)."

Christians were to share the gospel with the pagan world and convert it. There was an understanding that Christians were called to a higher way of life because they had received the fullness of truth from the One who came to bear

---

[30] Cap. 40, PG 24, p. 366.

[31] In Latin this work is referred to as Contra Gentes. It was written about 318 A.D.

witness to the truth (Jn 18:37). Furthermore, unlike the Jews, Christians saw the division between nations and the separation of peoples into believers and non-believers as something that would eventually end. They also understood that this separation was never God's intention but in fact, it was God's will that all peoples come to know Him.

In this new world, all division would cease and all would be one. As Saint Paul explained, in Christ there is "neither Jew nor Greek, there is neither slave nor free, there is neither male nor female; for you are all one in Christ Jesus (Gal 3:28)."

In all of this, Christians were inspired by their faith in the divinity of Jesus Christ, a belief expressed in various ways through both Tradition and Sacred Scripture.

It was this belief in the divinity of Jesus Christ and in the truth and preeminence of His teachings that first inspired the Apostles to proclaim the gospel "to the end of the earth (Acts 1:8)" and "make disciples of all nations (Mt 28:19)." What is interesting is that as he carried out these commands of Jesus, Saint Paul would come to see himself as "an apostle to the Gentiles" (Rm 11:13).

From what has been said, it is evident that the distinction between those who embraced the teachings of Jesus Christ and those who did not has existed since the Church began. This distinction also explains the need for a word to refer to those peoples who did not know or accept the Christian belief that Jesus the Christ is in fact God the Son. That word was first Gentile and later pagan.

For centuries, the Church used the word pagan in a very broad sense to refer to all non-Christian religions. In a more narrow sense, the word was used to refer to all non-Christian religions except those which trace their roots back to Abraham, that is, to Judaism and Islam. Regardless of how it was used, the word pagan implied a certain imperfection. It suggested incompleteness, and it indicated that non-Christian religions lacked a full understanding of God and of man's relationship with Him.

In more recent times, use of the word pagan in reference to non-Christian peoples has declined due primarily to the recognition that most non-Christians are also people of good will. Rather than continuing to refer to them as pagans, which conveys a certain pejorative tone, the Church has chosen to return to Biblical terminology and refer to non-Christian peoples as "the nations" or simply "other religions." [32] It should be noted here that despite this change in terminology, the Church still regards all other religions as it always has, as lacking the fullness of truth found in Christ's revelation.[33]

---

[32] See the Decree on the Church's Missionary Activity, <u>Ad Gentes Divinitus</u>, Vatican II, December 7, 1965 and also the Declaration, <u>Dominus Iesus</u>, #22, Congregation for the Doctrine of the Faith, August 6, 2000.

[33] See Documents of Vatican II, <u>Lumen Gentium</u>, November 21, 1964, in particular #8. See also <u>Dominus Iesus</u>, June 16, 2000, in particular #20–22.

Chapter Three
REASONS FOR THE SEPARATION

Observing that Christians separated themselves from Gentile customs and practices is one thing, but understanding the reasons for this separation is something entirely different. Why did Christians separate themselves from the pagan world? What was so bad about it that caused them to withdraw from pagan culture and from its customs and practices?

Quite simply, it was not possible for Christians to live like pagans. When the Apostles began to proclaim the Gospel, they and their fellow Christians faced a world at odds with the teachings of Jesus. It was a world radically different from that which exists today, one much worse in many ways than our present world even with all of its flaws. The ancient pagan world was without any Christian influence on its morals and ethics, and this was especially true in the area of sexual morality. As was already mentioned, in pagan culture, contraception, abortion, infanticide, pornography, fornication, adultery, divorce, and homosexuality were widely practiced and accepted.

However, Christian sexual morality prohibited all of these practices. Christians were called to be monogamous. Sexual relations before or outside of marriage were forbidden. Christians married for life and were called to be faithful in marriage. They did not engage in homosexual relations. In addition, they welcomed and celebrated new life; they did not practice contraception, and they did not resort to abortion or infanticide. Quite simply, living like pagans was incompatible with life in Christ.

Even more, since pagan sexual morality affected nearly everything having to do with interpersonal relationships, especially those relating to the opposite sex, Christians had no choice but to break with the world in which they lived and to separate themselves from its customs, beliefs and morals.

It is interesting to note that on several occasions in the New Testament, the word Gentile is used not simply as a reference to non-Christians, but in a stronger, sharper way. In this way, the Greek word normally translated as Gentiles or peoples, "ἔθνη" (ethne), can be translated as heathen, pagan or unbeliever. In these cases, the individuals referred to are people leading immoral lives and living in ways incompatible with how Christians are called to live. Below are several examples:

In First Corinthians, Saint Paul admonishes the Corinthians in the strongest terms for allowing a man who was living with his father's wife to remain in their midst. Saint Paul said to them, "It is actually reported that there is immorality among you, and of a kind that is not found even among pagans (1Cor 5:1)." Here Saint Paul accuses the Corinthians of living in a way more base than those who did not know Christ!

In another place, also in First Corinthians, Saint Paul recalls the Corinthians' state of ignorance before they had come to know Christ. He writes, "You know that when you were heathen, you were led astray to dumb idols ... (1Cor 12:2)."

In his Letter to the Ephesians, Saint Paul once again admonishes these new followers of Christ for not living up to their calling as Christians. He writes to them, "Now this I affirm and testify in the Lord, that you must no longer live as the Gentiles (heathens) do, in the futility of their minds; they are darkened in their understanding, alienated from the life of God because of the ignorance that is in them, due to their hardness of heart; they have become callous and have given themselves up to licentiousness, greedy to practice every kind of uncleanness. You did not learn so in Christ! —assuming that you have heard about Him and were taught in Him, as the truth is in Jesus. Put off your old nature which belongs to your former manner of life and is corrupt through deceitful lusts, and be renewed in the spirit of your minds, and put on the new nature, created after the likeness of God in true righteousness and holiness (Eph 4:17–24)."

In First Thessalonians, Saint Paul wrote words of instruction, saying, "For this is the will of God, your sanctification: that you abstain from unchastity; that each one of you know how to take a wife for himself in holiness and honor, not in the passion of lust like heathen who do not know God ... (1Thess 4:3–5)."

Saint Peter also illustrates this distinction between those who follow Christ and those who do not. He wrote, "Beloved, I beseech you as aliens and exiles to abstain from the passions of the flesh that wage war against your soul. Maintain good conduct among the Gentiles, so that in case they speak against you as wrongdoers, they may see your good deeds and glorify God on the day of visitation (1Pet 2:11–12)."

In yet another example, Saint Peter illustrated this distinction between Christians and Gentiles when he wrote, "Let the time that is past suffice for doing what the Gentiles (heathen) like to do, living in licentiousness, passions, drunkenness, revels, carousing, and lawless idolatry. They are surprised that you do not now join them in the same wild profligacy, and they abuse you ... (1Pet 4:3–4)."

Both Saint Paul and Saint Peter took pains to point out that because of the revelations they had received from Jesus Christ, Christians now had a deeper understanding of things including God's plan for the human race. Thus they were not only called, but expected to lead a life different from the Gentiles (pagans) around them.

Because of these differences, Saint Paul declared, "Do not be mismated with unbelievers. For what partnership have righteousness and iniquity? Or what fellowship has light with darkness? What accord has Christ with Belial? Or what has a believer in common with an unbeliever? What agreement has the temple of God with idols? For we are the temple of the living God; as God said, 'I will live in them and move among them, and I will be their God, and they shall be my people. Therefore come out from them, and be separate from them, says the Lord, and touch nothing unclean; then I will welcome you, and I will be a father to you, and you shall be my sons and daughters, says the Lord Almighty (2Cor 6:14–18).'"

From a Christian perspective, there were two different ways of looking at life, and two different world views, the Christian and the pagan, and the two were profoundly incompatible. This meant it was not possible for there to be peace between the two because the world views of Christians and pagans had two profoundly different starting points. Pagan idolatry and pagan sexual morality simply forced Christians to withdraw from pagan society.

At the same time, it was the duty of every Christian to make the gospel known and to bring Christ to the pagan world so that it might be healed and so that man might be restored to the glory he had before the fall. This they did.

Over time and by the grace of God, Christianity came to dominate the world, and it gradually established a new culture with new customs and practices.

This new Christian culture changed the world. The worship of pagan gods was replaced by the worship of the one true God. Organized care for the poor and sick was instituted. The universal brotherhood of man was proclaimed which in turn led to the gradual abolishment of slavery. Christian sexual morality became the assumed starting point for evaluating sexual behavior. Its fundamental teaching that all human life was sacred led in turn to the rejection of contraception, abortion and infanticide. Its fundamental teaching that marriage must be both a faithful and a life-long commitment led to the elimination of polygamy and divorce. It also led to a much greater appreciation for the dignity of women. Finally, because sex outside of marriage was considered sinful, orgies, pornography and homosexuality declined.

Until recent times, these teachings and practices were the standards for judging sexual morality in all Christian nations. They were the direct result of centuries of Christian influence upon those cultures.

Chapter Four

THE WORLD TODAY:
EMBRACING A NEW PAGANISM

Of late, there has been a new development in America, namely, a rapidly growing number of people who intentionally and deliberately reject Christianity. They do not accept that Jesus Christ is the Son of God nor do they follow His moral teachings. Quite the contrary, they have chosen to deliberately and consciously reject Christian morals and ethics, and this is especially true in the area of sexual morality. The majority of these people are either former Christians or individuals whose near ancestors were Christians.

Rather than be offended by the term, some of these people actually want to be called pagans (which would be an accurate label since the term fits them quite well). Indeed, in their beliefs and morals, these new pagans bear a striking similarity to the ancient pagans who were criticized by Saint Paul and Saint Peter. In many ways, they represent the rearguard of the post-Christian culture that has been developing over the last several centuries.

This post-Christian culture has been promoted by various elites in Western society who regard Christianity as, at best, merely one of the world's "great" religions. They see Christianity as simply one religion among the many religions of the world, where each religion has its own perspective on faith and morals, but where none has an absolute claim on the truth. From the elites' perspective, it follows that no religion could ever claim preeminence over any other, nor could one see the others as somehow inferior or incomplete. It is ironic that the only belief system elitists regard as superior to any other is their own, and this points to a flaw in their logic. They maintain that no system can have an absolute claim on the truth, but consistency demands they include their own ideas as well.

Something Christians have believed since the Ascension of Jesus is that our Lord entrusted to His Apostles special revelations meant for the entire human race. As was already noted, this belief inspired Christian missionaries to traverse the globe, to suffer and even to die so that others might come to know the saving teachings of Jesus Christ.

Today however, many Christian leaders (both Catholic and Protestant) no longer believe that Christianity has special revelations for the world. Instead, they have been greatly influenced by the elitist viewpoint that no one religion is superior to any other. Hence their discomfort and embarrassment at the use of the word pagan, both in times past to describe non-Christians in general and even today, when referring to those who reject and attack Christianity in particular. Referring to these people as pagans would grant to Christianity a preeminence which they no longer accept.

A direct consequence of this loss of faith among Christian leaders (that Christianity has special revelations for the world) is a lack of missionary zeal. This loss has coincided with a loss of understanding regarding the unique role of Christ, and hence, of the need for conversion which they no longer see as necessary. A secondary consequence is that many people no longer turn to Christianity for answers to life's important questions.

While it is true there still exists a large minority of practicing Christians in America, their cultural influence is fast fading as the elitists, the new pagans and others from non-Christian backgrounds continue to exert more and more influence on society. Observing this transformation are the weak Christian leaders who have either acquiesced to it or remained silent in the face of it. With the fracture of Christian culture has come a new pagan culture in America that has not only aggressively challenged the former Christian culture but has in fact replaced it and become the dominant public culture.

While in times past, America's Christian culture shaped its sexual morality, that is no longer the case. Instead, our sexual morality is now shaped almost entirely by the new pagan culture. This culture has rejected almost all of the restraints our formerly Christian culture once imposed on sexual behavior. Thus, in the area of sexual morality, our new pagan culture with its contraceptive practices, casual sex, cohabitation, homosexual practices, divorce, pornography, and abortion has come to resemble in nearly every way the ancient pagan cultures that existed before the coming of Christ. In fact, with the help of technology, modern pagans have even exceeded their ancient counterparts in sexual depravity.

So what has been the Christian response to this new paganism? Are modern Christians following the example of the first Christians? Unfortunately, the answer is no. Instead, a rather large group of modern Christians have responded in ways quite different from their Christian ancestors. Rather than seeking to convert the new pagans while standing apart from their beliefs and practices, many of today's Christians have aligned their morals and beliefs with those of the new pagans. Nowhere is this behavior more evident than in the area of sexual morality.

It is a sad fact that large numbers of modern Christians have integrated and incorporated the sexual morality of the new pagans not only into their own lives, but in many cases, even into the faith statements of their Christian communities. In that sense, they are not just embracing but actually promoting the new pagan culture.

For example, the morality of contraception, sterilization and in vitro fertilization is rarely questioned by most Christian denominations. Cohabitation and divorce are tolerated. With regard to abortion, many denominations now consider it a woman's right. Some even cover abortion in their employee health care plans. In some denominations, homosexual unions are not only accepted among the lay faithful but even among the clergy. The first Christians would have recognized this behavior and been quite familiar with it, but they would have recognized it as being something practiced by pagans, not Christians.

Because many Christian communities have failed in their duty to uphold and teach God's plan for sex, many of today's Christians (who may be quite sincere and devout) know nothing of Christian teaching with regard to sexual morality. Neither do they understand how profoundly it differs from pagan sexual morality. They are simply ignorant of God's plan for sexuality and of how it should be lived out in their lives.

This ignorance has left them unable to distinguish the difference between Christian and pagan sexual morality. Consequently, they do not understand that Christians are called to live differently from how the pagans live, nor do they understand that every Christian is called to share his or her knowledge of God's plan with the nations (those who do not know Christ). This widespread ignorance of God's plan for sex is the primary cause and source of the unhappiness and pain many people experience in their sexual relationships today.

There are still some parts of the world where people live without the knowledge of modern medicine. In those areas, people still suffer from polio, malaria, leprosy and other diseases we have all but exterminated in the West. Even though we know what causes and cures these diseases (and have known for generations), these people still suffer from them because they do not know.

In the same way, because few people today know about God's plan for sex, they are suffering the consequences. This is true not only for the new pagans who have deliberately rejected Christ, but also for the many Christians who have never heard the truth about God's plan for sex. By not living as God designed or willed (even without knowing it), they too suffer the consequences.

So, what is to be done? In response to this new pagan world, some Christians, have chosen to retreat from it. Like the early Christians, they have recognized that living like pagans is incompatible with the life of a Christian. However, unlike the early Christians, they are not seeking to convert the pagan culture. Instead, they have isolated themselves from pagan society in nearly every way. Clearly, that is the wrong response.

The right response is to do exactly what the early Christians did. That is, to reject pagan morals and withdraw from all that is not holy, to live in the world while not being part of it, while at the same time making a sincere effort to share the gospel with the world and convert it. Pope Saint Pius X chose as his motto, "To restore all things in Christ." [34] When considering the state of our culture today, that is the approach Christians must take.

Here it should be noted that there will be and always has been a price to pay for serving Christ. That price is hatred by the world. As Jesus Himself said,

> "The hour is coming, indeed it has come, when you will be scattered, every man to his home, and will leave me alone; yet I am not alone, for the Father is with me. I have said this to you, that in me you may have peace. In the world you will have tribulation; but be of good cheer, I have overcome the world (Jn 16:32–33)."

Today, living as a faithful Christian, especially in the area of sexual morality, is to be different. It means being a witness to the truth, and doing so is to invite persecution not only from the new pagans but even more so from modernistic Christians. When people who are living a lie are confronted with the truth, they have one of two options. They can either convert and conform their lives to the truth, or they can reject the truth and attack the one who has presented it to them.

All Christians need to realize that by simply living their faith, they will be persecuted. At the same time, they should be of good cheer because Christ

---

[34] He took these words loosely from Saint Paul's letter to the Ephesians 1:10.

has overcome the world. Yes, there will be persecutions, but there will also be consolations. As Jesus said,

> "Truly I say to you, there is no one who has left house or brothers or sisters or mother or father or children or lands, for my sake and for the gospel, who will not receive a hundredfold now in this time, houses and brothers and sisters and mothers and children and lands, with persecutions, and in the age to come eternal life (Mk 10:29–30)."

This completes our examination of paganism and its influence on our culture and our thinking. We are now at last ready to look at God's wonderful plan for sex. In Part Two of this Book, we will see how Christians should talk about sex and also how sex is part of God's creation and is therefore good. We will then consider the sexual differences between men and women from a Christian perspective.

PART TWO

CHRISTIAN SEX

PART TWO: CHRISTIAN SEX

At first glance, the phrase "Christian sex" may seem rather odd. In fact, some devout Christians might even say it sounds a bit immoral. Furthermore, upon reflection, some might question whether such a thing even exists. After all, Jews have sex, Muslims have sex, Hindus have sex and even atheists have sex. So, how could there be such a thing as Christian sex? Sex is just sex right? In addition, modern pagans might add that even if such a thing did exist, Christians could save a lot of time and energy and easily summarize their beliefs about sex with just one single word: "NO!"

However, all of these ideas are wrong. Christian sex does exist. It is not odd, and it is not immoral. In addition, sex is not just sex. Quite the contrary, depending upon your definition of the word, and depending upon what you are doing, how you are doing it and why you are doing it, the meaning of the sexual act can be totally different from one case to the next.

For example, sex between a husband and wife as an expression of their committed love is something quite different from sex between an unmarried couple, and it is also quite different from sex between a man and a prostitute. While the physical act is the same in each case, the meaning is completely different. Differing circumstances change the meaning of what is done. So clearly, sex is not just sex. The what, the how and the why all make a big difference, and each can change the meaning of the act entirely.

Now, someone might say, "Ok, I get that point, but I still don't see what you mean by 'Christian sex.'" Once again, it needs to be said that what is done is shaped by the intention and perspective of those doing it, and Christians have some pretty clear ideas about sex, what it is for, how it is done and who can participate in it.

Going further, what makes Christian sex different from pagan sex or, for that matter, any other kind of sex is the Christian understanding of it, an understanding which differs greatly from that of the pagans. The difference is not so much in the mechanics but in the meaning of the act, in the circumstances that surround it, and in the respect Christians owe to their brothers and sisters in Christ. These things and others put Christian sex into an entirely different context from pagan sex. They raise it to a higher level and make it holy.

For a Christian, all of life is shaped by the teachings of Jesus Christ, and because one's sexuality is part of life, it too must be shaped by the teachings of Jesus Christ. Just as our faith transforms all we do and sanctifies it and makes it holy, so too our faith transforms the act of sexual love and makes it holy.

So, here is a definition: *Christian sex is that kind of intimate behavior which follows from a Christian understanding and teaching about human sexuality.*

In the chapters ahead, we are going to look at God's plan for sex and how it is revealed to us through His Holy Church and through the Sacred Scriptures. In so doing, we will see how God's plan for sex (which is synonymous with Christian sex) contrasts profoundly with the pagan ideas on the subject. We will also see how by living out God's plan (which is not always easy and sometimes even very difficult), we will find the greatest peace, happiness and enjoyment in life. So then, with all of this in mind, let us move on and see why Christian sex is far better than anything the pagans have to offer.

Chapter Five
SOME BASIC PRINCIPLES

Our discussion on Christian sex must begin with some basic principles, and here is the first: Things go better when you follow the directions. When a thing is used in the way that its maker designed it to be used, it always works better. A hacksaw works best when it is used to cut metal and not wood. Lipstick goes better on your lips than on your sleeve. Everything electronic works better when it is plugged in. Do not bake pizza without first removing the cardboard.

These examples point out that to get the most out of something, we first need to know what it is for and second, use it in the way that its maker intended. When we do that, things go better. On the other hand, when we use something in the wrong way, in a way not intended by its maker, things do not go as well. It is true that in some cases the thing may work fairly well even when it is misused, but then again, it might not work at all. The point is that everything has a purpose, and the intentions of the inventor or designer should not be taken lightly or ignored when using that thing.

Sex is no different than anything else in life. That is because sex also has a purpose which was established by its creator who is God. To put it another way, God invented sex, and it was God who established its meaning and purpose. That means we as human beings do not have the right or the power to redesign sex or to use it for purposes other than those God intended. In fact, that right belongs to God alone.

Because God invented sex, it also means (contrary to what modern pagans believe) that the purpose of sex is not self-defined; it is not subjective. In other words the objective (or real) meaning and purpose of sex does not change based on the subjective (or personal) intention of the user. Rather, both the meaning and the purpose of sex are unchanging. When sex is used properly, both its purpose and meaning remain the same for every single human person. To put it another way, the purpose and meaning do not change from one person to the next.

Here is a second principle: We are not free to engage in certain activities unless we have first acquired the skills associated with those activities. For example, if you have learned how to play the violin, you are then free to play it or not depending upon your mood. However, if you have never learned how to play the violin, you are not free to play it. If you know how to play chess, if you know the rules of the game, you are free to play it or not. On the other hand, if you do not know the rules of chess, you are not free to play the game.

In the same way, in order to use sex properly, you have to know what it is for and to have also acquired those moral virtues associated with its proper use. Without that knowledge, and without those virtuous habits, you will not be free to use sex properly and so, will not be able to enjoy it in the way God intended. On the other hand, knowing God's plan for sex gives you the freedom to use it (or not) as it was intended to be used by its Maker.

Today, most people do not think about sex with these principles in mind, and that is unfortunate. They do not understand that sex has a purpose and that its purpose was established by God. Sadly, this lack of knowledge and the failure to understand that sex has a purpose beyond physical pleasure has led to all sorts of problems. This is especially true for the pagans who either do not do much thinking about the meaning of sex or, if they do, have tried to redefine and redesign it. It is also true for many Christians who may have adopted (knowingly or unknowingly) many pagan practices when it comes to sex.

Ignorance is slavery. Because many people never consider that sex has a purpose nor of how God intended that it be used, they end up misusing it. The result is that they are dissatisfied with their sex lives, but at the same time, unable to identify what is wrong. Of course the reason for their dissatisfaction is that they are misusing sex. Furthermore, because sex involves such powerful emotions, they often end up being deeply hurt by their misuse. It is like someone playing with a grenade who has no idea it could blow up and is shocked when it does.

A final cautionary note. In the area of sexual morality, our pagan culture has been much more influential in shaping and forming beliefs and attitudes about sex than has Christianity. This is especially true with regard to widely accepted practices such as the use of artificial contraception, sterilization and most techniques used in fertility clinics. This is also true to a lesser extent with practices such as cohabitation, homosexual relationships and abortion, all of which are more controversial but still widely accepted. The assumption by many that these practices are moral and perfectly acceptable have skewed their understanding of God's beautiful plan for sexuality. Their assumptions have also made it impossible for them to grow to the heights of love God has planned for them.

For these reasons, the reader would do well to examine and then re-examine his or her assumptions about the purpose of sex and about the morality of these (and other) commonly accepted sexual practices. More than a few readers (even among those who consider themselves practicing Christians) are going to find their assumptions challenged by what follows. They may be surprised to find that what they have taken for granted and accepted without question is not Christian. Let us begin this re-examination by looking at how we talk about sex.

Christian Sex

Chapter Six
HOW TO TALK ABOUT SEX

Generally speaking, there is a right way and a wrong way to do everything, and that is also true when talking about sex. There is a right way to talk about it and a wrong way. Yet, most people have no idea how to talk about sex in the right way. In fact, it has probably never occurred to them that there even is a right way to talk about sex. Clearly, this is true for the modern pagans. However, today's Christians do not know how to talk about sex either, and that is unfortunate because it is absolutely essential that Christians know how to talk about sex in the right way, and for two reasons.

First, because how we talk about things reflects how we think about them. If we are not thinking about something in the right way, or if we do not have a proper understanding of it, then we cannot talk about it in the right way. With regard to sex, when someone has a mistaken idea about God's plan for it, that person will be unable to talk about sex in the right way. On the other hand, having a correct understanding of God's plan for sex allows us to talk about it correctly, which in turn helps reinforce correct thinking about sex.

Second, it is absolutely essential that Christians know how to talk about sex in the right way so they can explain what they believe and why. As Saint Peter put it, "Always be prepared to make a defense to any one who calls you to account for the hope that is in you (1Pet 3:15)." Here it should be noted that even if one understands something, he or she may not be able to explain it well or even at all, and this is certainly true with regard to God's plan for sex.

Many Christians have an innate understanding of what is right and wrong sexual behavior and live their lives accordingly, but they cannot explain why they live as they do. However, that is not an acceptable position. If Christians are to share the gospel and convert the world, it is essential that they know how to talk about sex in the right way. They must have the ability to explain to others why they live as they do.

To talk about sex in the right way, two extremes must be avoided: talking about sex all the time and never talking about sex at all. On the one extreme are some devout Christians who never talk about sex (at least not in public), and they do not think others should do so either. They would be appalled if a priest or minister were to discuss sexual matters from the pulpit. They consider these matters to be private in every respect. However, it is clear that the Church has never held this position. In fact, the Bible itself contains numerous references to sex.

At the other extreme are the modern pagans. They seldom stop talking about sex, and do not seem to care much when or where they talk about it. You can watch them talking about it on TV (which is saturated with implicit and explicit sexual content). You can listen to them talking about it on the radio. You can overhear them talking about it in restaurants, at the mall, at work, at school and just about anywhere people gather including places where children are present.

Besides their sexual references in conversation, modern pagan are also fond of sexual imagery. The Internet is overrun with their pornography. Tabloids in the grocery store checkout lanes are filled with sexual themes and images. We have all heard the phrase, "sex sells." You can see evidence of this as you stroll through the mall past clothing stores with provocative ads or drive down the highway past so-called "Gentlemen's clubs." None of this represents a Christian approach to sexuality nor do these subjects have any place in Christian conversations about sex.

All of us are assaulted with these sexual references on a daily basis. Whether it is in their conversations, in the sexually explicit advertising, in the sexual programming on TV or in countless other ways, modern pagans seem to believe that sex and sexual messages are meant for public consumption by people of every age group, from small children to great-grandparents. Furthermore, their sexual comments and discussions are so pervasive they are virtually impossible to avoid, and this has consequences for us all.

Whether we want to admit it or not, we have all been deeply influenced by our culture. We have become desensitized to how the pagans talk about sex. Because of its frequency, we hardly notice how all of these conversations and images have shaped our own perception of sexuality as well as our own behavior and conversations, but we should. That is because the way pagans talk about sex is the wrong way to talk about it. In fact, Christians simply cannot imitate the pagan way of talking about sex.

So what is the right way to talk about it? The answer lies in the middle between the two extremes described above. In other words, not too much and not too little. Also, the right way to talk about sex will acknowledge that sex has a meaning and purpose that goes far beyond physical pleasure. Proper conversations about sex will begin with the understanding that God is the one who has established its meaning and purpose. In addition, these conversations will be carried out with a certain respect and discretion. The Church's reflections on the Bible and what it says will give us direction on how to proceed from here.

As was mentioned, the Bible is full of sex. From the Book of Genesis where it states that "Adam knew his wife Eve (Gen 4:1)" to Saint Paul's First Letter to the Corinthians where he gives advice to husbands and wives about when to have conjugal relations (1Cor 7), sexual intercourse is mentioned dozens of times. Most of the time, but not always, it is within the context of marriage. However, there are also references to adultery, fornication and even to rape and incest.

Sexual morality is also a frequent subject in the Bible. For example, the Books of Leviticus and Numbers contain several chapters on the subject. In addition, Jesus Himself did not refrain from speaking about these matters. He once stated, "You have heard that it was said, 'You shall not commit adultery.' But I say to you that every one who looks at a woman lustfully has already committed adultery with her in his heart (Mt 5:27–28)." Finally, the early Christians also heard about sexual morality from Saint Paul who addressed issues such as fornication, adultery and marital rights.

Here it should be pointed out that Saint Paul's letters were read during Mass in the early Church, and so these topics were heard by the early Christian congregations who came together for "the breaking of the bread" each Sunday, "the first day of the week (Acts 20:7)." In all of this, we see that the Bible is not simply a book of innocence and love. Rather, in so many ways, God's inspired word is very much the story of human life with all of its joys and sorrows, the good as well as the bad.

So, we must be clear that the Church has never been silent when it comes to talking about sex and sexual morality, and that makes perfect sense because we as human persons are sexual beings right down to the very last cell in our bodies.[35] It is part of who we are; it goes with the territory. It is precisely because

---

[35] Each cell is either male or female in that each cell carries either the XY chromosome in men or the XX chromosome in women. That is why a true "sex change" is not

every human person in general and every Christian in particular is a sexual being that we need to understand our sexuality and how God expects us to use it. In order to do that, Christians should and must talk about sex from time to time. The issue then is not whether to speak about sex or not, but rather, how to speak about it. What is the proper way? What is the proper context?

Our first clue on how to do this comes from the Commandment, "Thou shalt not commit adultery (Ex 20:14)" and from its corollary, "Thou shalt not covet thy neighbor's wife (Ex 20:17)." God gave these commandments to the Israelites through Moses, and they were reaffirmed by Jesus when the rich young man asked what he must do to have eternal life. Jesus said to him, "Keep the commandments." When the man asked which ones, Jesus said, "You shall not kill, you shall not commit adultery ... (Mt 19:18)."

These commandments were also taught by Saint Paul to the first Christians. In his letter to the Romans he said, "Owe to no one anything, except to love one another; for he who loves his neighbor has fulfilled the law. The commandments, 'You shall not commit adultery, You shall not kill, You shall not steal, You shall not covet,' and any other commandment, are summed up in this sentence, 'You shall love your neighbor as yourself.' Love does no wrong to a neighbor; therefore love is the fulfilling of the law (Rom 13:8–10)."

At this point, for the sake of clarity, adultery needs to be defined. Adultery is when a person has sexual relations with someone who is married to another. However, the commandments which prohibit adultery also apply to more than just the physical act of sexual intercourse. By extension, they also prohibit sexual relations between two unmarried persons as well as actions by unmarried persons that are only proper between married couples, and sexual acts with one's self such as masturbation. Finally, it is clear that thoughts too must be controlled (for both married and unmarried persons). That means one cannot imagine having sex with someone other than his or her spouse. The reasons for these prohibitions will be discussed later.

Notice that the commandments place sexual relations within a certain context, and that context is marriage. It is in this context that the Scriptures speak about sex in favorable terms, whereas outside of marriage, sex is spoken of as something immoral. That means no Christian could ever engage in sexual

---

possible. To change one's sex would involve modifying every single cell in the body which is impossible.

relations outside the bounds of marriage without sinning.

Notice too that limiting sexual relations to marriage puts an end to nearly all of the conversations pagans have about sex. Pagans almost always talk about sex as if it were merely entertainment and nearly all of their conversations concern sex outside of marriage, but these kinds of conversations are out of bounds because they are about immoral things. Pagans have little or no interest in restricting their sexual relationships or discussions about sex to its proper context which is marriage. However, Christians must do so because God expects it of them.

Restricting discussions about sex to the context of marriage leads to an important guideline on how to talk about sex: *It must be done with a certain discretion and with a recognition that sex is a private thing, an intimate and personal thing between a husband and wife.*

Indeed, if Christian sexuality is ultimately about the intimate expression of love between a husband and wife, then it is no one else's business. No Christian married couple engages in sexual intercourse in public. They do not perform sex acts on TV or in the movies (or watch them for that matter). To do so would be a violation of the personal and intimate self-gift of one to the other. That gift belongs to no one else. Indeed, not only is this kind of love not expressed in public, it is also not discussed in public. What wife would not feel violated if her husband were to discuss her body with other men in a bar? What husband would not feel violated if his wife were to discuss his body with the other girls at work? Sex was not meant for public consumption. It was not designed by God to be a spectator sport. To repeat, a proper approach to Christian sexuality will maintain a certain modesty and discretion.

Within the context of marriage, discussions about sexual love and love-making between a husband and wife are appropriate. Here one could look to the Song of Songs for confirmation. This Book of the Bible has been interpreted by Jews as a symbol of God's love for His people and by Christians as a symbol of Christ's love for His Church.

However, the symbol for this love is spousal love, that is, the love between a bridegroom and bride, between husband and wife, and this symbol includes the sexual dimension. This love is intense, deep and personal; it is also physical. The Song of Songs gives us an inside view of this love between spouses. We hear their conversations, words meant not for the outsider, not for others but for the beloved.

There is an intimacy. The husband describes his wife and her body, and the wife does the same with her husband. They speak of each other's characteristics, such as their eyes and hair but also of her breasts and thighs, and of his legs. The Scriptures present this as intrinsically good. Obviously, all of this is a reality known and familiar to lovers, but not to outsiders.

Notice something more. Even here, as we are allowed to look in on this couple and their lovemaking, not all is revealed to us. Something is still left to the imagination. She invites him into her secret chamber, a euphemism for sexual intercourse. That deepest intimacy where the two become one flesh is a symbol of God's spiritual union with the soul which is deeply personal and something not to be shared with others.

Furthermore, there are also many symbols of fruitfulness. It is springtime. There are flowers. The fig tree puts forth figs, and the vines are in blossom. Human sexual love is not meant to be barren but fruitful. In fact, one translation has the husband praising the beauty of his wife and among other things he says to her, "Your belly is a heap of wheat, encircled with lilies (Sg 7:2)" perhaps an image of pregnancy, the fruitfulness that results from their intimate love for each other.

All of these terms of endearment are private. They would never be uttered in public and would embarrass the beloved if they were. However, we are given the opportunity to eavesdrop, if you will, so that we may see that this kind of lovemaking and conversation is not wrong, but in fact good when it is between husband and wife.

Furthermore, this passionate, physical and intense love whereby the two become one flesh, something married couples experience, is in fact a great mystery and, as Saint Paul said, is "a reference to Christ and the Church (Eph 5:32)."

At this point, it should be clear that outside of marriage and the intimate conversations married couples have with each other (which are presented as good in the Song of Songs), any discussion about one's sex life that would betray one's partner in marriage or that would imply sexual actions outside of marriage or that would call attention to our sexual parts, is wrong. That is because the only reason one would do so would be to reveal thoughts and actions to others that should only be revealed to one's spouse.

Furthermore, it should also be clear that any discussion about sex must be done with a certain reverence, discretion and maturity. There should be an understanding that when sex is properly respected, it has a private and intimate dimension to it which makes public discussions about it and about one's intimate relationship out of place. In that sense, the instincts of devout Christians are more correct in their reluctance to talk about sex than are the pagans who talk about it all the time. Sadly, pagans have no grasp of this concept. They are constantly talking about sex primarily because they are incapable of distinguishing the holy from the profane.

In conclusion, sex is not meant for public consumption. It is not a spectator sport. Rather, sex is a deeply personal thing. Consequently, there should always be a natural reticence when talking about sex, a holy modesty. This is especially true for Christian people, but it is true for others of good will as well. Making love to one's spouse is among the most intimate of acts. It is a sign of the self-gift a husband and wife bestow upon each other. That is why a couple's love-making should not be discussed with others, at least not by those who truly love each other.

In the end, talking about sex in the right way is part of living a virtuous life and is something which is holy and pleasing to God. Throughout the rest of this book, we will discuss sex with these principles in mind.

Chapter Seven

SEX IS PART OF GOD'S CREATION AND GOD'S CREATION IS GOOD

In the first chapter of the Book of Genesis, the very first book of the Bible, it says, "God created man in His own image, in the image of God He created him; male and female He created them (Gen 1:27)." Here is revealed to us a fundamental truth, namely, that God who is the Creator of heaven and earth and of all things is also man's Creator. Man too is part of God's creation.[36] As the Psalmist says, "Know that the Lord is God! It is He that made us, and we are His; we are His people, the sheep of His pasture (Ps 100:3)."

Genesis also reveals to us a second truth: God created man in His own image. It is in the soul that man resembles God. Furthermore, man is the only creature with whom God plans to share His divine nature (2Pet 1:4). In that sense, man has a unique place; he alone has been set apart from all the rest of God's material creation.

However, man is not an exact copy of God. Rather, man is different from God (and from the angels) in that he has both a soul and a body. God and angels are called pure spirits because they have no physical parts; they have no bodies. Man, on the other hand, has a soul, a spiritual part like God and the angels, but he also has a physical body, a part like the animals and the rest of God's creation. Because he has both a soul and a body, man is said to be a composite being.

Philosophers tell us that God's essence is to exist. The Scriptures go further and explain that God "dwells in unapproachable light (1Tim 6:16)" and that God is both light (1Jn 1:5) and love (1Jn 4:8). If we are to live with God in heaven and to share in God's divine nature, we must live as we were created to live, and that means living as God lives. More to the point, just as

---

[36] Here I want to avoid the debate over evolution, intelligent design and creationism. While of great interest, the question of exactly how God created man is not important for the purpose of this discussion. What is important is that God created man. If true, it means God is ultimately responsible for both man's existence and his design which then allows us to ask the question, "Why did God create man as He did?"

God is both light and love, we too must be light and love to the world. Only then will we find true peace and happiness.

We can express and share God's light and love in spiritual ways such as praying for others and setting a good example. However, we can also express God's light and love through our bodies. As part of God's plan, our bodies are not simply an afterthought. They are not like some kind of container for the soul. Rather, our bodies are part of us. When we are hungry we do not say, "My body's stomach is hungry." We say, "I am hungry." When we are at the barber shop, we do not say, "The hair on my body's head is being cut." We say, "I am getting a haircut." When a husband engages in sexual intercourse with his wife he does not say, "My body is engaged in sexual intercourse with my wife's body." He says, "I am making love to my wife." From this, it should be clear that what we do with our bodies makes a difference because it is we who are doing it.

In considering the human body, there are certain things everyone has in common. We all have eyes and ears. We all have a heart and lungs, and we all have feet and hands. There are also some differences. We come in various shades or colors, black, white, brown and so on. Some people are shorter and some taller. Hair colors differ. These variations are all superficial and are examples of non-essential differences.

However, there is one essential difference, and that difference was noted above in the passage from Genesis. There we are told that God not only created us in His image, but that He also created us male and female. Again, while this difference is most obviously physical, no man says, I am a person with a male body, but rather, I am a male. Likewise no woman says, I am a person with a female body, but rather, I am a female.

The fact that God created us male and female also means that sex and sexual differences are part of God's creation, and these sexual differences are good. Upon completing His work, God surveyed all that He created. As He did so, we are told that "He saw everything that He had made, and behold, it was very good (Gen 1:31)." In the New Testament, Saint Paul reaffirms this when he writes, "Everything created by God is good (1 Tim 4:4)." As part of God's creation, this means sex is good too. Consequently, it should never be seen as something dirty, bad or unseemly (with one proviso, and that it is within its proper context which is marriage).

Because we have bodies, part of human love of necessity will be physical. It is going to involve our bodies. There will be touching, caressing, kissing, embracing and engaging in sexual intercourse, and the Bible addresses all of these things. While the Bible is primarily about our relationship with God, it is also about human life and human love. It is about how God would have us interact with each other. Consequently, the Bible does not avoid sexual topics. In fact, it contains numerous references to sexuality. The Bible tells it like it is.[37]

For example, in the Book of Genesis, we are told, "a man leaves his father and mother and cleaves to his wife, and they become one flesh (Gen 2:24)." This is a reference to sexual intercourse where the two are physically joined together as a sign of their love for each other. Their union of bodies is an expression of their union of hearts. Jesus Himself refers to this approvingly when He quotes from this passage of Genesis and then adds to it by saying, "So they are no longer two but one flesh. What therefore God has joined together, let not man put asunder (Lk 19:6)."

The science of immunology provides a fascinating modern-day confirmation of this two in one flesh reality. Our immune system is designed to fight off intruders in our bodies. A key means of doing this is its ability to distinguish us from them, self from non-self. That is how diseases are overcome, and that is why our bodies reject organ transplants. However, during sexual intercourse something remarkable happens. The husband's sperm contains a mild immunosuppressant which alters the wife's immune system just enough so that her body sees the sperm as part of herself. In other words, she and

---

[37] In all there are dozens of times in which sexual intercourse is mentioned or referred to in the Bible. Often these references to sex are obscured by the translators who use euphemisms for the actual Biblical words. Thus, sexual intercourse is translated as to know, to lie with, to have relations, conjugal rights, intercourse, goes in to her, go in unto her, lie with her, sleep with her, went into her, had carnal relations and so on. The practice of referring indirectly to sexual things reflects the influence of those who believe sex should hardly be discussed if at all. However, as was mentioned, that is an extreme position. Obscuring the sexual references in the Bible also obscures God's word to us by obscuring the fact that we have been created male and female and that sex is part of life. This undue modesty can also give the impression that sex is not good but somehow "dirty." Finally, it hides the times when God sometimes uses the graphic image of sexual infidelity (as in the case of an unfaithful spouse or a prostitute) to symbolize the spiritual infidelity of His people Israel.

her husband are truly two in one flesh and their children are the fruit of that union! [38]

The Bible also tells it like it is in another way when it speaks disapprovingly of sexual intercourse outside of marriage. We see this with King David who was aroused by the sight of Bathsheba, the wife of Uriah the Hittite. We are told that he then sent for her, and she came to him and "he lay with her (2Sam 11:4)." For this act of adultery, he was punished. In another place, the incestuous rape of Tamar by her half-brother Amnon is mentioned (2Sam 13). In yet another place, the unfaithfulness of Samaria and Jerusalem are compared to harlots "whose breasts were pressed (caressed) and whose virgin bosoms handled (fondled) (Ez 23:3)." It goes on to say that Jerusalem did not give up her harlotry "for in her youth men had lain with her and handled her virgin bosom and poured out their lust upon her (Ez 23:8)."

The Bible speaks of kissing as a sign of love between husband and wife, "O that you would kiss me with the kisses of your mouth! For your love is better than wine (Sg 1:2)." It also mentions kissing in adulterous affairs as when a woman goes to her lover and "kisses him (Prov 7:13)." A kiss can also be used to deceive or betray as can be seen in the case of Judas. Thus when Judas kissed Jesus in the Garden of Gethsemane our Lord said, "Judas, would you betray the Son of man with a kiss (Lk 22:48)?"[39] Judas had used this physical sign of love dishonestly, not as a sign of love and affection, but in an attempt to hide his true intentions from Jesus.

The Bible speaks about our sexual parts and our sexual development. It mentions the male genitalia when it refers to circumcision, the physical

---

[38] "Canada and Same-Sex Marriage," by Donald DeMarco, Ethics and Medics, December 2002, Volume 27, Number 12.

[39] A kiss is a physical sign of the unseen love and devotion a man has for a woman (and vice-versa). Consequently, when a man kisses his beloved, that kiss reveals to her the unseen love which he has for her, and reassures her that her trust in him has not been misplaced. That is why when the physical signs of love are used to deceive and betray, they are so hurtful. The one betrayed does not normally suspect or interpret the sign as something dishonest. Thus the profound hurt when one discovers that physical signs of love have been used to deceive. The more intimate the sign, the more intense the hurt. Most hurtful of all is when that physical sign is sexual intercourse, the most intimate physical sign of love.

sign of the covenant God entered into with Abraham (Gen 17:9–14). In that operation, the foreskin of the penis is cut away. It mentions those who have been maimed or who have physical imperfections including men whose testicles are crushed or whose penis (male member) has been amputated (Deut 23:1). Men with these conditions are to be excluded from the assembly of the Lord. There was knowledge in the ancient world that a castrated man could not father a child. Eunuchs, those who had been castrated, are mentioned in four books of the Bible, particularly in the Book of Esther. Saint Paul speaks of those who insisted on maintaining the practice of circumcision after the New Covenant was established. In exasperation with them, he wished they would go the whole way and "castrate themselves (Gal 5:12)."

The Bible implicitly refers to erection and ejaculation when it speaks about a man being unclean if there is a discharge of semen (seed), and it specifies how he is to be purified (Lev 15: 16–18). It also speaks of these things in the case of Onan who in the act of intercourse withdrew from his deceased brother's wife and spilled his semen on the ground (Gen 38:9).

The Bible talks about how a woman develops at puberty. In the Song of Songs, a little sister is mentioned who as yet "has no breasts (Sg 8:8)." In the Prophet Ezekiel, Jerusalem is compared to an abandoned baby girl upon whom God took pity. God said to her, "Live, and grow up like a plant of the field. And you grew up and became tall and arrived at full maidenhood; your breasts were formed, and your hair had grown ... (Ez 16:6–7)."

The Bible speaks of a woman's monthly cycle and her menstruation. In the Levitical law we read, "When a woman has a discharge of blood which is her regular discharge from her body, she shall be in her impurity for seven days (Lev 15:19)." A man was not to have relations (uncover her nakedness) with a woman while "she is in her menstrual uncleanness (Lev 18:19)." [40]

There was clear knowledge that children were the result of intercourse. For example, we read that, "Adam knew Eve his wife, and she conceived and bore Cain (Gen 4:1)." "Cain knew his wife, and she conceived and bore Enoch (Gen 4:17)." In describing himself, Solomon says, "I also am mortal, like all men ... from the seed of a man and the pleasure of marriage (Wis 7:1–2)."

---

[40] A woman's menstrual period and her time of purification is often translated in obscure ways including "having her sickness," "menstrual impurity," and even "having her flowers." See note 37.

When the Angel Gabriel announced to Mary that she would conceive a Son, our Lady replied, "How can this be since I have no husband (Lk 1:34)."[41]

The Bible speaks of pregnancy and childbirth. During pregnancy, the wife of Manoah was instructed to "drink no wine or strong drink (Jgs 13:4)."[42] The pains of childbirth are mentioned as punishment for the sins of Adam and Eve. God said to Eve, "I will greatly multiply your pain in childbearing; in pain you shall bring forth children (Gen 3:16)." A woman's pain at childbirth is mentioned in numerous places. For example, "I heard a cry as of a woman in travail, anguish as of one bringing forth her first child (Jer 4:31)." "She was with child and she cried out in her pangs of birth, in anguish for delivery (Rev 12:2)."

The Bible often speaks of breast feeding. In the persecutions of Antiochus, an Israelite mother appeals to her son to be faithful to the Lord and says, "My son, have pity on me. I carried you nine month in my womb, and nursed you for three years, and have reared you and brought you up to this point in your life (2Mac 7:27)." When Pharaoh's daughter found Moses in the river, she said to his mother, "Take the child away and nurse him for me (Ex 2:9)." After Hannah gave birth to Samuel, she "nursed her son, until she weaned him (1Sam 1:23)." In praise of the mother of Jesus, a woman from the crowd called out to Him and said, "Blessed is the womb that bore you, and the breasts that you sucked (Lk 11:27)!"

The Bible makes implicit references to menopause when a woman is too old to conceive. When God promised Abraham that his wife Sarah would conceive and bear a son, we are told Abraham said to himself, "Shall Sarah, who is ninety years old bear a child (Gen 17:17)?" When Sarah heard this, she too laughed because in her advanced age, "It had ceased to be with [her] after the manner of women (Gen 18:11)." When the Angel Gabriel announced to Zechariah that he and his wife Elizabeth would have a son, Zechariah replied, "How shall I know this? For I am an old man, and my wife is advanced in years

---

[41] Literally, "How can this be since I do not know man?" Other translations are, "How can this be seeing that I have no husband?" "How can this be since I have not had relations with a man?" "How can this be since I am a virgin?"

[42] This same advice is given to women today so as to not harm the unborn child's development.

(Lk 1:18)." However, this came to pass, and when the angel spoke with the Blessed Virgin, he informed her, "Behold, your kinswoman Elizabeth in her old age has also conceived a son and this is the sixth month with her who was called barren. For with God nothing will be impossible (Lk 1:36–37)."

The Bible also mentions and praises virginity (when a man or a woman has not had sexual intercourse). It refers to marriage when "A young man marries a virgin (Is 62:5)." It mentions the daughter of Jephthah "who had never known a man (Jgs 11:39)." Virginity is associated with the miraculous birth of our Savior and with the Incarnation, "A virgin shall conceive and bear a son (Is 7:14)."[43] Israel is described as the virgin daughter of Zion (Is 23:12, 37:22), a term of praise and endearment.

As can be seen, the Bible does not hide the sexual realities of life. Rather, it refers to them in a matter of fact way as it does with all things that are part of human life. Furthermore, within the context of marriage, sexual intercourse is not only mentioned, but also affirmed as something that is both part of God's creation and also something that is good.

This is how Christian sex should be viewed. Sex is part of life. It is something natural and good because it is part of God's creation, and God's creation is good. Consequently, when necessary and in its proper context, sex can be discussed without shame or embarrassment. The Bible serves as our model for this.

---

[43] Some translations use "young woman" here instead of "virgin," but the Septuagint, the Greek Bible used by the Jews, translates the Hebrew word used here as "virgin" as does Saint Matthew in his Gospel (1:23). This passage obviously refers to the Virgin Mary.

Chapter Eight
SEXUAL DIFFERENCES

God never does anything by accident. Unlike us, He does not have second thoughts; He does not change His mind. With God, all is deliberate, and everything is done on purpose.[44] That means man did not come about by chance. Quite the contrary, our existence has a cause and is the result of a divine plan that was quite deliberate. Thus God declares, "Before I formed you in the womb I knew you (Jer 1:5)." From this, it is also clear that the distinctions between male and female were no accident. From the beginning, it was God's plan that human beings would also be sexual beings, and they would come in two basic models, male and female.

While men and women have the same dignity or worth, that is about the only thing they share equally. In virtually every other aspect of their being, men and women are different, and these differences are not trivial. They exist not only at the sexual level but also on the physical, emotional, and psychological levels. These differences are also the source of most human interaction in that nearly all men find women fascinating and vice-versa. At the same time these differences can be very frustrating. For example, what woman has not at one time or another placed her hands on her hips in exasperation and said simply, "Men!" The implication being that men are quite beyond all help or understanding. Likewise, what man (when there are no women around), has not said in total bewilderment, "Women, there's just no understanding them!" As these words are uttered, his male friends can be seen nodding solemnly in agreement.

At this point, a brief review of the feminist movement would be helpful. Before the rise of modern feminism, everyone knew and admitted that men

---

[44] One can point to passages in the Bible where God appears to change His mind. The conversation between God and Abraham over the destruction of Sodom is one example (Gen 18:16–33). However, this and similar examples are not meant to teach about God's knowledge of the future or His unchanging nature. Rather, they are meant to illustrate certain qualities of God (in this case His great mercy) in ways that are easier to understand.

and women were different. It did not have to be proved; it was part of our lived experience. However, all that changed in the 60s and 70s. Those decades gave rise to the equal rights movement. At first the driving force was simple, equal pay for equal work. As the movement gained ground, it began to call attention to other important issues such as job discrimination and more athletic opportunities for girls.

In the movement's early days, women were limited in how far they could advance in a "man's world." Job discrimination prevented women from entering many fields and careers. There were very few women doctors, lawyers, judges, professors or politicians. High school and college athletics offered limited and underfunded programs for girls and young women.

Over the years, legislation outlawing discrimination on the basis of sex was passed, and the movement's main goals have become accepted by nearly everyone. On the other hand, as progress was made on the movement's core issues, certain philosophical issues also arose and began to be promoted. These would prove divisive both within and outside of the movement.

Many feminists began to exhibit a certain bitterness and anger. These individuals were no longer just concerned about pay and equal employment opportunities. The more radical feminists also desired power. They maintained that had it not been for male oppression, women would have achieved equal if not greater things than men. Men were no longer seen as partners in a just society or even in marriage. Rather, men were the problem. They were holding women back. From this point of view, men were seen as hardly necessary. "A woman needs a man like a fish needs a bicycle" became a popular feminist slogan.[45]

Radical feminists asserted that virtually all behavioral differences between the sexes were the result of cultural conditioning. Thus, part of the movement came to include an effort to erase all sexual distinctions. The Equal Rights Amendment was proposed as a way to provide legal remedies for this.[46]

---

[45] This phrase first used by Irina Dunn, was popularized by Gloria Steinem and later by the band U2.

[46] Section 1 stated, "Equality of rights under the law shall not be denied or abridged by the United States or by any State on account of sex." The amendment was nearly ratified by the required 38 states. However, passage stalled at 35 states and later on, five states rescinded their approval.

Another corrective to the supposed cultural conditioning was to give little boys dolls to help them be more nurturing and to give little girls toy trucks and cars to help them be more assertive.

One unfortunate result of this kind of thinking was the integration of high school sports when an equivalent girls sport was unavailable. In those cases, girls were allowed to play in boys' sports. Thus, even high school wrestling was integrated forcing boys to wrestle those girls who demanded access to that sport. School boards, coaches and parents seemed oblivious to the obvious physical contact that was inevitable and to the embarrassment of boys who had been taught not to touch girls in certain places.

Feminists also devalued motherhood. In their view, bearing children and caring for babies prevented women from advancing in the world of men. The unfair burden of pregnancy had to be overcome. Abortion was touted along with better and more effective means of birth control to level the sexual playing field.[47] Without babies, a woman could be as free and liberated as any man. Those women who stayed home to raise their children were viewed as second class citizens by many feminists and were made to feel as such. When asked what they did, stay at home moms hung their heads and said quietly, "I'm just a housewife."

It has now been several decades since society began to live out the feminist experiment, and that time has given us a chance to evaluate the real life consequences of its theories. Modern women have now entered every male preserve, and they have found that behaving like men (as did their feminist mothers and grandmothers) is deeply unsatisfying. Most would rather behave like women, and be treated as such. The desire to have children is no longer looked on with disdain. Yet the struggle to find ways to balance family and career remains.

In a positive development, women have added a feminine perspective in formerly male arenas such as corporate board rooms, the practice of medicine and law, higher education, civic and business organizations and politics. On

---

[47] To this day, older feminists continue to insist on the absolute right to abortion without any limitations, even for late term pregnancies where the baby is viable outside of the mother. The views of Supreme Court Justice Ruth Bader Ginsburg and former Senator Hilary Rodham Clinton on abortion clearly exemplify this attitude.

the other hand, the so-called sexual freedom women gained through abortion and birth control has led to increased STD rates and emotional scars left by the surgical removal of those "products of conception."

These gains by women have come at a cost to men. While women have preserved certain female activities and organizations such as the League of Women Voters and women religious orders, they have also insisted that exclusively male clubs and organizations be open to them as well. This has left men with no place to go for exclusively male company including such unlikely places as football locker rooms and Marine Corps boot camp.

It is also interesting to note that the successful effort to advance women's rights has left men lagging behind in graduation rates and college enrollment. Women are increasingly better educated, and consequently, more employable in the modern technical workplace than men. No longer able to act as the family's provider, men's self-esteem has suffered. Many seem to have been left without any clear purpose in life.

This perceived emasculation has caused more than a few men to become resentful of feminine success in the workplace. This is particularly true in jobs which are physically demanding and where standards were lowered to accommodate women. Examples include public safety work and the military. Violence against women has increased as the traditional family has become a thing of the past.

It needs to be said that sexual differences are not so much the result of cultural conditioning as they are of biology. As modern science has studied the physiological reasons behind why men and women think and act as they do, the data has confirmed what nearly everyone in the past already knew: men and women really are different. The good news is that many modern women are much more open to hearing this than their feminist mothers and grandmothers.

To return to the main point of this chapter, not only are men and women physically different, but we also think and behave differently. We see the world differently, and we respond to things differently. These differences (while not found universally in every individual) go to the very essence of who we are as men and women. They also explain why men and women often find it difficult to communicate.

Behavioral scientists have noted these differences which can be stated in general terms. For example, men tend to look at things abstractly. Women tend to personalize things. Men tend to consider the big picture. Women tend to see the details. Men tend to focus on things and stuff. Women tend to focus on people. Men tend to see themselves in terms of what they do and to find fulfillment in their jobs. Women tend to see themselves in terms of who they are and to find fulfillment in their connections to others (particularly their families and friends). Men focus their attention on one thing at a time. Women find it easier to multitask. Men are more aggressive while women tend to be more passive. Men are more individualistic. Women are more relational. In conversations, men tend to generalize and overlook non-verbal signals. Women tend to focus on the individual and readily pick up on nonverbal cues.

Sexually, men are more visual. Men are attracted to the physical aspects of sex whereas women are more interested in the relational dimension and whether or not they are loved. An astute observer once remarked, "men love sex like women love babies, and women love sex like men love babies." Here we might say that men are external and women are internal. This last point is also interesting in that it pertains to the body and the sexual organs as well, and this leads to one final observation about the differences between men and women. By themselves, they are incomplete.

In general, the things man designs and makes for his own use are complete in and of themselves. Cars, washing machines and iPods do not need anything else for them to do what they were made to do. A car will get you to where you want to go. A washing machine will wash your clothes. An iPod will play your music. They were designed for these particular functions, and they do them well.

With regard to men and women, it is true that they are also complete in many ways. Both men and women's respiratory systems function independently of the other. Both men and women can walk and move about without the other. Both can think and reason independently apart from the other. In fact, the basic man and the basic woman can do most things without the other. However, in one remarkable area this is not true.

Both are incomplete when it comes to their sexual organs. Both the man and the woman have sexual parts which do not work by themselves. In fact, without the opposite sex, human sexual parts have no purpose. More to the point, neither the man nor the woman can reproduce without the other, nor can they express their love in a sexual way or even experience sexual pleasure as it was meant to be experienced. By themselves, they are incomplete.

Furthermore, this incompleteness is not simply limited to the physical/ sexual dimension. It also shows up in how men and women think, act and react. Indeed, men and women complete each other in many ways. She helps him see how people are feeling while he helps her to consider things in an abstract way. He helps her to see the big picture, and she helps him with the details. He does things out of love for her. She loves him for the things he does. Men and women need each other and are completed by each other.

In this complementarity lies the clue as to why God created man as He did. Therein also lies the reason why He made us incomplete. At first glance, one might say it was for the purposes of reproduction, but that is not the whole story. God did not have to make us sexual beings for there to be new life. He could have made it possible for new human life to come about in any number of ways. God could have made each of us directly from nothing, or He could have made us like potatoes or amoebas which can reproduce asexually, but He did not.

Rather, God made us male and female because He has different parts for us to play and different roles for us to perform. Note here that roles are not the same as jobs. A job is something we do and can be done by either sex (with some limited exceptions). Roles go beyond culturally assigned tasks such as being a breadwinner or providing meals. While the task of breadwinner is traditionally assigned to men and the task of providing meals to women, these things can also be done by either sex. So roles are more than jobs or tasks. Roles go to the very essence of who we are. A job or task is about what one does whereas a role is about who one is. In that sense, roles are not interchangeable.

That men and women cannot exchange roles is clear. For example, no man could ever make someone a good wife and no woman could ever make someone a good husband. No man will ever make his child a good mother and no woman will ever make her child a good father. The reason is that these are not jobs but roles which are sexually defined and determined. Men can be husbands and fathers but not wives and mothers. Women can be wives and mothers but not husbands and fathers. The two roles cannot be reversed without doing serious harm to all concerned.[48]

---

[48] The practice of calling the other partner in homosexual relationships "husband" in the case of two men or "wife" in the case of two women is to redefine the words husband and wife. That new definition would refer to a relationship where either a

At this point, having explained how to talk about sex, that sex is part of God's creation, that sex is good, and finally, that men and women were created for different roles in the human family, we can now at last look at God's plan for sex and the reason why He made us sexual beings. We shall begin doing so in the next and following chapters.

---

man or a woman could refer to their spouse/partner as husband. Similarly either a man or a woman could refer to their spouse/partner as wife. Because it erases the sexual roles, this new definition would tell us less about the other's partner than do the traditional definitions of husband and wife. If this practice becomes widely accepted, when a man says, "I am a husband," one would next have to ask whether he has a wife or a male lover. Similarly, when a woman says, "I am a wife," one would next have to ask whether she has a husband or a female lover.

Christian Sex

PART THREE

GOD'S PLAN FOR SEX

PART THREE: GOD'S PLAN FOR SEX

Along with their ancient counterparts, modern pagans believe the main reason for having sex is pleasure. This explains why modern pagans freely engage in sexual activity without limits, either within or outside of marriage, either alone or with others. Their one and only rule (which they often violate) is that sex should be "safe" so that no one gets hurt. In practice, this means sexual activity which could lead to unwanted pregnancies or sexually transmitted diseases should be avoided. Otherwise, anything goes.

For their part, Christians acknowledge that sex is by nature pleasurable but that sexual pleasure is not the main reason for having sex. Enjoying the taste of food is not the main reason for eating. We eat to nourish our bodies and to stay alive. In a similar way, enjoying the pleasure of sex is not the main reason for having sex. Rather, Christians believe God created sex for other, higher reasons than simply pleasure. These reasons are love and life.

In God's plan, sex is meant first to be a physical sign of the love between husband and wife. In addition, God meant that sex be the source for new human life, namely, children whose very existence comes from an act of love between a husband and wife. So, the main reason for sex is not pleasure; rather sex is for love and life. One might say that pleasurable sex is like tasty food; it is a kind of added bonus for those who live out God's plan for sexual intimacy. Pleasure goes with sex, but it is not the main reason for having sex.

Unfortunately, modern pagans have rejected God's plan for sex and refuse to use it as God intended. Nevertheless, because sex plays such a powerful part in life, pagans who misuse it frequently end up deeply hurt by their misuse. The same could be said for many of today's Christians who have been greatly influenced by the pagan culture and who are ignorant of God's plan for sex. They too have been hurt by their unintended misuse of sexual intimacy.

Knowing God's plan for sex is liberating. It gives one freedom to use sex in the way God intended. Furthermore, Christian sex will always be more enjoyable than others kinds of sex. In Christ we find the fullness of revelation about ourselves and about what God expects of us. That means informed

Christians will have the clearest and most precise understanding of God's plan for sex. That understanding will allow them to use sex to its fullest potential, in a way which will bring about the most enjoyment.

As was mentioned previously, to get the most out of something, you first need to know what it is for, and then you need to use it in the way it was designed to be used. Things always work best when you follow the directions. So too with sex. Knowing God's plan for sex and then using it as He intended always works best. With that in mind, let us now examine God's plan for sex in more detail by looking first at the nature of love.

Chapter Nine
THE NATURE OF LOVE

Few English words have as many levels of meaning as does love. That is what makes love so hard to define. Try asking the question, "What is love?" Most people will pause for a moment or two and then reply, "I know what love is but I can't explain it." Some would go on to say that love is a feeling, and others that love is when you care about someone. However, love is more than a feeling. Love is actually a decision to seek out and acquire what is good.

Consider the different ways in which we use love. A young child might say, "Grandma, I love ice cream." A few moments later as grandma prepares a dish of ice cream, that same child might say, "Grandma, I love you!" A young man might say, "I love football." A young woman might say, "I love my cat." Later, that same young woman might ask that same young man, "Do you love me?" In response (without looking up from the game), he might say, "Of course I love you." A mother might say to her children, "I love you more than anything." While on a north woods camping trip, a man might say, "I just love it up here!" Once home, that same man might say to his wife, "You are the best thing that ever happened to me; you are the love of my life." In prayer, one might simply say, "I love you God with all my heart." Saint John tells us "God is love, and he who abides in love abides in God, and God abides in him (1Jn 4:16)."

What is clear from these different ways in which love is used is that love is always linked to what appears good. We love what we judge to be good. No one ever loves what is bad or evil. Instead, we avoid what is bad, and we flee from what is evil.[49]

---

[49] There are times when someone may choose what is objectively evil. However, in those cases, that person has decided that what is bad or evil is a relative good. In other words, they focus on satisfying their immediate desires and not on the big picture. Someone on a diet knows they should not have another piece of cake, but the cake is so good, and they want another piece. So the will sends new instructions to the intellect to recalculate the good of the diet versus the good of another piece of cake. This is called rationalizing, where the truth is overlooked or ignored so that

Jesus once gave His disciples this command, "Love your enemies, do good to those who hate you (Lk 6:27)." Obedience to this command is only possible because, even in our enemies and in those who have done evil, even in those who have deformed and defaced the image of God, there still remains some good. Were there no good at all, love would be impossible. That is why we cannot love the demons or the damned souls. There is no longer any good in them.

With regard to what is good and therefore, what can be loved, there are two categories. First, there are those things which everyone agrees are good. These things are intrinsically good; they are good by their very nature. Health is one example. Everyone agrees that having one's heath is a good thing whereas losing one's heath is a bad thing. Other things such as truth, life, courage and so on are also judged by everyone to be good. The goodness of these things does not depend upon personal opinion or majority vote.

Besides things which are intrinsically good, there are those things we judge to be good based upon personal preferences and tastes. For example, some people like the color blue whereas others prefer yellow or red. Some people like the country whereas others like the city. Some people like baseball and others like hockey. These are examples of relative goods. Their goodness depends upon personal opinion.

In determining what is good, an informed conscience is necessary, and an informed conscience requires both knowledge of and reflection on God's laws. His laws are the standards by which all judgments on the goodness of human actions must be based. God's laws are revealed to us through His creation (the natural law) or through revelation (Divine positive law). One who is knowledgeable of God's laws is said to have an informed conscience.

The process by which we determine what is good always involves our intelligence. By it we determine what is good for us, and love is a response to that good. Seen in this way, love is not so much a feeling as it is a decision. Love is not so much an emotion as it is a choice. We choose to love that which is good, and we may even choose to love those things or persons which appear to others as unlovable. The stray dog, the wayward son and even our enemies, but we can only love them because we see in them some good.

Here then is a definition: *Love is the attraction to that which is good.* This

---

what is objectively bad or evil can be chosen by the will as a relative good.

definition of love works for nearly all of the ways in which we use the word.

That said, it is clear that there is a big difference between loving ice cream and loving your grandma. There is a big difference between loving football and loving your wife. There is a big difference between loving God's creation and loving God.

When we love things such as food or activities or pets, we recognize some good in them, and we desire to have them. Acting on our desires, we take the necessary steps to acquire those things we love. Thus we eat ice cream, or we go skiing, or we buy a pet cat.

On the other hand, when we love another person, when we see them as good, we cannot own or acquire that person as we do things. It would be wrong to keep someone in a cage like a pet canary. It would be wrong to force or compel another to stay with you. It would be wrong to make someone your slave. Clearly, doing so could never be the right way to love another person. It would not respect that person's human dignity. Instead we would be using that person for our own selfish interests.

At one time or another, most of us have been used by someone. Those times were more than a little unpleasant. In them was a recognition that advantage was taken of us and that we were used. We realize that we were just stepping stones. We were deceived and not loved. The bitter feelings and the sense of injustice simply confirm that we were created for love. We are not just chopped liver.

To love another demands that you first respect them as a child of God, as someone whose dignity and worth is equal to yours. All people have this dignity, even the poorest most insignificant person in the world, even a newly conceived child in the womb, even an elderly person with dementia. This dignity comes from the fact that every single human person has been made in God's image and likeness and that we were all purchased with a price and that price was the Blood of Christ (1Cor 6:20). "For Thou wast slain and by Thy Blood didst ransom men for God (Rev 5:9)."

Even atheists who do not accept these principles would agree that we must respect the personal autonomy of others. To disregard the dignity of others or to use them or treat them as a thing or an object is never right and is not love, and is in fact a sin.

Here then is a moral principle: *We can use things, but we can never use people.* To love others, one must begin with the recognition that they too are children of God.

When we recognize the goodness of others, we are naturally drawn to them, and this is not surprising. Human beings are not like grizzly bears or wolverines. We are not solitary animals. Rather, man is a social animal. Normal human beings need and desire interaction with others. Newborns and very young children need human touch for them to fully develop.[50] When we are alone, we seek the company of others; we crave the love of others, and there is a very good reason for this. It is because we are made in God's image and likeness (Gen 1:26).

By His very nature, God is a community of persons, the Father, Son and Holy Spirit. That means no person in God has ever been alone. Man, made in God's image and likeness, reflects this divine society but with a difference. Since God is infinitely perfect and lacks nothing, it means God is social by nature and not by necessity. On the other hand, man who lacks the perfection of God, is social by necessity; man needs others.

Man also reflects that God is love in that he was created out of love and for love. That is why man can only find true fulfillment when he is loving others. That also explains why Jesus said to His disciples, "A new commandment I give to you, that you love one another; even as I have loved you ... (Jn 13:34)." Man would be a very poor image of God if he were to live in isolation, alone and apart from other human beings. In fact, that kind of lifestyle would be a precursor to hell where there is no love at all.

As was mentioned, we are naturally drawn to those we love. We desire to be close to them, and to please them. We are happy when they are happy, and we are sad when they are sad. As love deepens and grows, there is a kind of union of hearts that grows and deepens between those who love and care for each other. There is a spiritual bond which develops. Even our language reflects this. We say some people are soul-mates. We say I love you with all my heart and soul.

Fathers and mothers love their children with this kind of love. Deep friendships also exhibit this kind of love. It explains a mother's happiness at her daughter's wedding and a father's pride at his son's graduation. It also explains why we cry when someone we love has died. It is because we have

---

[50] "How Important Is Physical Contact with Your Infant?" by Katherine Harmon, Scientific America, May 6, 2010.

been wounded deep in our souls.

Love is also expressed in giving of oneself to another. Whether the gift is some thing, or time spent with another, or our prayers, our gifts freely given (and not with the hope for some gain) are all signs of love. Thus parents give of themselves for their children. Friends give of themselves for their friends. Priests and ministers give of themselves for their flocks, and Christ gave of Himself for the world. All interpersonal love is like this.

Love looks to the other and not to the self. Love seeks the good of the other and not the good of the self. Love involves the self-donation of the one who loves to the one who is loved. When a man loves a woman, he thinks about what would make her happy. He is happy when she is happy. A man in love will sacrifice his interests in favor of those of his beloved. He will make great sacrifices to please his beloved and is delighted when he has been successful. Likewise, a woman in love will do the same for the man she loves.

The greater the love, the greater desire one has to express that love and to give more and more of one's self to the other. Gifts given are more carefully chosen or prepared and even then seem inadequate for the one who is loved. Time spent with good friends is delightful and never too long. Monks and nuns in love with God spend long hours at prayer and sacrifice without concern for themselves. "Love does not consist in feeling great things but in knowing great deprivation and great suffering for the Beloved."[51]

At first glance, love would appear to go against one's self-interest. Yet upon further reflection, that is not the case. We were made in God's image and likeness, and since God is love, it is in loving that we find fulfillment and peace. When love seeks the good of the other, there is never a loss. Rather, as one gives, the gift of love is often reciprocated. Love begets love. Thus, in the loving concern for another, more is gained than is lost. Truly, "it is more blessed to give than to receive (Acts 20:35)."

Thus far, we have considered the nature of love apart from sex. That is because most interpersonal love is not sexual in nature. Fathers and mothers love their children. Grandparents love their grandchildren. Friends can have a deep and abiding affection for each other. Yet none of these loving relationships are ever expressed in a sexual way.

This is something modern pagans fail to understand about love. They

---

[51] Saint John of the Cross, Maxim 165.

equate sexual pleasure with love. Consequently, they do not grasp that love for another can at the same time be very deep and yet not sexual. In fact, it is quite possible and normal to have a loving relationship without it also being a sexual relationship.[52]

In reality, God has designed marriage to be the one and only place where the love for another can be expressed in a sexual way. Marriage is the only loving relationship which is also a sexual relationship. Conversely, that means no sexual relationship outside of marriage can ever be loving in a true sense. Let us now see why this is true and how God meant sex to be the unique physical sign of the love which exists between husband and wife.

---

[52] It is also possible to have a sexual relationship without it being a loving relationship. Having sex with a prostitute or sexual assault are two clear examples.

Chapter Ten
SEX IS FOR LOVE

In the Book of Genesis God said, "It is not good that the man should be alone; I will make him a helper fit for him (Gen 2:18)." These words (and those which follow) give us clues regarding the kind of relationships man can enter into. From them we see that man was not made to be alone. Man was made for love.

When God said He would make man a "suitable partner" or "a helper fit for man," He implied that unsuitable partners or unfit helpers could also exist. This became evident as God went on to present the various creatures He had made to the man in order for him to name them.

But "for the man there was not found a helper fit for him (Gen 2:20)." Among all of the animals and birds, none of them were found to be suitable partners for the man. The reason is none of them were made in God's image and likeness.[53] None of them had either an intellect or a free will. Consequently, they could neither know nor love as man does.

It is true that animals can respond to love and affection. In response to affection from their owners, dogs wag their tails and cats purr. However, animals are not capable of friendship in the truest sense of the word because friendship involves sharing in the things proper to one's own nature, and with regard to man, that is something animals cannot do.[54] This is why none of God's creatures were found to be suitable partners for the man.

---

[53] Being made in God's image and likeness is man's distinct privilege; it has been given to man alone because only man was created to share in God's divine nature (2Pet 1:4).

[54] In our pagan society which is often bereft of love, pets and other animals are often substitutes for the missing relationships that should exist between people. This explains why so many people refer to their pets as family members and treat them as children, as their little boys and girls, and so on. It is the craving for human love along with the hurt from failed relationships that cause people to turn to animals for affection. This tendency is seen more often in women than men.

It was then that God created woman. With the woman's creation, the man was no longer alone. When God presented her to the man, he exclaimed, "This at last is bone of my bones and flesh of my flesh; she shall be called Woman because she was taken out of Man (Gen 2:23)." Now at last there was a suitable partner and a fit helper for the man. The woman was able to do what the animals could not do. She could know the man's love for her, and she could also choose to return that love.

We see evidence of this when the man declares, "This at last is bone of my bones and flesh of my flesh."[55] His words express his joy at no longer being alone. Now he is both known and loved. His words also indicate that the loving union between the man and the woman would be expressed, not just in a spiritual way, but also in a physical way, a way intended to be unique to married couples.

Indeed, after the man states "this at last is bone of my bones and flesh of my flesh," the Scriptures declare, "Therefore a man leaves his father and his mother and cleaves to his wife, and they become one flesh (Gen 2:24)." To become one flesh means to be joined bodily through sexual intercourse. Furthermore, to become one flesh reunites a man and woman and restores the state they had before being separated at the woman's creation. Incomplete as individuals, they are now once again made whole. They are no longer incomplete.

That the love of husband and wife should have a physical dimension to it is not surprising. After all, human beings are creatures composed of body and soul. This means our love for one another must be expressed both spiritually and physically, in both the soul and the body. In fact, we cannot make our love known to the other without some physical contact. Without us speaking,[56] gesturing, listening attentively, or touching, the other person would not be able to know what is on our minds and in our hearts.

We make our love known to others whenever we smile, wave, or say hello

---

[55] It is important to note that Adam and Eve were married, and this fact is clear from the scriptures. For example, we read that Adam "called his *wife's* name Eve because she was the mother of all the living (Gen 3:20)." We also read that, "Adam knew Eve his *wife*, and she conceived and bore Cain (Gen 4:1)." In fact, Adam and Eve were the very first married couple.

[56] Even writing, emailing or texting still involves speaking through the medium of written words.

to people we know. Good friends have "heart to heart" talks. Mothers hold their babies and coo to them. Grandchildren hug their grandparents, and boyfriends and girlfriends hold hands. Furthermore, the deeper the love, the closer and more intimate the physical contact. Parents will kiss their children but not their co-workers. A man will embrace his fiancée but not some cashier at the convenience store. A husband and wife also express their love with physical contact, and this contact is the most intimate of all. A married couple becomes physically one by uniting their bodies through sexual intercourse, an act unique to marriage.

Notice how this deeper union of hearts develops and ultimately leads to marriage. As a man's love for a woman grows, so too does his desire to please her. He does things for her. He spends time with her. He gives her things. In the end, he decides to risk everything; he decides to offer her the most valuable thing he has, namely himself. He will offer to her all that he is in the hope that she will be pleased with his gift and it will delight her. So he approaches her, filled with excitement and hope, but also with anxiety and trepidation and asks, "Will you marry me?"

For her part, if she loves him, she is delighted with his offer and accepts it. Likewise, implicit in her acceptance is her gift to him. Included in her "Yes" is her resolution to give her most valuable possession to him, namely herself, all that she is, and this is only right. Her gift must complement his gift. Her gift must be equivalent to the one she has just been offered and accepted. Were she to accept his gift of self, yet offer something less than her whole self in return, it would be disproportionate. She cannot give less than her whole self.

To be able to give one's whole self to another requires a complete trust in them. We are open and honest with those whom we trust, but we are only totally open and honest with those whom we trust completely. Only then do we feel confident that we can reveal to the other person what is on our hearts and minds, our innermost hopes and fears. This kind of revelation leaves one vulnerable to profound hurt if someone were to betray the trust that was placed in them. It explains why we only reveal ourselves completely to those whom we trust completely.

It is interesting to note that before the fall, Adam and Eve had this sort of trust for each other. In the Scriptures, we are told that they were naked and were not ashamed because they had nothing to hide from each other (Gen 2:25). Their nakedness symbolized their complete trust in each other, a trust which made their complete gift of self to the other possible. In a similar way, when a husband and wife engage in sexual intercourse they are naked and their nakedness symbolizes that in their hearts, they have nothing to hide from each other. In marriage there is a total openness, which also means total vulnerability. There is nothing hidden from the other.

Once a couple's love has grown to the point that they desire to be one, all that remains is for them to make a formal declaration of their love. This declaration takes place at their wedding when they exchange their marriage vows before God and His Church. With their formal declaration of love complete, their love can then be ratified or consummated by the union of their bodies. Sexual intercourse is the physical sign of their oneness in heart and soul; it is an expression of their total gift of one to the other. Note well that in all of this there is a proper order. The union of hearts is completed only with the exchange of vows. Only then, after the vows have been exchanged, can the union of bodies take place. It is only within marriage that sexual intercourse becomes a true and real sign of the union of hearts. Let us examine in more detail why this is so.

In God's original plan for the human race, marriage is the most fundamental institution, and central to all family life. Furthermore, God meant for marriage to be a holy thing. In Hebrews it states, "Let marriage be held in honor among all, and let the marriage bed be undefiled; for God will judge the immoral and adulterous (Heb 13:4)." That marriage is a great thing in God's plan is attested to by the fact that Jesus worked His first miracle at the wedding in Cana (Jn 2:1–11). God never does anything by accident; everything is planned. Thus, this miracle, worked at the request of the Blessed Virgin Mary, was deliberate. It was intended to emphasize the importance of marriage in God's plan.

In speaking about marriage, Saint Paul directs husbands and wives to be subject to one another out of reverence for Christ (Eph 5:21). In other words, both must willingly and lovingly give up their self-interests for the good of the other and the good of their marriage. However, they will do this in different ways that are appropriate to each as a man or as a woman. As single people, both the man and the woman were free to make their own decisions without regard for anyone else. But as a married couple, they must now consider the needs and desires of their spouse. Only by doing this will the two be able to grow as one.

Thus, husbands are told, "Love your wives, as Christ loved the Church and gave Himself up for Her (Eph 5:25)." Just as Christ died to sanctify the Church so that "She might be holy and without blemish," so too husbands are to die for their wives that they might be holy and without blemish in the sight of Christ.

This means a husband must sacrifice his independence and freedom for the good of his wife and his marriage. He must also put the needs of his wife and family ahead of his own. His spousal love demands that he sacrifice all, even his very life so that his beloved might get to heaven. He gives of himself so that one day she will be able to "stand before the throne and before the Lamb, clothed in a white robe with a palm branch in her hand (Rev 7:9)."

Wives are told, "Be subject to your husbands, as to the Lord (Eph 5:22)." This means a wife must willingly and lovingly submit to the authority of her husband. A wife must sacrifice her independence and freedom for the good of her husband and her marriage. This does not mean that the husband can order his wife around or insist that she do what he commands as a master might do with a servant. Rather, it means that after both have discussed things and considered each other's points of view, if there is still an impasse or a disagreement, the wife would graciously defer to the authority of her husband. Wives whose husbands love them as Christ loved the Church should never fear being subject to their husbands in such a way because such husbands would never ask of their wives anything they did not think was good for them and for their marriage.

By willingly submitting to the authority of her husband, the wife acknowledges that there is a hierarchy in marriage and that one body cannot have two heads. That is what Saint Paul meant when he said, "the husband is the head of the wife as Christ is the head of the Church (Eph 5:23)." Her spousal love demands that she sacrifice the independence she had as a single woman so that her beloved might get to heaven. Saint Peter also makes this clear when he says, "Likewise you wives, be submissive to your husbands, so that some, though they do not obey the word [of God], may be won over without a word by the behavior of their wives (1Pet 3:1)."

God designed sex to help the husband love his wife as Christ loved the Church. He also designed sex to help the wife be subject to her husband. That is why after Saint Paul tells husbands to love their wives as they do their own bodies, he quotes from Genesis and says, "For this reason a man shall leave his father and mother and be joined to his wife, and the two shall become one flesh (Eph 5:31)." Being one flesh by being united bodily through sexual intercourse helps both the husband and wife realize they are meant to be one in heart and mind. It reminds them that they must work together for the good of the whole and that in so doing, they will grow in love. God designed sexual intercourse for this very purpose. Sex is meant for love.

Finally, in concluding his comments on marriage, Saint Paul points out that sex is not only a physical sign of the love and spiritual union between the spouses, it is also a sign of a far more significant union. In a mysterious way, marriage is also meant to be a sign of the union between Christ and His Church. As Saint Paul says, "This mystery is a profound one, and I mean in reference to Christ and the Church (Eph 5:32)."

****

Modern pagans see no reason to link sexual intercourse to marriage. That is because they do not see its deeper meaning as a sign of the union of hearts. Instead, their focus is almost exclusively on sexual pleasure which can be found both inside and outside of marriage. At the same time, modern pagans like to think that when they are "having sex" outside of marriage, they are still somehow "making love."

That sex has something to do with love should come as no surprise, and here the pagans are on to something. After all, the phrase "making love" is a common euphemism for "having sex." However, these two expressions are not equivalent. The phrase "making love" implies a certain generosity and concern for the other. One who makes love is giving something to the other. In marriage, it is a sign of the total gift of one person to another.

On the other hand, "having sex" implies a certain selfishness and lack of concern for the other. One who has sex is taking something from the other. One who has sex does not love the other but instead uses the other for his or her own selfish pleasure and satisfaction. In marriage when there is not a complete gift of one to the other or when people have sex outside of marriage, sexual intercourse always involves taking advantage of the other and using the other on some level. To see why this is so, consider the following possibilities.

Suppose a man promised in his marriage vows that he would be 99.7% faithful. In other words, that he might have sex with someone else just once a year. Other than that, he would be completely and totally faithful. No self-respecting woman would be satisfied with this kind of promise. Similarly, if it was the woman who made this sort of promise, no clear-thinking man would go along with it, and the reason is not hard to understand.

A husband who promised to be anything less than 100% faithful to his wife has only offered part of himself to her. To promise anything less than total fidelity is to say that she is not good enough for him. In other words, that she is inadequate to meet all of his needs. To make that kind of promise is to say to his wife that he needs something more than what she can give him, but she has already given all that she has, namely, her whole self. She has nothing more to give. Love could never grow in that kind of a relationship.[57] Clearly, anything less than total fidelity would not be loving the wife but simply using her, and that is hurtful in the extreme.

In a similar way, if a man agreed to marry a woman for a certain length of time but not for life, say for ten years (perhaps with an option to extend the marriage for another ten year after that), he would likewise be using the woman and not loving her. Again, the man would only be giving part of himself. By promising to be faithful for only a certain period of time, he would be hedging his bets in the event someone more interesting came along. If that occurred, he could then leave his wife for that new person when their commitment was up.

A woman who promised anything less that 100% fidelity or who only promised to marry a man for a certain length of time would not be loving the man but simply using him. She would be in the same position as a man who did this.

It is clear that without life-long fidelity, the union of hearts is not possible and neither is true love. Without life-long fidelity, either one or both would end up using the other. Then sexual intercourse would become a false sign and in fact a non-verbal lie. True love is possible only when there is a commitment to life-long fidelity. Anything less would not be loving the other but rather using the other. This explains why marriage requires a commitment that is

---

[57] This also explains why polygamy can never lead to true love. A husband with more than one wife would be a husband divided. His heart would not belong to one woman but would be shared by however many wives he had. He would end up using and not loving his wives. This explains the Muslim attitude towards woman who in theory are respected but in practice are treated as second class citizens.

both faithful and life-long.

The necessity of life-long fidelity in marriage is also affirmed in the Scriptures. The sixth commandment states, "You shall not commit adultery (Ex 20:14)." Jesus Himself declares, "What therefore God has joined together, let not man put asunder (Mk 10:9, Mt 19:6)." These commands affirm the structure of marriage outlined above, a structure which God has designed so that love can grow.

Outside of marriage, sexual intercourse is always a selfish act and a sin. Outside of marriage it becomes a kind of fraudulent body language. It would be similar to the handshake of a false friend or the smile of an enemy.

The most serious misuse of sexual intercourse outside of marriage is adultery. Married persons who have sex with someone not their spouse sin gravely, and their acts of adultery are in no way love. Rather, they are acts of betrayal. The act of adultery says to the other, you have given me everything, all that you are, but I have found you wanting and went elsewhere to be satisfied. That revelation is always devastating to the other and explains why adultery is so destructive to a marriage.

Sexual intercourse between unmarried persons is called fornication; it too is a selfish act and a lie. That is because no promises have been made and no vows have been exchanged. It is simply two people using each other. This is most clear when someone engages in sex with a prostitute. That act is simply a commercial transaction, an exchange of money for sexual pleasure where no commitment and no love are involved.

However, even when there is some level of commitment, as for example sex between those who are cohabiting, it still reduces to two people using each other for their own ends. Because a commitment to a life-long, faithful union is lacking, so too is complete trust and that makes true love impossible. Since both parties are free to leave at any time, no true union of hearts can exist.

Even when couples are engaged, if they are having premarital sex, they are still using each other (but to a lesser extent). While they plan to wed, they have not yet done so. Until they actually give themselves to each other in marriage, until they actually exchange their vows, they still have the freedom to call off the wedding. They can still change their minds and marry someone else. However, after the vows have been exchanged and the two have become one, there is no longer that possibility. There must be a union of hearts before there is a union of bodies, and the union of hearts takes place when the vows are recited.

Because the physical union of husband and wife is meant to be a sign of their union in heart and mind, sexual intercourse makes no sense outside of marriage where no complete union exists. While some relationships involving sexual intimacy do have a certain level of love and commitment, without a commitment to fidelity and a life-long union, these relationships will always entail at least one using the other, if not both. That explains why sexual relationships outside of marriage can never be entered into by Christians (or by others who seek true love). True love can be found only in marriage which requires the total gift of the man to the woman and of the woman to the man.

Chapter Eleven

SEX IS FOR LIFE

The Book of Genesis tells us that after God created Adam and Eve, He blessed them and said to them, "Be fruitful and multiply, and fill the earth and subdue it ... (Gen 1:28)." It is noteworthy that God's words here are in the form of a command. His words were not simply suggestions or proposals presented to Adam and Eve for their consideration. Rather, God gave the two of them a job. The earth was empty, and God ordered them to fill it with other human beings. They were to have children and grandchildren so that the earth might be populated. From this we see that married love was meant to be fruitful and that children, the fruit of married love, would be the means by which the human race would continue into the future.[58]

It's interesting that the Bible often uses the image of fruit-bearing plants and their produce as an analogy for women and childbearing. Thus we read that "the fruit of the womb is a reward (Ps 127:3)." We are told that while in Egypt, "the descendants of Israel were fruitful and increased greatly (Ex 1:7)." We hear Saint Elizabeth declare to the Blessed Virgin Mary, "Blessed are you among women and blessed is the fruit of your womb (Lk 1:42)!" Furthermore, to be fruitful implies not less of something but more. Just as a fruitful vine produces many grapes or a fruitful harvest yields thirty or sixty or a hundred fold, so too a fruitful womb produces abundant life.

In order that Adam and Eve might succeed in carrying out His command, God gave them power over the earth and all it contained. They were to tame the earth and subdue it. They would have dominion over the birds of the air and over all creatures on land and in the sea, as well as all the plants. By using the things of the earth, they would have food, clothing and shelter, and they would be able to raise and support their family.

But the question remained, how would this new life come about? How

---

[58] Here note again, that Adam and Eve were married. The commission of bringing new human life into the world was given to married couples. There is no scriptural evidence nor any in Christian tradition that allows for procreation outside of marriage.

would Adam and Eve be fruitful? They themselves were the result of God's own handiwork. God had no help in creating them, nor did He need any. However, God was now charging Adam and Eve with the task of bringing new human life into the world. They were the ones commanded to be fruitful and multiply. However, their fruitfulness would differ in two significant ways from how God had created them.

First, the creation of new human life would now come about in a physical way. It would be by means of sexual intercourse, that most intimate, physical expression of love between a husband and wife. In that physical act where the union of hearts is expressed in a bodily way, God placed the potential for new human life.

In this new way of creating human life, the father and mother would each contribute part of the material that goes into making up the body of their child. This material is analogous to the dust of the earth from which God fashioned the body of Adam or the rib of Adam from which God fashioned the body of Eve. In this way, the couple's role in the creation of new human life bears a certain similarity to the way God created the bodies of Adam and Eve.[59]

However, the contributions of the father and mother, while necessary in God's plan, are not sufficient by themselves to bring about new life. It is true that the human body is formed from the genetic material contributed by the parents, but for new human life to come about, something more is needed. Because the human soul is spiritual and beyond man's ability to create and

---

[59] Let us suppose (as most biologists maintain) that God used animals as the material source (or cause) for the bodies of our first parents. This does not create a problem for the Christian understanding of man. Precisely because our souls are spiritual, each human soul must be directly created by God, and there are several ways God could have done this. He could have created our bodies out of nothing. He could have designed us so that new human life would come about asexually. Humans could have reproduced by simply dividing as do simple organisms or by growing sprouts like potatoes that could be cut off to become a new person. However, Genesis says that God created Adam from the dust of the earth which means God did not create Adam out of nothing but rather used materials which He had previously made to fashion Adam's body. Many Christians assume that this dust was unformed. However, there is no problem with God having used dust that had already been formed into a living, non-human being for Adam's body. What is important to understand is that if this were the case, that non-human being would become a human being not gradually, but the instant that God created the soul of Adam.

because each person is unique, God must directly act to create that soul. Only when He does so will a new human person bearing His divine image come into existence. This explains why the word procreation rather than reproduction more aptly describes the creation of new human life. Procreation is only used with regard to human generation. It implies creation with God. Animals reproduce, but only human beings procreate.

The second way in which the creation of new human life differs from the way in which God created Adam and Eve is this. God no longer creates alone. Instead, God now partners with married couples to bring new life into the world. God now shares His creative power with the husband and wife. In that sense, God gives the married couple a great power, and this new power is something far greater than even the power over life and death. One might call it a "God power." That is because married couples are able to decide whether or not a new human being will even exist, and not just in this world, but for all eternity.

In essence, when it comes to the question of new human life, God has submitted His creative power to the consent of the husband and wife. If a couple says "Yes" to new life, if they are open to life, God may create a new life. However, if they say "No" to life, even if God had planned to bless them with a child, He will not violate their freedom and create new life against their will. This freedom to accept or reject life is clear in God's command to Adam and Eve. While they were directed to be fruitful, God did not remove their freedom to say "No." The same could be said for every couple.

Here one might object that some couples who have said "No" to life still conceive. It may appear that in these cases of "contraceptive failure" or in the rare instances where conception occurs after sterilization that God has violated the couple's freedom. However, that is not the case. God always respects our freedom, but God has also bound Himself to the laws of His creation. That means when a couple conceives against their will, God has not violated their freedom to say "No." Rather, it simply means that the couple has failed to adequately understand the laws of nature and some essential step required for the prevention of conception has been overlooked.

It cannot be overstated how significant is the gift of fertility that God entrusts to married couples. There is essentially nothing man can make here on earth that will last forever. However, the children that parents accept and bring into the world and who are judged worthy of heaven will live with God forever. They will exist for all eternity. Married couples would do well to frequently reflect on this fact.

New human life always enriches both the family of God and the family of man. Through it, heaven is filled with the saints who stand before God's throne in joyful praise. Because no one person could ever do or know everything required for a decent life here on earth, new human life makes life easier for all. Tasks are shared. Things are invented. Learning is advanced. At the same time, new human life also enriches each individual family.

New life is the primary fruit of married love and enriches both the life and love of husband and wife. Rather than dividing their love into thirds, a child expands its parent's love. Now there is not only the love between spouses, but also the love between father and child and the love between mother and child. Later, love will continue to grow between generations and between relations. The love between grandchildren and grandparents and the love between cousins are examples of this.

While it is certainly true that raising children requires sacrifices, the graces received in cooperating with God will always outweigh those sacrifices. Even in those cases where children turn out to be disappointments or sources of pain for their parents (as Cain was for Adam and Eve, Absolom for King David, and Eli's two sons, Hophni and Phinehas), there is still the consolation couples receive by doing God's will and accepting His gift of fertility. Jesus said, "Whoever does the will of my Father in heaven is my brother and sister and mother (Mt 12:50)." Couples who are open to life and willing to accept children from God are always pleasing to Him. They are part of His family, and God will reward those who serve Him.

That children are blessings from God is a constant theme in the Bible. This is clear from the Psalms where we read, "Lo, sons are a heritage from the Lord, the fruit of the womb a reward (Ps 127:3)." Also, "Blessed is everyone who fears the Lord ... Your wife will be like a fruitful vine within your house; your children will be like olives shoots around your table (Ps 128:1, 3)." And, "Praise the Lord! ... He gives the barren woman a home making her the joyous mother of children (Ps 113:1, 9)." Below are some further examples in which children are described as blessings:

* When He established a covenant with Abraham, God said, "Behold, my covenant is with you, and you shall be the father of a multitude of

nations. No longer shall your name be Abram, but your name shall be Abraham; for I have made you the father of a multitude of nations. I will make you exceedingly fruitful; and I will make nations of you, and kings shall come forth from you (Gen 17:4–6)."

* God promised the chosen people that because they were obedient and had kept His ordinances, He would keep His covenant with them; He would "multiply them;" He would bless "the fruit of their body and the fruit of their ground." He also promised, "You shall be blessed above all peoples; there shall not be male or female barren among you, or among your cattle (Deut 7:14)."

* For many years, Rachel, the wife of Jacob was childless. At one point she cried out to Jacob, "Give me children or I shall die (Gen 30:1)." At last God remembered her and opened her womb and she conceived and bore a son, Joseph. Rachel then said, "God has taken away my reproach (Gen 30:23)."

* Hannah, the wife of Elkanah, was childless and for that she wept and was sad. After many prayers she conceived and bore a son, Samuel. She later went back to the temple and worshiped because the Lord had granted her prayer for a son (1Sam 1:27–28).

* Saint Elizabeth who was childless rejoiced after conceiving Saint John the Baptist and proclaimed, "Thus the Lord has done to me in the days when He looked on me, to take away my reproach among men (Lk 1:25)."

On the other hand, those who do not have children are considered cursed. Others were sometimes punished with sterility for their infidelity. For example:

* Because of their idolatry and plots, the Prophet Jeremiah cursed Israel and prayed, "let their wives become childless and widowed (Jer 18:21)."

* After Michal ridiculed King David for dancing before the ark of God, she was punished and "had no child to the day of her death (2Sam 6:23)."

* The punishment for immoral sexual unions is to die childless. (Lev 20:20, 21).

* As punishment for Israel's sin, the Prophet Hosea declares, "Ephraim's glory shall fly away like a bird – no birth, no pregnancy, no conception (Hos 9:11)!"

As can be seen, part of God's plan for sex involves procreation which is intrinsically linked to sexual intercourse. Love and life go together. This means openness to life must be an essential part of married love. Children are meant to be the natural result of love making. While married couples are free to reject this part of God's plan, doing so will always be an offense against God and His generosity. Couples who reject their gift of fertility not only reject the power to decide if new life will come about, but they also reject the trust God has placed in them. In addition, they reject the blessings of any children God had planned to give them.

For a married couple to reject their fertility would be similar to a skilled surgeon declining to perform surgery to save a life or a farmer refusing to plant crops to feed the hungry. Someone who has the power and ability to do good but refuses to do so out of selfishness commits a sin of omission. In a similar way, couples who decline to partner with God in bringing new life into the world, also sin.

There is also another more subtle problem for couples who reject the gift of fertility. To say "No" to life is also to say "No" to love. As was mentioned previously, when a couple marries, each gives to the other his or her whole self. At the same time, the gift given must be totally accepted, otherwise one spouse (or both) will end up using the other.

To see this, consider what would happen if a man said to his wife, I will accept your gift to me as long as you remain young and beautiful. However, if you put on a little weight or start going grey, I'm going to start looking for a new wife. Similarly, consider what would happen if a woman said to her husband, I will accept your gift to me as long as you are healthy, but if you come down with a debilitating illness, I will leave you. It would be impossible for love to grow in either of these relationships.

Quite simply, the human person cannot be divided into parts. We have spiritual, intellectual, emotional, physical and sexual dimensions to us, but these all come together in one package. When a man gives himself to a woman in marriage, he gives all that he is, including his fertility, his power to father a child. Similarly, when a woman gives herself to a man in marriage, she gives all that she is, including her fertility, her ability to conceive a child.

One cannot give everything to the other except for his or her fertility and one cannot accept everything from the other except for his or her fertility. If a husband said to his wife, "I love all of you except your fertility; I don't want that," he would be rejecting an essential part of her. Similarly, if a wife said to her husband, "I love all of you except your fertility; I don't want that," she would be rejecting an essential part of him. How could either one not feel the rejection of something which goes to the very core of who we are? To reject the beloved's fertility would be to harm and damage the union of hearts. Doing so not only impedes the growth of love, but over time it can kill love altogether. To reject the gift of fertility is to be selfish with God, selfish with one's spouse and to reduce love to the use of the other.

Finally, to reject one's fertility (except in the case of total abstinence) is often accomplished by means of some drug or operation that does harm to the body. In both cases, this violates the fifth commandment, "You shall not kill (Ex 20:13)."

God's plan is that love and life must be kept together and not separated. Keeping them together opens one up to God's blessings. Separating them always has negative spiritual, moral and physical consequences. In God's plan, sex was made not only for love but also for life.

****

Modern pagans reject the idea that sex is for life.[60] In fact, they severed the link between love and life long ago. For them, having sex is all about pleasure, and babies are not part of the equation. Pregnancy is simply an obstacle to be overcome so that pleasure can be maximized. This attitude is made clear by their willingness to kill unborn children through abortion or abortifacient drugs. It is seen by their widespread use of contraception and sterilization. Finally, for those pagans who do have children, it is revealed by their tiny families and by not having children until they are "ready."

Modern pagans make no distinction between procreation and reproduction. They fail to appreciate the privileged position they have as partners with God in creating new life. They do not reflect on the marvelous power they have received to contribute the material for new life, nor that without their consent, God will not create new life. They believe they have absolute power over their fertility and are responsible to no one for how they

---

[60] Recall that it has been nearly a hundred years since Margaret Sanger founded the Birth Control League.

use it, including God.

Modern pagans do not believe that children are gifts from God, and most are not open to life (except on their own terms). Consequently, they scoff at the idea that married love was meant to be fruitful. They think it ridiculous that mankind should "Be fruitful and multiply." To them, babies are expensive and annoying, and children are burdens which restrict their freedom and finances. So, whatever children are to pagans, they are certainly not blessings.

Often, pagans who do have children see them as a kind of accessory to their materialistic relationships. When all is said and done, once they have all they want and are settled and secure in their jobs, then perhaps, they might consider having a child or two. Other pagans simply reject the idea of having any children at all. Some have joined organizations such as "Childless by Choice" and "Childfree Life." There they find support for their selfish and voluntary decision to remain barren.

While modern pagans have separated sexual intercourse from procreation in their minds, this has proved much harder to accomplish in practice. As was mentioned previously, human beings come as an integrated package, and it is only with great difficulty (if at all) that their parts can be separated in any real way. This explains the huge amount of time and energy that has gone into devising ways to prevent sexual intercourse from leading to pregnancy.

Nearly all of these methods cause physical harm, especially to women who must take pills and shots which alter the body's natural function. Incurable diseases are contracted by engaging in supposedly "safe sex." Both men and women have resorted to surgical sterilization which mutilates the body and disables a healthy bodily function. Sadly, many women have resorted to abortion when their "family planning method" failed to prevent pregnancy.

Besides the physical harm, these methods also cause emotional harm as both men and women use each other for their own gratification. They encourage cohabitation where couples never marry and have children. They also harm marriages as a kind of ennui creeps in and stifles love. This in turn harms society as homes and families are broken apart when love dies and these marriages fail. Finally, there is the spiritual harm which alienates souls from God because of their disobedience to His command to increase and multiply.

By rejecting how God has made them and attempting to separate love from life, pagans end up using instead of loving the other. In so doing, they destroy any hope of ever experiencing real love. When love and life are separated, even in the most committed relationships, some element of use will creep in to erode and destabilize that commitment.

****

Christians must beware of false ideas regarding sex and procreation. They need to realize that in subtle and not so subtle ways, the idea that love and life can be separated has been promoted for decades. It would be very surprising if this idea has not influenced their thinking and attitudes about procreation in some way.

For example, most Christians (but not all) see fertility as God's gift and children as God's blessings, but blessings in only very limited numbers. For many, fruitfulness generally means just two children, and four or five would be considered a huge family. Furthermore, when planning their families, many start from a materialistic position. They think having a baby should take place only after careful consideration, proper planning and adequate financial reserves have been built up. In that sense, they have unwittingly accepted the idea that they are in total control of their fertility and that it all depends on them. They forget that they are in fact partners with God in bringing new life into the world, and that He will help provide for them.

Because love has been divorced from life for so long, few Christians now believe that each and every act of sexual intercourse must remain open to the possible conception of new life. Most would consider this to be an extremist position. Instead, they accept the idea that an act of intercourse can be rendered infertile if they do not want children at that time. This infertility can be either temporary as when contraceptives are used or permanent if sterilization is chosen.[61]

Certainly no faithful Christian would ever consider joining an organization like Childless by Choice or Childfree Life. However, not a few belong to Planned Parenthood which promotes all of the pagan ideas about sex that have been described earlier.

Our pagan culture's attitudes about sex have deformed our understanding about the life-giving end of marriage. It would not be wrong to say that many

---

[61] These issues will be addressed in Chapter 14 "Family Planning." At that time, moral family planning methods that do not separate love and life will be discussed.

Christians have unwittingly accepted both its practice of planning their families without consulting God in prayer, and of temporarily or permanently separating love and life by contraceptive use or sterilization. Christians should keep in mind that there is no scriptural evidence to support these positions, nor is there any in Christian tradition. In God's plan, love and life must always be kept together. To separate love and life, even on an intermittent or temporary basis, is to go against God's plan.

At this point, Christians should be asking themselves several questions. Where do I get my ideas about love and life? Are they scriptural? Are they consistent with the teachings of Jesus and of His Church? If not, what must I change so that love can grow in my life?

Chapter Twelve
THE DEFINITION OF MARRIAGE AND THE DEFINITION OF FAMILY

While there are many definitions of marriage and family circulating in our pagan culture, nearly all of them fall short of what Christians believe about marriage and family. For that reason, Christians need to have their own definitions of marriage and of family, definitions that incorporate all of God's teachings regarding love and life. The definitions used by Christians should bring all of the various elements of God's plan for sex together in a concise and understandable form. In point of fact, Christians do have these kinds of definitions, and two of these will be used as the basis for our concluding remarks on God's plan for sex. Since families begin with marriage, we will look first at the definition of marriage and then at the definition of family. Our first definition, that of marriage, follows below:

> Marriage is a covenant, by which a man and a woman establish between themselves a partnership of the whole of life. This covenant is by its nature ordered toward the good of the spouses and the procreation and education of offspring. Finally, between baptized persons, this covenant has been raised by Christ the Lord to the dignity of a sacrament.[62]

Our definition begins by noting that marriage is more than a contract. Rather, marriage is a covenant. Just as God established covenants with Abraham, Noah and David, so too when a man and a woman marry, they establish a covenant between themselves and also with God. This distinction between a covenant and a contract is significant. Contracts are conditional whereas covenants are not. In general, contracts involve an exchange of goods or services whereas covenants involve an exchange of persons. The fulfilling of one's contractual obligations is linked to the other party fulfilling his or her contractual obligations. Thus, if the first party fails to fulfill his contractual obligations, the second party is no longer bound to his contractual obligations.

---

[62] Code of Canon Law, 1983, C. 1055, §1

If someone takes out a loan to purchase a car, he or she agrees to pay monthly installments for a certain period of time. In return, the car dealer gives that person the keys to the car. If payments are not made, the dealer (or bank) can then repossess the car.

Marriage is not like taking out a loan. In marriage, the vows a man and a woman make to each other are unconditional. One does not say to the other, "If you don't get sick, then I will take you as my lawful spouse." The man does not say, "As long as you don't go gray, I will take you as my lawful wife." The woman does not say, "If you don't snore, then I will take you as my lawful husband." Rather, both bride and groom make unconditional promises to each other. The man says, "I take you for my lawful wife, to have and to hold, from this day forward, for better, for worse, for richer, for poorer, in sickness and in health until death do us part." The woman says, "I take you for my lawful husband, to have and to hold, from this day forward, for better, for worse, for richer, for poorer, in sickness and in health until death do us part."

Marriage vows are intended to make clear that future events (which in most cases cannot be foreseen) have no bearing on the promises each spouse makes to the other. That is why the vows are not stated conditionally. They are stated without any conditions or reservations.

The Christian view of marriage is in marked contrast with that of the state. The state looks upon marriage as a contract only. In fact, even less than a normal contract because with no fault divorce, one party can simply leave the marriage without any legal consequence or remedy for the other. Unlike every other contract, one party can simply break the contract and the other has no legal recourse.

Next, our definition states that marriage is between a man and woman, and here the definition highlights another feature of marriage. Christian marriage is by definition between one man and one woman. Marriage is not between two men or two women, nor is marriage between groups of people. So called "gay marriage" or same-sex unions are excluded from this definition. Christian marriage does not admit multiple spouses either. Polygamy is not allowed.

While our definition calls marriage a partnership, it is a special kind of partnership. It is a "partnership of the whole of life" and not simply a part of life. In life, there are any number of relationships. At work, there are relationships between the employer and the employees, and there are relationships with one's coworkers. Church members have a relationship with each other as brothers and sisters in Christ. In the family, there are relationships between parents and children, between siblings, between grandparents and grandchildren and so on. The closer the relationship, the greater the love and the more that is shared. However, all human relationships differ from marital relationships in one significant way. Marriage is the only human relationship that, by design, is also a sexual relationship. In that sense, in a consummated marriage, a partnership of the whole of life also includes the gift of one's body to the other.

That marriage is a partnership of the whole of life also means that marriage must be entered into freely. There can be no coercion with regard to the consent that is given on the part of either party. There can be no force or fear involved. Marriage is a partnership not a dictatorship. One party does not have the right to dominate the other, nor should one party fear the other. To compel another to marry or to use force or fear to coerce them into marriage is not a partnership and would not be the proper medium to grow either trust or love.

To be able to enter into marriage freely also implies the ability to give consent. This means both the man and the woman must have a certain level of maturity as well as an understanding about the nature of marriage. For their consent to be valid, they must clearly understand what they are doing and the implications of the consent they are giving. These conditions prevent certain people from marrying such as children who lack the maturity and knowledge to give informed consent and those who suffer from severe mental retardation.

Similarly, there are some people who are incapable of giving consent due to mental illness. Even though they are adults and may understand full well what marriage is and the commitment marriage requires, because of some neurosis or trauma or other problem, they are rendered incapable of keeping commitments. Were they to attempt to enter into marriage, their consent would be impaired and not valid. A valid marriage requires both the understanding of what marriage is and the ability to give consent to what marriage is.

A partnership for the whole of life also means that the matrimonial covenant continues in force from the point at which the vows are exchanged until one's spouse dies. At that point, the remaining spouse is no longer bound by his or her vows. That marriage involves a life-long commitment means that even desertion or infidelity does not release innocent parties from the promises they have made to God and to their spouse. Once the vows are exchanged, they remain in force until one or the other dies.[63] Note also that marriage is a temporal or earthly covenant. As Jesus said, "In the resurrection they neither marry nor are given in marriage, but are like angels in heaven (Mt 22:30)." This also means there will not be sexual intimacy in heaven.

A partnership of the whole of life means both husband and wife are faithful to each other, and this means more than just physical fidelity (not having sexual intercourse with someone else). Married persons give themselves totally to the other, and this must include how they act and behave and even how they think. Going out with someone of the opposite sex, flirting, dating, and even daydreaming about someone else are not appropriate behaviors for married persons. These things all involve infidelity at some level.

All of the things discussed thus far, that marriage is a covenant, that it is a sexual relationship, that it is entered into freely, that it is between a man and a woman, and that it involves a life-long and faithful commitment, all of these things might be called the properties or characteristics of marriage. They are a description of what marriage is. Our definition now turns to the ends or purposes of marriage which explain why marriage is as it is.

There are two reasons for marriage, and they are closely connected. The first is for the good of the spouses. As God said, "It is not good for the man to be alone (Gen 2:18)." (Nor is it good for the woman to be alone.) We were made in God's image and likeness, and as such, we were made for love. Husbands and wives are to help each other. They are to assist each other on their journey through life to heaven, and they are to love each other. That is what is meant by the good of the spouses.

The second reason for marriage is children. From the physical expression of love in sexual intercourse, children are conceived and born into the world. In this essential part of God's plan, the husband and wife cooperate with God in bringing new life into the world. Parents are also entrusted with the

---

[63] In that sense, the marriage covenant is similar to the covenants God established with the Israelites. Even in those times when the Israelites were unfaithful, God still remained faithful. Here it should be noted that to remain faithful does not always mean one spouse can continue to live with the other. There are times such as desertion or the danger of abuse where remaining together is no longer possible. In those times one spouse can separate from the other, but that does not mean that spouse can also remarry. Marriage vows remain in force until death parts them.

responsibility and authority of raising and educating those children. Primarily, this means teaching them about God and His love for them. It also means teaching them how to get to heaven by loving God and their neighbor. Secondarily, it means teaching them life skills so that they might succeed in the world and use their God-given talents for good and for the betterment of humanity.

Finally, our definition notes that marriage between the baptized is also a Sacrament.[64] In the Sacrament of marriage, the husband and wife receive special graces from God to aid and assist them in their married duties and in keeping their vows to each other.

****

We are now ready to look at the nature and definition of family. Our definition follows below:

> "A man and a woman, united in marriage, together with their children, form a family."[65]

Our definition notes that Christian families begin with and are built upon marriage. When a man and a woman have exchanged their marriage vows, they become a new family. Furthermore, as the basic social unit, families serve as both the foundation and the building blocks of every society.

All earthly relationships not built on marriage are only families in an extended sense. For example, residents in a group home may be referred to as a family but only in the sense that they live together in close proximity. Their relationships are not founded on marriage. Similarly, in a certain paternalistic way, large corporations might refer to their workers as their corporate family, but again this is an extension of the word family and hardly resembles a family

---

[64] Note here that Catholic and Orthodox Churches regard marriage as a Sacrament between two baptized persons who are free to marry, and this includes marriages between two baptized Protestants. Protestant denominations generally do not regard marriage as a Sacrament. Instead, most Protestant denominations regard marriage as the first institution designed by God. In Protestant theology, marriage represents the highest example of the relationship between Christ and His Bride, the Church, and as such, is a holy thing.

[65] <u>Catechism of the Catholic Church</u>, Second Edition, 1997, #2202.

built on marriage.

Other relationships between cohabiting couples (who may have children) and between homosexual couples (who may also have children) more closely resemble families than the above examples. However, while these relationships usually include sexual intimacy, they lack a life-long commitment and a promise to fidelity, and in the case of homosexual relationships, they also lack a partnership between a man and a woman. Again, because these relationships are not founded on marriage, they cannot be said to be families in the truest sense.

Broken families and blended families where divorce has left one spouse alone with the children or where there has been remarriage after divorce are more problematic. Also problematic are single parent families where a child is being raised outside of marriage. Sadly, these are all cases where the family has been damaged or harmed, usually by sin.[66] In all of these cases, a man and a woman are not united in marriage, and so, the family is deformed in some way.

A different case is when a spouse has died leaving the other with children to raise. These are true families in that they were founded on marriage.

Our definition of family continues by speaking of children. Families begin with a man and a woman united in marriage. Later, most families are blessed with children who are the fruit of married love. While some married couples are not blessed with children (either because of age or some other reason), this does not make these couples any less a family. Inasmuch as the family begins with marriage, couples without children are as much a family as are any other married couples.

Finally, it should be pointed out that only human beings can be members of a family. Today, many people regard their pets and other animals as family members. Some even go so far as to refer to them as their "boys and girls" or as their "children." However, pets and other animals are, by definition, not family members.

Modern pagans do not accept the above definitions of marriage and of family, nor do they regard marriage as an important and essential societal institution. This has led them to ignore marriage altogether and simply live together or to expand the definition of marriage to include remarriage after

---

[66] In some cases, divorce was pursued against the wishes of one spouse. When that happens, the innocent spouse has done nothing wrong and is guilty of no sin.

divorce and homosexual unions. Modern pagans have also expanded the definition of family to include virtually every grouping of people under one roof, a list too long and varied to discuss here.

PART FOUR

SOME PRACTICAL POINTS
FOR MARRIED COUPLES

Part Four: Some Practical Points for Married Couples

Living out God's plan for sex is both enjoyable and challenging. Knowing that you are living according to God's plan brings great peace and happiness. It also allows God to fill your soul with His grace, and God is very generous with those who are generous with Him. In fact the more generous we are with God, the more generous He is with us. God can never be outdone in generosity. At the same time, the blessings of married life will also come with crosses, and that should not surprise those who follow Jesus Christ. Our Lord once said, "If any man would come after me, let him deny himself and take up his cross daily and follow me (Lk 9:23)."

As with everything else in life, one's sexuality will be a source of both joy and sorrow. Couples will have the happiness of sharing everything, including physical intimacy. They will also have to abstain from sexual intercourse on occasion and sometimes even for extended periods. There will be the joys and blessings that come with children. There may also be times when God blesses them with a child they did not plan or expect. On the other hand, sometimes their desire for a child will remain unfulfilled.

Every couple will be called to practice marital chastity. That means even in marriage, there are limits to what is morally acceptable behavior. One cannot do just anything. Couples need to know what these limits are and what sort of things they can and cannot do. Living a sexually moral life is another matter. That requires being considerate of one another; it will also require self-control and discipline sustained by prayer and God's grace.

Then there are questions about children. How many should we have? What does it mean to be open to life? What are moral ways to plan our family? Is contraceptive use within marriage morally acceptable? Can I be sterilized?

A very difficult cross is that of infertility. There are many couples who long for a child but for one reason or another have trouble conceiving. What can they do to have children in a way that is both moral and ethical?

Finally, since parents have an obligation to see to the education of their children, how do they take care of their children's education in sexual matters?

How do they form their children with Christian values?

These and similar issues will be faced by every couple as they seek to live out God's plan for married love. In the chapters which follow, these issues will be discussed in the context of Biblical teaching and Christian Tradition.

Chapter Thirteen
SEXUAL PRACTICES WITHIN MARRIAGE

Once their vows have been exchanged, married couples have the right to enjoy each other's bodies and to engage in sexual intercourse. However, marriage does not give couples license to do whatever they please sexually. Just as single people must practice the virtue of chastity according to their status, so too married couples must practice the virtue of chastity according to the married state.

Saint Paul says this to all Christians, "You were called to freedom, brethren; only do not use your freedom as an opportunity for the flesh, but through love be servants of one another (Gal 5:13)." The Apostle's counsel applies just as much to married couples as to anyone else. Simply put, his words are just another way of saying that husbands and wives must never be selfish with each other but must always be loving and generous, and that also includes when they are intimate.

With regard to their love making in general, Saint Paul gives some very clear directives to husbands and wives. In his first letter to the Corinthians, he writes,

> "The husband should give to his wife her conjugal rights, and likewise the wife to her husband. For the wife does not rule over her own body, but the husband does; likewise the husband does not rule over his own body but the wife does (1Cor 7:3–4)."

These words should serve as a reminder to husbands and wives that when they exchanged their vows, they gave themselves to each other. In a very real sense, they no longer belong to themselves. Rather, each belongs to the other. That is why a husband can point to his wife and say, "There is my wife." She is his wife and not the wife of someone else. He has accepted her gift of self, and she is now his "to have and to hold."[67] She belongs to him. Similarly, that is

---

[67] The legal phrase "To have and to hold" is found in deeds where property is transferred from one owner to another. It is used to begin the sentence describing the rights of the new owner. In the marriage vows, it also has the idea of conveying

why a wife can point to her husband and say, "There is my husband." He is her husband and not the husband of someone else. She has accepted his gift of self, and he is now hers "to have and to hold." He belongs to her.

This gift of self includes the body. Motivated by love, each has the desire to please the other and make them happy. To that end, the wife gives her body to her husband for him to enjoy. Likewise, the husband gives his body to his wife for her to enjoy. Husband and wife no longer rule over their own bodies, but their spouse does. In that sense, each has given "conjugal rights" to the other. This means when the wife would like to make love, the husband should not refuse. Likewise when the husband would like to make love, the wife should not refuse. Deliberate refusal would not only be selfish but even sinful because one spouse would be withholding something that rightfully belongs to the other.

There are times when requesting sex would not be loving. These may include the need to avoid pregnancy for a time. They may also include less serious reasons such as illness or fatigue. Saint Paul also says there are times when couples may agree to abstain for a period of time. He says,

> "Do not refuse one another except perhaps by agreement for a season, that you may devote yourself to prayer; but then come together again lest Satan tempt you through lack of self-control (1Cor 7:5)."

From this we see that moderation also applies to sexual intercourse. Just as we might fast from food or drink at certain times (during the season of Lent for example), so too by mutual agreement a couple may decide to fast from sexual intercourse for a time. However, notice that Saint Paul says this kind of abstention must be by mutual agreement. One cannot say to the other, I have decided to abstain from sex during Lent and consequently, so will you. One cannot unilaterally deny to the other his or her conjugal rights.

In all of these things, there must be respect for the other. Married couples should never forget the great dignity to which they have been called. They should remember that their union is a sign of the union between Christ and

---

something from one party to another. In this case the item is not property, but a person. The woman gives herself to the man and becomes his wife, and the man gives himself to the woman and becomes her husband. In that sense, each now belongs to the other.

His Church. No doubt, that is the inspiration behind these words from the Letter to the Hebrews,

> "Let marriage be held in honor among all, and let the marriage bed be undefiled; for God will judge the immoral and adulterous (Heb 13:4)."

Here the marriage bed represents more than just a piece of furniture. It refers to that place where the husband and wife give themselves to each other and become physically one. Their unity of bodies symbolizes their unity of hearts, and this unity should never be defiled or dishonored. Hebrews warns that those who defile the marriage bed and who violate the covenant of love between husband and wife will be judged by God.

Clearly, adulterers defile the marriage bed; they violate their vows and make a mockery of all that is sacred within marriage. The immoral also defile the marriage bed.[68] They do so by introducing into it intentions, actions or things which do not belong there. Those things also defile the marriage bed.

With regard to love making in particular, the Church has no specific rules. There is not nor will there ever be any official document listing every acceptable and unacceptable sexual practice. There will never be a manual one can consult as to when or where or how to make love. In fact, no complete list could ever be compiled because people are so different in their interests and behaviors. Instead, just as in other areas of life, the Church sets forth principles which are then applied to specific circumstances.

While Christian couples have broad freedom in their lovemaking, they should be wary of introducing practices into their love life which are common among the pagans. Many of these practices are odious to God because they separate love from life. Other pagan sexual practices are either demeaning or unnatural or both. These practices harm love and thereby diminish the enjoyment that should be present with intimacy. However, given their prevalence, it would be surprising if, in all innocence, certain of these practices have not crept into the love life of many Christians. A rule of thumb: Be careful of "defiling your marriage bed." If something makes you uncomfortable

---

[68] The Greek word used here is πόρνος (pornos). Pornos means a sexually immoral person. This word is also related to the Greek words for prostitute and fornication. It is also the root word for the English word "pornography."

or does not seem right, it probably is not.

Here another word of caution is in order. Because they have misapplied Biblical and Church teaching, some Christian authorities have created confusion about certain points of sexual morality. Furthermore, because many Christian denominations fail to properly apply Godly and Biblical principles, they have also given incorrect answers to questions concerning sexual morality within marriage. In fact, as we shall see, both sometimes speak approvingly of pagan sexual practices which are not appropriate for anyone, let alone for Christians.

****

In their efforts to keep their sex lives interesting, modern pagans have made a kind of science of the sexual act, even an industry of sorts. They have their sex experts, sexologists, their open and rank discussions of sexual techniques, practices and aids, and stores that cater to their deviant behavior. In their quest for pleasure, modern pagans are a lot like drug addicts who need a little stronger fix each time to get the same high. This explains their need to keep trying new techniques, places, and costumes. It explains grocery store magazines with cover stories such as "Twenty Great Sexual Techniques Guaranteed to Please Your Partner."

The pagan motivation for sexual intercourse is pleasure, and motivation makes all the difference. Pagans who embrace these ideas are motivated by lust; they have sex not for love, but for pleasure. What they do and what they expect are based upon their own selfish interests. They care little for how the other feels. They are not interested in pleasing the other but only in pleasing themselves. That is why when they are intimate, they are really only having sex and not making love.

Unwittingly, in their quest for pleasure, they have eliminated both love and life from sex, the very reasons why God made sex. All their efforts to maintain and increase their sexual pleasure have left them with a loveless, lifeless sex, an endless and boring merry-go-round leading nowhere. In his study on disease in the ancient world, A.T. Sandison writes, "The study of sexual deviation is, therefore, very largely the study of sexual activity divorced from love."[69] His

---

[69] <u>Diseases in Antiquity</u>, "Sexual Behavior in Ancient Societies," Don Brothwell and

observation about sex in the ancient world is just as true today as it was then.

While sexual pleasure is very much a part of making love, for the Christian married couple, love is the motivation behind all they do, and this includes those times when they are intimate. Their union of bodies should be a sign of their union of hearts. While they may not be thinking about this in the midst of the delights and pleasures of making love, nevertheless, love should be the underlying motivation behind what they are doing. As they prepare for love making, they should keep these things in mind.

As couples make love, as they share their bodies, all of the senses are engaged, sight, touch, taste, smell and hearing. Like preparing savory food, the wife will delight in making herself beautiful for her husband. As the wife gives herself to her husband, she does so out of love for him. She will think about how she can please and delight her husband by how she looks, the fragrance she wears, what she says and so on. Out of love, she will allow him to touch her and hold her in ways that delight him. Similarly, the husband will delight in making himself attractive for his wife. He will allow her to touch him and hold him in ways that delight and please her. His desire will be her enjoyment.

Both husband and wife will be pleased when the other is happy and takes pleasure in their gift of self. There will be a concern that each has been satisfied when they make love. The pleasure they derive from their touches, kisses, embraces, smells and so on results from their efforts to please each other, and those efforts are in turn motivated by their love for each other.

Christian couples should feel no qualms about enjoying the pleasures of sex. It is something quite natural and is part of God's creation. As such, it is also good. In fact, sexual pleasure is simply one fruit of the couple's love for each other. Writing on that subject in the previous century, Pope Pius XII made some comments which are still valid today. He said, "The Creator Himself ... established that in the [generative] function, spouses should experience pleasure and enjoyment of body and spirit. Therefore, the spouses do nothing evil in seeking this pleasure and enjoyment. They accept what the Creator has intended for them. At the same time, spouses should know how to keep themselves within the limits of just moderation."[70]

A.T. Sandison, 1967, p. 734.

[70] Pope Pius XII, Discourse, October 29, 1951.

With all these things in mind, there are a number of principles that will help you keep the love in your love-life. These principles will also help answer most questions about what is proper behavior when making love. Finally, they will help set guidelines for what it means "to keep within the limits of just moderation when making love." They are as follows:

* The end does not justify the means.

* In sexual intimacy, love and life must never be separated.

* The husband and wife must always respect each other's dignity.

* Unnatural or injurious practices are always immoral.

With regard to the first principle, one can never use a bad means to achieve a good end. You cannot rob from the rich in order to give to the poor. In marriage, this principle means couples may not use immoral means to heighten or achieve orgasm. For example, watching pornography as foreplay or using sex toys or other things to arouse or stimulate yourself or your spouse is wrong.[71] Pornography is a lie and introduces other parties and images into the intimate union of spouses. While making love, what spouse could possibly be thinking only of the other after having just watched pornography? Rather than making love, he or she is more likely just having sex. In their thoughts as well as their actions, couples must be making love to their spouse and not to another. True love demands this.

With regard to the second principle, keeping love and life together simply means a couple can never deliberately set aside one or the other reason for sex either during the act of sexual intercourse itself, before engaging in the act or after the act has been completed. If their lovemaking is going to end with sexual climax of either or both, this must take place within sexual intercourse where the husband's sperm is deposited into the wife's vagina.

To embrace love but without the life-giving end of marriage would be to

---

[71] It would be unacceptable for healthy people to use drugs or artificial or mechanical devices in foreplay or as a substitute for the sexual act. However, when there is some medical issue, a doctor may prescribe medication or some treatment or perform surgery if necessary in an effort to cure the problem. As with any other part of the body, if medical attention is needed to restore proper function to the sexual organs, this is perfectly acceptable.

use the other. Doing so would always be wrong. Thus, couples cannot resort to anything that prevents new life. This would include mutual masturbation, withdrawal where the husband withdraws from the wife before ejaculation, the use of condoms or other barrier methods that prevent the sperm and egg from meeting or the use of spermicides and similar agents. Couples cannot use contraceptive drugs that would render the woman temporarily infertile. Finally, they cannot resort to sterilization which renders them permanently infertile.

All of these things reject the life-giving end of sexual intercourse and end up with one spouse (or both) rejecting the other's fertility and in so doing, using the other. Couples who have serious reasons for avoiding pregnancy may do so, but they must use moral means that do not separate love and life. This topic will be discussed in more detail in the following chapter.

To embrace life but without the love-giving end of marriage is the other side of the same coin and is also always wrong. Thus, couples cannot seek to achieve pregnancy outside of sexual intercourse. This would include any technique which involves fertilization outside of the wife's body, any technique which uses eggs or sperm from someone other than the husband or wife, and the use of surrogate mothers. By extension it would also include a prohibition against donating sperm or eggs to someone else. This is harder to understand since a good thing, a baby, is the desired end. However, these methods eliminate the love-giving end of marriage and reduce procreation to a laboratory procedure. The end (having a baby) is a good thing, but that end does not justify using immoral means. This topic will be discussed in more detail in the chapter on infertility.

With regard to the third principle, both the husband and wife must respect each other's dignity in all things. In all that they do, they must love one another and never use one another for their own sexual gratification. Therefore, Christian couples cannot introduce behaviors or things into their love life which demean them or would result in them using one another to satisfy their own selfish desires. One spouse should never ask the other to do something which is demeaning or which the other finds uncomfortable.[72]

---

[72] If what is asked is not intrinsically wrong, then one should try to come to the point where he or she can do what is asked as a loving response to the other. This would be similar to visiting in-laws one does not particularly like out of love for one's spouse.

Even when both agree to some practice, if it is disrespectful or demeaning, they cannot do it.

To understand this one needs to realize that all things have an intrinsic meaning, and they retain that meaning in spite of what individuals may say or believe. For example, a dollar bill is a form of legal tender, money in other words. If someone were to say it was a goldfish, most people would say, "No, what you have there is a dollar." Even if that person insisted the dollar really was a goldfish, that would not make it so. Things are what they are and do not change just because we want them to change. We do not live in Alice's Wonderland or Dorothy's Oz. Our culture does not like the idea of objective standards and definitions. Yet, placing everything in personalistic and subjective terms does not change the intrinsic meaning of those things.

With this in mind, one can see why dressing like a prostitute, a playboy bunny or doing something similar is always demeaning. To take a specific example, playing the role of a prostitute is beneath the dignity of a daughter of God, and no husband should ever ask his wife to do so. Even though some couples might argue that having the wife dress like a prostitute as part of their foreplay is not demeaning for them, that is not the case. Even in the privacy of their bedroom, those whom Christ has purchased with a price must still behave according to their dignity as sons and daughters of God.

Lastly, with regard to the fourth principle, couples cannot engage in unnatural or injurious practices. To go against nature is to go against God's intended design for the body. Whenever parts of the body are used for something other than their proper purpose, the action will be immoral. Going against nature rejects God's plan, misuses the body and also fails to show respect for it as a temple of the Holy Spirit. Consequently, even when there is mutual consent, what is unnatural is not allowed.

Unfortunately, today many unnatural and violent sexual practices have been revived by modern pagans. What was until recently considered deviant behavior and what caused disgust and revulsion whenever it was mentioned is now considered quite normal and discussed openly and calmly by many people. Examples include bondage, anal intercourse and oral sex. Sadly, there are even Christian authorities who permit some of these practices as part of marital foreplay.[73]

---

[73] For example, see <u>Sacraments of Community and Renewal</u> (Volume 3), by Fr.

Some of these authorities hold that since the Church has not made any official statement about these things and since the Bible does not specifically condemn them, these practices must be morally acceptable. However, this approach is backwards. Neither the Bible nor the Church could ever anticipate everything we will ever face in life, nor is that their purpose. Rather, the Bible contains principles which we must apply to our lives, and Church teaching is similar.

The right way to evaluate the morality of something is to start with general principles and then apply them to specific situations. For example, the Bible says nothing about passive euthanasia, surrogate mothers or the use of weapons of mass destruction. However, starting with our Lord's teaching that we must love one another, Christian theologians have rightly concluded that all of these things are not loving and therefore immoral. Similarly, just because the Bible does not specifically prohibit the use of oral sex or anal intercourse as part of marital foreplay, it does not mean engaging in these activities is morally acceptable.

In point of fact, from its beginnings, the Church has condemned these practices. The first Christians knew about anal intercourse and oral sex because they were widely practiced by the pagans. These practices were denounced in the Letter of Barnabas which dates from the early 100s. In that letter, those who engaged in anal sex were compared to rabbits and those who engaged in oral sex to weasels.[74] Writing at the end of the Second Century, Clement of Alexandria compared those who engaged in sodomy, pederasty, and unfruitful

---

Nicholas Halligan, O.P., 1974, where he allows anal sex as part of foreplay (p. 199); In Pursuit of Love: Catholic Morality and Human Sexuality by Fr. Vincent Genovesi, S.J., 1986, where he allows oral/genital contact as part of foreplay (pp. 242–243); Sex and the Marriage Covenant: A Basis for Morality by John F. Kippley, 2005, where he allows oral/genital contact as part of foreplay (p. 45); Good News about Sex and Marriage (revised edition) by Christopher West, 2007, where he allows oral/genital contact as part of foreplay (p. 93) and the remote possibility for the moral use of anal sex (p. 94); Holy Sex, by Gregory K. Popcak, 2008, where he allows oral/genital contact as part of foreplay (pp. 197–198, 220) and where he allows anal sex as part of foreplay (p. 248).

[74] Letter of Barnabas, Chapters 10:6 and 10:8;

sex as hyenas.[75] At the time, it was believed these animals engaged in deviant and unnatural sexual practices.

Christian opposition to these practices has been consistent and continuous throughout the centuries. Today's Christian authorities who favor these practices seem unaware of this. It is true that most moral theologians prior to mid Twentieth Century wrote about these subjects in Latin, and few of their works have been translated into English. However, that does not mean their teachings are any less significant for the people of today.[76]

Saint Thomas Aquinas (1125–1274) speaks in general of these sins against nature.[77] Saint Alphonsus Ligori (1696–1787) divides the sin of sodomy into two kinds, the first involves sexual acts between people of the same sex which he calls *sodomis perfecta*. The second involves sexual acts between a man and a woman which he calls *sodomis imperfecta*.[78] Because there is no possibility for conception and because these acts are contrary to nature, he states that they are always gravely sinful.

Within marriage, moral theologians make no distinction as to whether sodomy was engaged in as part of foreplay or simply as a substitute for natural intercourse. They judge all such acts morally wrong for the same three reasons they are wrong outside of marriage, namely, the act is contrary to the end of marriage which is children, the act is unnatural in that the husband's penis is inserted into the wife's rectum and finally, there is the real possibility of semen

---

[75] Instructor by Clement of Alexandria, Book II, Chapter 10:83 and 85–88.

[76] A sampling of works in which these sexual practices are addressed includes: Theologia Moralis by Saint Alphonsus Liguori (1696–1787), the first complete edition appeared in 1755 and the ninth edition in 1785; Theologia Moralis in Compendium Redacta by A. Konings, 1877; A Manual of Moral Theology by Rev. Thomas Slater, S.J., 1908, (the book is in English except for the section on sins against marriage which is in Latin); Summarium Theologiae Moralis, by Rev. Antonio Arregui, 1919; Institutiones Morales Alphonsianae, by Rev. Clemente Marc and Rev. Francis Gestermann, 1927; College Moral Theology by Anthony F. Alexander, 1957 (this work is in English). See also the magisterial text: Response of the Sacred Penitentiary, April 3, 1916 (DS 3634).

[77] Summa Theologica, II–II, Q 154, A. 11.

[78] Theologia Moralis by Saint Alphonsus Liguori, Book 4, 466.

being ejaculated outside of the vagina.

Directly addressing the question as to whether the husband sins mortally by beginning intercourse in wife's rectum but completing it in the vagina, Saint Alphonsus calls this "true sodomy" and not legitimate sexual intercourse.[79] He concludes by stating that this as well as genital/anal touches by the husband to his wife are also immoral.

Various moral theologians have also directly addressed the morality of oral/genital contact. Again, because it is against nature and because of the real possibility of semen being ejaculated outside of the vagina, they have concluded that acts of this sort, even as part of foreplay, are immoral.[80]

When analyzing the morality of these acts, earlier moral theologians concluded that even within the context of marriage, acts against the natural order, acts which are deliberately opposed to the generation of children, and acts which induce ejaculation outside of natural intercourse are immoral. In so doing, these theologians were simply reaffirming the judgment of the first Christians.

In one sense, the Church should not have to make pronouncements on every single thing because some things should be obvious. For example, we can determine what is natural from what is unnatural by functionality. The throat was made to swallow food and drink, not swords. The veins were made to circulate blood, not heroin. The ear was designed for hearing, not as a place to store marbles. Similarly, in sexual matters, we can determine what is moral by simply considering the proper function of the body part in question.

For example, the hands are naturally designed for touching and holding. That means couples can use their hands to caress and touch the body, and their hands can be used to help stimulate arousal and to facilitate intercourse. Moral theologians also agree that after intercourse, if the wife has not achieved orgasm, she can touch herself (or she can allow her husband to do so) to achieve orgasm because for the woman (as for the man), orgasm pertains to

---

[79] Ibid., Book 6, 916.

[80] Institutiones Morales Alphonsianae, by Rev. Clemente Marc and Rev. Francis Gestermann, 1927, #2111, c, p. 615. Saint Alphonsus says it seems to be a new kind of venereal pleasure against nature (*videtur nova species luxuriae contra naturam*). See Book 6, 935.

the completed act of sexual intercourse.[81]

The rectum was designed to expel feces; it was not designed for sexual intercourse. The tissue is too sensitive and susceptible to injury, and the practice is unsanitary. There is also good evidence this practice can cause cancer.[82] The mouth was designed to hold food and drink; it was not made for genital contact. It was not intended to be a receptacle for the penis, nor was the penis designed to be stimulated by the woman's mouth or tongue. Similarly, the man's tongue was not designed to be inserted into the woman, and a woman's genitals were not designed to be stimulated by the man's lips or tongue. Semen was not designed as food and was therefore not intended to be eaten. By considering functionality, it becomes obvious that anal intercourse and oral/genital contact go against nature and are therefore immoral.

Love-making can never involve deliberately injurious practices such as beating, cutting, burning or other masochistic activities. These are always perversions done in an effort to make loveless sex entertaining in some twisted way. They are never acceptable for Christian couples under any circumstances.

In conclusion, couples have wide latitude in their love-making. They have great freedom in their thoughts and actions, as well as in how and where they make love. That said, when they are making love, the husband and wife should enjoy each other as husband and wife, and that is true even in their thoughts where there can never be some imaginary third person involved.[83] Also, in their love-making, Couples can never do anything which is degrading, unnatural or harmful, and this is true even if both have agreed to practices of this sort. In whatever they do, each must always respect the God-given dignity of the other.

One final point. Couples may engage in lovemaking where sexual intercourse is not the intended purpose. Thus kissing, even passionately, and

---

[81] Theologia Moralis by Saint Alphonsus Liguori, Book 6, 919; Institutiones Morales Alphonsianae, by Rev. Clemente Marc and Rev. Francis Gestermann, 1927, 2111, 2°.

[82] "The Vatican and Same-Sex Unions" by Donald DeMarco, Ethics and Medics, November 2003, Volume 28, Number 11.

[83] See A Manual of Moral Theology by Rev. Thomas Slater, S.J., 1908, p. 365, where he states it is sinful to have relations with one's spouse while thinking of another.

touching or embracing, even sensuously, is perfectly acceptable. So too is gazing on the body of your spouse, thinking about the body of your spouse or listening to your spouse talk about intimate things. All of these things are acceptable within marriage as long as they do not lead to orgasm outside of natural intercourse.[84] However, as with drinking too much, if a couple does not intend to engage in intercourse, they need to know their limits and stop before things become too passionate.

****

As they strive to live a chaste life, married couples will also face external threats to their marriage. Consequently, living chastely will mean anticipating threats from outside and having plans for how to deal with them.

The first and best defense to temptation is personal prayer. At the beginning of each day and throughout the day husbands should pray for their wives and wives should pray for their husbands, and both should pray for their family. They should ask that God bless them and keep them safe. They should also ask that God help them personally to be faithful to the vows they have made to each other before His altar. Couples should also pray together each day. They can do this at meals and also before they go to sleep or at some other convenient time during the day.

They should also admit that they are weak and need God's grace to resist temptation. As Jesus said, "Temptations to sin are sure to come (Lk 17:1)." They should not be so naive as to think that the devil will not tempt them or that they can resist these temptations on their own. That is the very reason for the sacramental graces God gives in marriage. They are there to help the couple keep their marriage vows.

To preempt temptations, always wear your wedding ring.[85] This will serve as a reminder to you that you are no longer a single person and that you can no longer behave as one. Your ring will also be a sign that you are married

---

[84] Theologia Moralis by Saint Alphonsus Liguori, Book 6, 933; Theologia Moralis in Compendium Redacta by A. Konings, 1877, #1651, 3°, p. 297.

[85] Some men who work in heavy construction or in other occupations where a ring might be hazardous should get a chain and wear their ring around their neck.

and unavailable to those who may be looking for a relationship. Dating, flirting, and even thinking about members of the opposite sex in a sexual way are not appropriate for married persons. As Jesus said, "Every one who looks at a woman lustfully has already committed adultery with her in his heart (Mt 5:28)." This verse would also apply to a woman who looks lustfully at a man in her heart.

Be very careful of Internet relationships. At first they seem to offer a safe place to go where someone will "listen" to your problems. Soon you are chatting about very personal things or about problems in your marriage. Complaints about your spouse are met with sympathy. Feelings begin to develop. Then meetings are arranged. Many people have become infatuated with those they have met online, with people they have never even met in person. Some have even abandoned their husbands or wives and children to go and live with their Internet lovers.

Avoid going to places where you know you will be tempted. Do not be alone with persons of the opposite sex; do not go out to lunch or spend time at a neighbor's home or even at the house of a best friend when his or her spouse is not at home. For example, a wife should not be alone with the husband of her best friend (or even a brother-in-law) and vice-versa. When it is necessary for a husband to be at the home of a woman (whether she is married or single) when she is alone to say, fix the plumbing, he should go with someone else such as his wife or a friend who can act as a chaperone of sorts. These precautions might seem unnecessary or extreme, but they are based upon the sad outcomes of real life experiences. Men always have a soft spot for a woman in need, and women in need are grateful for their help and attention. However, what starts as a sincere desire to help can often end up as something neither of them intended nor wanted. The devil will never cease to capitalize on the opportunities we give him.

Be aware that certain people will not care whether you are married or not. These people are experts at lying, flattery and expressing false empathy. They will watch for times when you are at your weakest, when you are depressed or struggling with your spouse over some issue. Then they will move in with a listening ear and an empathetic smile. They will take your side and tell you that you deserve more and pretty soon you are at a place you never thought you would be.

So, a word to the wise. Assume that you will be tempted at some point in your life and make preparation for that time by having an exit strategy. When someone approaches you or makes a pass at you, show them your ring and tell them you are not interested. If they persist, tell them to get lost. If they persist at work, tell them you will make a sexual harassment complaint with Human Resources. If necessary, quit your job or even move to some other town. These kinds of temptations must be confronted immediately. If not, they will quickly become a source of great shame and pain.

We all change a little every day. When couples are together, they change together, but when they are separated, their paths begin to diverge. So beware of long separations. Saint Paul warned against abstaining from marital relations for too long lest "Satan tempt you through lack of self-control (1Cor 7:5)." Couples who are separated for long periods of time because of work (truck drivers, those who work on ships, those who travel for work, those in the military, etc.) should take special care to cultivate unity. Ideally, couples who are separated should make changes in their lives so they can work together or travel together and so on. When that is not possible, they can still take advantage of email, Skype or Facebook to stay in touch. Obviously, these things are not substitutes for being there in person, but virtual connectivity can help bridge distances.

Living chastely within marriage requires a conscious decision to do so, a decision that should be renewed on a daily basis. The pagan world contains many temptations. In addition, we all suffer from the effects of Adam's fall. However, married couples should take heart. God has promised that He will be with them. If they do their part, He will do His to make their marriage a success. With prayer and prudence and the help of the Sacrament they will not fail. It was Jesus who said, "What God has joined together, let not man put asunder (Mk 10:9)."

Some Practical Points for Married Couples

Chapter Fourteen

FAMILY PLANNING

Imagine living without your car or your cell phone or even without a land line. Imagine living without cable or even without a television. Imagine living without electricity. Most of us cannot. We cannot imagine living like that because doing so would be so different from the kind of life we live. We know what it is like when our car is in the shop for a day or two or when the power is out for a few hours, but a whole life without our car or electricity is unimaginable.

Now try to imagine life without artificial birth control. Again, most of us cannot. Take the pill for example; it has been around since 1960. That means only a woman born around 1945 or before could have experienced life without it (for at least some of her reproductive years). Only a woman born around 1920 or before could have lived all of her reproductive years without the pill having been available at all. A time when the pill was not available is beyond the living memory of the vast majority of women (and men). Quite simply, the pill is as much a part of our lives as are phones, cars or televisions.

In our culture, access to contraceptives is nearly universal. If she is not using it herself, virtually every woman knows someone, a sister, cousin, aunt, friend, coworker, colleague, neighbor and most probably her mother (and perhaps even her grandmother) who is using or has used some form of birth control. Contraceptive drugs, devices and products are just a normal part of "fertility care." While there are a few people who do not use birth control for religious or philosophical reasons, they are viewed as rather extreme, like people who voluntarily live without electricity or cars.

Along with pagans, most Christians view contraceptive use as a non-issue. Except for a tiny group of Protestants and those Catholics who follow Church teaching, most Christians use birth control without a second thought. However, Christian couples need to take a second look (or more likely a first look) at this issue. When they do, they may be surprised to find there is a significant difference between the prevailing view on birth control held by today's Christians and the practices of the early Church.

A significant feature of the early Church was its pro-family and pro-natal stance. This was in stark contrast to the pagan world described earlier. Any practice that harmed a child in the womb was rejected. So too were the pagan practices used during that time to prevent conception and birth. These would have included inserting devices or medicines into the vagina to kill the sperm or block the path of the semen to the uterus. They also would have included anal intercourse, withdrawal and mutual masturbation. Some of the earliest written evidence of this comes from Clement of Alexandria who wrote in the late second century. He said,

> "... the seed (semen) ought not be wasted nor scattered thoughtlessly nor sown in a way it cannot grow."[86]

Church Fathers who said much the same included Saint Augustine, Saint John Chrysostom, and Saint Jerome, and they were not alone.[87] Throughout the Middle Ages, Church teaching remained unchanged, and it did not change during the Reformation either.[88] In fact, leading Protestant reformers were no less harsh in their condemnations of artificial birth control than were the Fathers of the early Church. For example, Martin Luther wrote,

> "[T]he exceedingly foul deed of Onan, the basest of wretches ... is a most disgraceful sin. It is far more atrocious than incest and adultery. We call it unchastity, yes, a sodomitic sin. For Onan goes in to her; that is, he lies with her and copulates, and when it comes to the point of insemination, spills the semen, lest the woman conceive. Surely at such a time the order of nature established by

---

[86] <u>Instructor</u> by Clement of Alexandria, Book II, Chapter 10:91 (translated by S. Wood).

[87] <u>Marriage and Concupiscence</u> by Saint Augustine, 1:15:17; <u>Homilies on Romans</u> by Saint John Chrysostom, 24; <u>Against Jovinian</u> by Saint Jerome, 1:19. For other examples from the Fathers see the tract, <u>Contraception and Sterilization</u> published by Catholic Answers.

[88] The Reformation refers to that time which gave birth to modern Protestant denominations. It began in 1517 with Martin Luther's protests against the selling of indulgences and other serious abuses which existed in the Catholic Church at that time.

God in procreation should be followed. Accordingly, it was a most disgraceful crime ... Consequently, he deserved to be killed by God. He committed an evil deed. Therefore, God punished him. "[89]

John Calvin wrote,

"The voluntary spilling of semen outside of intercourse between man and woman is a monstrous thing. Deliberately to withdraw from coitus in order that semen may fall on the ground is doubly monstrous. For this is to extinguish the hope of the race and to kill before he is born the hoped for offspring."[90]

Christian opposition to the pagan practice of birth control continued until the early 1900s. Before that time Catholics, Orthodox and Protestants were all united in their opposition to it. It was simply a core teaching of Christianity.

In its opposition to birth control, the early Church merely embraced and affirmed the Jewish belief that children are God's blessings. For example, Psalm 127 proclaimed, "Lo, sons are a heritage from the Lord, the fruit of the womb a reward (Ps 127:3)." This teaching was accepted wholeheartedly by the early Church.

Following the Torah's teachings, the Jews were open to life. Jewish law prohibited sexual relations during menstruation. In that sense, Jewish beliefs and practices were ordered towards the conception of children even with regard to when a couple could have sexual relations. Thus we read in Leviticus, "When a woman has a discharge of blood which is her regular discharge from her body, she shall be in her impurity seven days ... (Lv 15:19)." Furthermore, "if any man lies with her, and her impurity is on him, he shall be unclean seven days (Lv 15:24)."[91] The time a woman was ritually impure coincided with the time she was almost always naturally infertile. The only scriptural account of

---

[89] Luther's Works, Volume 7, pp. 20–21, as quoted in The Bible and Birth Control by Charles D. Provan, 1989, p. 14.

[90] Calvin's Commentaries on Genesis, 38:8–10, translated from the Latin as quoted in The Bible and Birth Control by Charles D. Provan, 1989, p. 15.

[91] See also Lv 20:18 and Ez 18:6 where a man is praised who does not "approach a woman in her time of impurity."

an act against conception occurred when Onan withdrew from intercourse and spilled his seed. For that he was punished with death (Gen 38:8–10).

So, the question is not whether the Church has ever opposed artificial birth control, but rather, how did artificial birth control become so widely accepted among Christians? The answer lies partly with a desire to help couples with legitimate reasons for postponing pregnancy and partly due to human weakness stemming from original sin. When a couple had serious reasons to postpone pregnancy, some form of birth control seemed like a reasonable solution. That is exactly what Margaret Sanger and her confederates proposed when she formed the American Birth Control League back in 1921. Not many years after this, in 1930, the Anglicans became the first Protestant denomination to give approval to the limited use of contraception.

Once the Anglicans had approved contraceptive use in principle, other Protestant denominations began to follow suit and dropped their objections. At the same time Protestant opposition was eroding, the narrow reasons for using birth control were being expanded. Serious reasons to postpone having a child became less serious ones which in turn became trivial reasons and finally no reason at all other than not wanting a baby. By the mid Twentieth Century, the last of the Protestant opposition to artificial birth control was crumbling, and pressure was mounting on the Catholic Church to follow suit.

By the mid-1960s, many Catholic priests were already telling parishioners that they too could use contraception. These priests fully expected the Church's position would be changed. In 1963, a commission was established by Pope John XXIII to study the issue of contraception, and its membership was later expanded by Pope Paul VI. By 1966, the commission had finished its work, but its conclusions had not yet been released. Then, in 1967, before the Pope had issued his decision on the Commission's work, its conclusions were leaked to the press. The majority report took the position that contraception was not intrinsically evil, and this conclusion by the majority only heightened expectations that Church teaching would soon change.

In 1968, in the face of withering criticism for continuing to hold to the traditional Christian teaching on birth control, Pope Paul VI issued a document titled Humanae Vitae (On Human Life). It reaffirmed the Church's long-held stance on the issue. In it, the Pope wrote "every action that, either in anticipation of the conjugal act or in its accomplishment or in the development of its natural consequences, would have as an end or as a means, to render procreation impossible" was to be excluded as a means of birth control.[92] Also excluded was "direct sterilization whether perpetual or whether of the man or of the woman."

However, by the mid-1970s, even with Pope Paul VI's encyclical letter condemning contraception, Catholic opposition had all but collapsed. As use of birth control became virtually ubiquitous within all marriages, Christian or not, objections from religious leaders gradually died down until nary a peep was heard from any Christian pulpit, whether Catholic or Protestant. Nevertheless, Pope Paul VI's reaffirmation of the traditional teaching continues to be the official teaching of the Catholic Church.[93]

What seemed like a good idea at the time has not been without consequences. In fact, one might argue that with regard to birth control, the law of unintended consequences has struck with a vengeance. The great Twentieth Century English essayist G.K. Chesterton once quipped, "They insist on talking about Birth Control when they mean less birth and no control."[94] His remark more or less sums up our present situation.

****

Birth control has never been a Christian practice, and the reason is because birth control rejects the life-giving end of marriage. As was explained previously, God designed sex for love and for life, and everything about our sexuality is built around those two things. Neither one nor the other can be rejected without serious moral and natural consequences. There are limits to man's dominion over his body and its functions. He does not have absolute reign.

In God's plan, sexual intercourse was designed to be the way in which

---

[92] Humanae Vitae, 14. Some would say being open to life means simply being open to children at some point in your marriage. Thus, couples could use contraceptives for some part of their marriage. However, this position is wrong. Each act of intercourse must be open to life. If couples use their marriage rights during the fertile time, they must be prepared for the conception of a child.

[93] See Catechism of the Catholic Church, Second Edition, 1997, #2370 and #2399.

[94] "Obstinate Orthodoxy," The Thing by G. K. Chesterton, 1930.

new life comes about, but that is not all. It is also part of God's plan that new life come about only with the couple's consent. Husband and wife must say yes to the possibility of new life. Furthermore, God has given this power over new life to couples not only for their benefit but also for the benefit of society at large. Consequently, to deliberately reject the life-giving end of sex, to reject this power, is to reject God's plan for sex and to misuse His creation. Couples who do so sin against the generosity of God. In effect, they are saying to God, "I don't want to be part of your larger plan. I would rather live independent from you and your plans."

By using birth control, couples not only harm their relationship with God, they harm their spousal relationship as well. Marital love demands a total acceptance of the gift each spouse gives to the other. Those who choose to contracept say to the other, "I don't want all of you." A husband says to his wife, "I don't want the part of you that could conceive a child." A wife says to her husband, "I don't want the part of you that could father a child." Both say to the other, "I want some of you, but not all of you; I don't want your fertility." This rejection of an essential part of the other (even by mutual agreement) recasts marriage into a contract with conditions rather than a covenant without conditions, and that cannot help but stifle love.

Using the other is always an obstacle to deeper love. It blocks and prevents love from growing. Sexual intimacy becomes less intimate and even our language reveals this. When having sex, people speak of using "protection" or "taking precautions" with "barrier" methods and "spermicides." That language sounds more like a couple is making war rather than making love. The question to ask is this: Why would a husband and wife have to protect themselves from each other? Is a husband somehow an aggressor or is the wife somehow a threat? Why would one need protection unless he or she was not making love but instead just having sex (or at least making love but without giving himself or herself totally to the other)?

Contraception does not help marriages grow stronger but weakens them. Usually, women are the ones who must make sure that "nothing bad" happens when they have sex (where nothing bad means getting pregnant). Because of this, many women feel used. Instead of making love, couples just have sex. In that sense, engaging in contraceptive sex is like dumping a bucket of water on a campfire. It may not put it out, but it certainly dampens the intensity.

Contraception has also had a societal effect by making it easier to stray. With it, adultery becomes thinkable and premarital sex common. By making sexual promiscuity easier, it makes loving just one person harder. Contraception has contributed to our divorce culture, and to single parent homes. In that sense, it harms children too.

Besides the moral, spiritual and relational consequences, birth control also has harmful natural consequences. By design, birth control is intended to prevent conception and the subsequent birth of a baby. To do that, a number of modern methods have been added to the arsenal of very old ones. Ancient societies avoided conception by withdrawal, anal intercourse, the use of certain plants which had contraceptive or abortifacient qualities and the use of crude condoms. Today, these methods are still with us in one form or another. To these have been added hormonal contraceptives such as the pill, the Depro Provera shot and the contraceptive patch. Also added have been devices such as the diaphragm, the IUD and the female condom. Finally, there is less invasive surgical sterilization for both men and women (ancient societies had only castration).

All these methods fall into one of three types. The first are barrier methods which prevent the egg and sperm from meeting and hence prevent conception. These include condoms and the diaphragm. Barrier methods do not endanger new life and generally do not harm the woman physically. However, these methods do deprive the woman of the various benefits she would have received from the chemicals found in the seminal fluid.[95] The second type are hormonal contraceptives which can endanger new life and which can also harm the woman physically. Hormonal contraceptives prevent ovulation and hence the possibility of conception (most of the time). Finally, the third type includes methods which prevent implantation after conception or which cause drug-induced abortions. These include the IUD and the drug RU486 (Mifeprex). These last methods should really be classified as abortifacients because they can and do work by causing the death of a newly

---

[95] Chemicals found in the seminal plasma include testosterone, estrogen, prolactin, opiod peptides, oxytocin, serotonin, melatonin, and norepineprine. Seminal fluid acts as a natural anti depressants and has other benefits that reduce anxiety, improve sleep quality and increase energy and concentration. These benefits for the wife are all negated by condom use.

conceived child."[96]

Hormonal contraceptives work by tricking the woman's body into thinking she is in the early phase of pregnancy. When a woman is pregnant, natural hormones suppress ovulation (where an egg develops and is released into the fallopian tube). By supplying artificial doses of estrogen and progesterone, the woman's cycle is interrupted and ovulation does not take place.

However, occasionally what is called "break-through ovulation" occurs. This happens when the contraceptives fail to suppress ovulation and an egg still develops. When this happens, conception can take place in the normal way. This explains why some women have experienced "contraceptive failure" while on the pill and become pregnant even when taking it as directed. This happens more often to younger women whose bodies are stronger and healthier and as such, more able to overcome the effects of the pill.[97]

To deal with break-through ovulation, hormonal contraceptives have another little known feature. They also prevent the uterine lining from building up, and this is important because the lining is designed to envelope and nurture the new baby. Thus, in the event of break through ovulation and subsequent conception, the new and very tiny baby is unable to implant in its mother's womb. Having no place to live and grow, it then dies. In effect, the result is an early abortion. Surprisingly, even with the drug companies best efforts, about 3 to 5% of women on the pill will still become pregnant over the

---

[96] Note that conception is defined as that point at which the sperm and egg unite and form a new cell and a new human being. Conception and fertilization are really two words for the same reality. Implantation is when the new baby implants in its mother's womb and begins to grow inside her. To make the various forms of hormonal contraceptives more palatable, some companies have been using the word conception in reference to what is really implantation and then saying that their products prevent conception when in fact conception has already taken place. In reality, their products prevent implantation and thus kill the newly conceived child. They are in fact abortifacients.

[97] In the past, it was simply assumed that many teenage girls who became pregnant while on the pill were not taking the pill as directed. However, more recent studies indicate that these girls were telling the truth when they said they were taking the pill every day. It was simply the case that their bodies were strong enough to override the pill's harmful effects and do what they were designed to do, namely, produce an egg.

course of a year of normal sexual activity.[98]

At this point, pro-life women (and their husbands) should have grave concerns about continuing to use hormonal contraceptives. It is quite possible that they have conceived a child (unknowingly), but their child has died through the abortifacient effects of these drugs.

Besides concerns over the abortifacient nature of these drugs, many women also experience serious side effects. Hormonal contraceptives are designed to disrupt the natural events which take place in the woman's body during her menstrual cycle. In essence, these drugs make her body malfunction. Unlike most medications that are designed to correct something and heal the body, hormonal contraceptives do just the opposite by disrupting the body's natural function. The challenge for drug companies has always been to design a product that keeps the side effects of this disruption to a minimum.

Whenever we introduce unnatural things into our bodies, there will be consequences. Each part of the body has its own purpose and function, and we cannot change these functions without doing some harm. For example, wearing high heels causes sore feet and aching backs because they force the body into an unnatural posture. Excess drinking impairs the function of the brain to guide motor skills and results in slurred speech, an unsteady gait, and diminished mental abilities. Going against God's plan for sex and separating love and life is no different. To prevent conception, couples must do things to change the way their bodies are designed to work. Doing so often causes harm, and this has become more and more evident as medical science has advanced.

The workings of human sexuality are both complicated and fascinating. Some things are obvious such as our physical differences. For example, men have beards and women do not. Studies indicate that other things are more subtle, so subtle in fact that they are beneath our conscious knowledge. For example, when a woman is ovulating, there are many changes to her body. One change is that her pupils become slightly more dilated than normal, and men who looked only at pictures of a woman's eyes and no other part of her face subconsciously picked up on this. These men also found women who were

---

[98] Failure rates of contraceptive methods are calculated based upon the percentage of women who become pregnant while using that particular method over the course of one year of normal sexual activity.

ovulating to be more attractive than those who were not.[99] Another change has to do with the sense of smell. A woman smells different when she is ovulating from when she is not. Men are able to perceive these changes subconsciously. This is the time for new life, and like bees to a flower, men are more attracted to women when they are fertile.[100]

During ovulation women are also more interested in sex, and they subconsciously pick out men who are genetically different from them by how the men smell. This naturally leads to healthier children who are less likely to have genetic defects. On the other hand, women who are on hormonal contraceptives cannot smell these differences in men. This ability apparently goes dormant when a woman is pregnant or when she is taking drugs that mimic the effects of pregnancy. Consequently, women on hormonal contraceptives end up marrying men who are genetically similar to themselves more often than those who are not. In addition, when they go off the pill, their husbands do not smell "good" to them and are less attractive![101]

Women using hormonal contraceptives face many other known side-effects. These include serious issues such as heart attacks and blood clots; they also include less serious things such as weight gain, depression, headaches and nausea. One of the most serious side-effects is an increased risk of breast cancer.[102] These side effects are serious enough that long-term use of the pill is not recommended for any woman, nor is it recommended for women over forty years old.

At this point, husbands might ask themselves, if I really loved my wife,

---

[99] Incognito — the Secret Lives of the Brain, by David Eagleman, 2011, pp. 4–5.

[100] Ibid., pp. 90–95.

[101] "Pheromones and Common Scents" by Sr. Renee Mirkes, Ethics & Medics, November 2011, Volume 36, Number 11. Pheromones are produced in the apocrine glands and are subconsciously detected by the vomeronasal organ, part of the olfactory system.

[102] "The Pill and Breast Cancer Risk" by Timothy P. Collins, M.D., Ethics and Medics, March 2007, Volume 32, Number 3. The link between the pill and breast cancer is well documented. Why this fact remains largely unknown probably has to do more with ideological reasons than a true interest in women's health.

why would I ask her to take a drug that would hurt her? Is not my role to protect her and care for her? Is that not what love demands?

Sterilization is seen as a practical solution for couples who have all of the children that they want. While sterilization has the same result as birth control, it is not birth control. Rather, sterilization is a form of mutilation. Sterilization violates of the fifth commandment by deliberately harming the body. In male sterilization, the tube through which the sperm travels, the vas deferens, is cut. In female sterilization, the fallopian tube through which the egg travels is cut. This is commonly referred to as getting snipped or fixed. In reality, nothing is repaired, and nothing is fixed. Rather, something is broken.

Paradoxically, doctors who perform sterilizations are in the curious position of going against the most fundamental rule of medicine and that is "Do no harm." By disabling perfectly healthy sexual organs which are doing exactly what they were designed to do, doctors are harming their patients. In reality, it's hard to see how sterilization would be any different than deliberately severing the Achilles's tendon, amputating a thumb or any other surgery where harm is done to healthy parts of the body.

As can be seen, separating love and life has not been without consequences. Things always work best when you follow the directions and when you use them for their intended purpose. In 1968, Pope Paul VI predicted that widespread problems would develop in societies that embraced contraceptives. Among these were "conjugal infidelity and a general lowering of morality," the loss of respect for woman where man would "come to the point of considering her as a mere instrument of selfish enjoyment, and no longer as his respected and beloved companion." The Pope also predicted that governments would impose methods of contraception upon their peoples.[103] Here, the forced sterilizations in India and the one child policy in China come to mind. Forty-six years later (2014), Pope Paul VI looks very much like a prophet. Clearly, artificial birth control is one of those practices which defiles the marriage bed (Heb 13:4).

****

Christians are not opposed to family planning. In fact, no one disputes

---

[103] <u>Humanae Vitae</u>, Pope Paul VI, #17.

there have always been couples with serious reasons for delaying pregnancy. However, family planning must be done with the right intention, and it must also use moral means. To plan their families, couples must keep in mind that sex is for both love and life and not just one or the other; these two ends cannot be separated. Additionally, in bringing new life into the world, couples must see themselves as partners with God. While their fertility is a gift from God, it does not belong to them alone. God is also involved inasmuch as He creates each new soul. Finally, couples must have serious reasons for avoiding pregnancy.

Once a couple marries, they have the right to engage in sexual intercourse, but not the obligation (except to consummate their marriage). To put it another way, couples do not have to use their marital rights, but when they do, they must keep love and life together.

One way to delay the conception of a child is to abstain from marital relations altogether, and this is not as rare as it might seem. As couples grow older, not a few experience medical problems that make sexual intercourse difficult or even impossible. Occasionally, this can also happen with younger couples. While choosing to abstain from marital relations is permissible (although difficult), it must always be by mutual consent.

A better way is by using one of several methods of Natural Family Planning (NFP), all of which keep love and life together.[104] NFP is the Christian alternative to the pagan practice of artificial birth control. NFP requires no pills, no shots and no equipment. It is, as its name implies, natural. Furthermore, modern NFP is also very effective. Its method effectiveness is 97 to 98% and its user effectiveness is 93 to 94%.[105]

NFP works by observing the signs a woman's body produces when she

---

[104] These include the Creighton Model pioneered by Dr. Thomas Hilgers, the Couple to Couple model, and the Billings method among others. Their differences might be compared to different vehicles. Whether you are driving a car or a pickup, both will get you where you want to go but in a different style and with more or less bells and whistles.

[105] Note that modern methods of NFP should not be confused with the rhythm method which might be called the Model T of Natural Family Planning. It was your grandmother's method of NFP. Some opponents of NFP continue to confuse people by calling it rhythm.

is ovulating. Because these signs are consistent and do not vary much from one woman to the next, virtually any woman can learn NFP. This includes those women whose cycles are irregular. While learning from a professional instructor is recommended, home study courses are also available.

Using these signs, a woman is able to know when she can conceive and when she cannot. This fertile period lasts between five and eight days. The unfertilized human egg can live for up to a day and the sperm for around three to five days. Thus, if a couple were to have intercourse on the days surrounding ovulation, they could conceive a child. Any time before or after those days, conception is not possible. By taking advantage of the naturally infertile time, a couple can avoid pregnancy without doing anything to prevent life.

Some argue that NFP is no different than artificial birth control. However, the two are not the same. While it is true that in both cases the intention is to avoid pregnancy, the means used to achieve that end are entirely different. In the case of NFP, the couple does nothing to separate love from life. They simply do not use their marital rights during the fertile time. On the other hand, contracepting couples do separate love from life during the fertile time and in so doing reject the life giving end of marriage. This is not just a case of splitting hairs. As was noted, the end does not justify the means. It makes a difference how something is done.

NFP is not hard to learn, but living it out does require self-discipline. By nature, it is harder to remain apart during the fertile time. Using NFP will require sacrifice, but there are also benefits to this sacrifice. Couples who use NFP notice that they grow closer by sacrificing. They learn how to express their love for each other in ways other than sexual intercourse. Their communication skills grow, and they also discover a greater appreciation for the life-giving power God has entrusted to them. Each month they must discuss and consider whether or not God is calling them to have another child. Couples report a greater satisfaction in their love-life and are more appreciative of the time when they can come together again and be one flesh. Some describe it as a kind of monthly honeymoon. Finally, the divorce rate among NFP users is very low. These positive consequences, along with knowing they are living as God wills, serve to enhance a couple's love making and make it more enjoyable.

The power to bring new life into the world, the gift of fertility, is something which should be held in great respect by both husband and wife. It is a gift. It is also something God has designed for the good of society as a whole. It is necessary for the continuation of the human race. As such, couples should embrace their fertility as a way of serving both God and humanity. They should never renounce or reject their fertility, nor should they see it as a burden or a trial that must be accepted grudgingly or somehow overcome. Their generous acceptance of it will bear fruit not only in this life, but also in the next.

TWO RELATED ISSUES

The gift of fertility is mutual property. That means one cannot unilaterally decide to have children or not to have children. Just as a couple owns their home together, so too their fertility belongs to both together. A wife may want another child, but she cannot secretly plan to conceive. Her husband must be part of the decision. Similarly, the husband cannot simply announce to his wife that he is done having children. Doing so would be similar to one spouse selling the family home without telling the other.

Sometimes, one spouse will insist on using contraception. One might say to the other, I am going on the pill or I am going to use a condom or I am getting sterilized. When this occurs, it places the other spouse in a difficult position. When one spouse contracepts or gets sterilized against the wishes of the other, is the innocent party somehow tainted by the other? When they engage in sexual intercourse made sterile by the sin of one, does the other sin too?

The short answer is no. An act of intercourse deliberately made infertile by one spouse against the wishes of the other is always intrinsically evil. However, the innocent spouse does not sin when having intercourse and may cooperate under the following conditions: The innocent spouse does not unite his or her will to the will of the other, that is, the innocent spouse does not want to make the act infertile. The act is not already intrinsically wrong in itself, that is, by its very nature (as is the case with anal intercourse or withdrawal). The innocent spouse has a proportionately grave reason for cooperating in the act (examples may include a desire to preserve harmony in the marriage, a desire to strengthen the marriage by means of marital intimacy or the difficulty in resisting temptations against chastity apart from any intimacy at all). Finally, that over time the innocent spouse does what he or she can (through prayer, dialogue and charity) to dissuade the other spouse from sinning.[106]

There is one significant exception. If the contracepting spouse is using a method where conception can still take place (such as the pill or the IUD) and an early abortion could occur, or that spouse would resort to abortion inducing drugs or to abortion itself if conception did take place, then the innocent spouse must abstain from intercourse in order to protect the life of any child that might be conceived.

****

There are some people and some religions who do not believe in NFP or in any type of family planning at all. They believe in "supernatural family planning" where God decides when and how many children they will have. However, that is an extremist position. Couples who hold this position assume no responsibility for their fertility. In that sense, they do not accept God's desire that they partner with Him in bringing life into the world.

Through modern medical science, God has given us knowledge about human fertility, and just as in every other area of life, we have an obligation to use that knowledge for good. To say you should remain ignorant and leave family planning entirely up to God would be like walking around with your eyes closed while praying for God to keep you safe. God will not answer prayers like that, and you will probably end up bumping into something and getting hurt. When that happens you cannot blame God for your injury. God has given us eyes, and He expects us to use them. Likewise, once we have knowledge of how our fertility works, we have a responsibility to use that knowledge wisely.

A couple who may not be ready for another child but refuses to use NFP cannot blame God if they conceive. They acted irresponsibly by not using the moral means God gave them to postpone pregnancy. By contrast, it may be that God is calling a couple to have another child, and they too are longing to have another child, but because they do not know when they can conceive and so do not have intercourse during their fertile time, that child whom God intended to create and which they ardently desired will not be conceived. That

---

[106] <u>Vademecum for Confessors Concerning Some Aspects of the Morality of Conjugal Life</u>, 3. Pastoral Guidelines for Confessors, 13–14, February 12, 1997. <u>Casti Connubii</u>, Pope Pius XI, #53–59 (DS 3716–3718).

couple cannot then conclude God did not want them to have a child at that time.

Years ago, the health benefits of proper nutrition and exercise were unknown. Today, doctors urge their patients to eat right and exercise as part of a healthy lifestyle. While doctors cannot force their patients to do these things, everyone knows these things are good for us.

Similarly, the Church does not require that couples use NFP, nor does it even require them to learn how to use it. However, prudent couples should do both. Doing so gives them a certain freedom. With their knowledge of NFP, they can participate more fully with God in bringing new life into the world.

Chapter Fifteen
BEING OPEN TO LIFE AND FAMILY SIZE

God's plan is that married couples cooperate with Him in bringing new life into the world. It is also part of God's plan that they be fruitful where "fruitful" has the sense or connotation of abundance. Recall God's command to Adam and Eve, "Be fruitful and multiply, and fill the earth and subdue it (Gen 1:28)." But since fruitfulness is not defined, we are left to ask, what does it mean to be fruitful? How many children must a couple have to satisfy God's command? Is there some optimal number? Furthermore, must couples be prepared to have children at any time during their fertile years or can they legitimately postpone pregnancy for a time or even for the duration of their fertile years? These questions will be addressed below.

Even before He created us, God knew all about us, even our future. As the Psalm says, "For it was you who created my being, knit me together in my mother's womb. I thank you for the wonder of my being, for the wonders of all your creation. Already you knew my soul, my body held no secret from you when I was being fashioned in secret and molded in the depths of the earth. Your eyes saw all my actions, they were all of them written in your book; every one of my days was decreed before one of them came into being (Ps 139:13–16)." God spoke in similar words to the Prophet Jeremiah, "Before I formed you in the womb I knew you, and before you were born I consecrated you ... (Jer 1:5)."

We have always been in God's mind and in His thoughts, and so too have our children (and for that matter, even our grandchildren and our great-grandchildren). While God has yet to create them, they too have always been in His mind. That means God already knows how many children He wants to give you. So to be open to life means cooperating with God in bringing these children to life. It means willingly accepting all of the children God wants to give you.

Being open to life is an essential part of Christian marriage and of Christian family planning. Since God has already "planned" their families, Christian couples should make a serious effort to discern what God's will is for them. They should not begin their married life having already decided on the number of children they will have without also seeking out God's will. Their decisions about family planning should only be made after prayer, and with a prudential assessment of their family's welfare. Things they should consider will include their physical and psychological health, their finances, and the needs of children already born.[107]

Being open to life also means seeing children as God's blessings and gifts. As with the anticipation of any gift, there is always a certain excitement and delight when considering the possibility. One wonders what it might be and when it might come. In that sense, anticipating new life is appealing because new life is both a gift from God and an absolute good. Couples who are open to life will find their fertile years an exciting experience as God's plan for them unfolds and is revealed in the children they conceive. Each month will come with questions. Is this a time when we should seek the blessings of another child? Is God calling us to raise up a new soul for His honor and glory?

While scriptural fruitfulness has the sense of abundance, it does not mean having as many children as possible. Rather, it means accepting the children God has planned for you. For some couples this may be one or two or even none, and for others it may be ten or twelve. We see this openness to life lived out in the families of the Bible. There we find married couples whose families came in all sizes and compositions.

For example, Abraham and Sarah had only one son, Isaac (Gen 21:2). So too did Zacariah and Elizabeth, Saint John the Baptist (Lk 1:57). Isaac and Rebekah had twin sons, Jacob and Esau (Gen 25:24). Jesse and his wife had eight sons (1Sam 16:10–11). Jethro (also known as Reuel), the father-in-law of Moses, and his wife had seven daughters (Ex 2:16). Job and his wife had seven sons and three daughters (Job 1:2). The widow of Naim had only one son (Lk 7:11). During their ten years of married life, Ruth and her first husband had no children at all (Ruth 1:4–5). Manoah and his wife had only one son, Sampson (Jgs 13:24). So too did the Shunammite woman and her husband whose only son was born through the intercession of the Prophet Elisha (2Kg 4:17). The courageous mother mentioned in Second Maccabees had seven sons, all of whom died during the persecution of Antiochus Epiphanus (2Mac 7:1). Philip the evangelist had four daughters (Acts 21:9).

---

[107] Humanae Vitae, 10; Gaudium et Spes, 50.

The widow of Zarephath had only one son (1Kg 17:12). Lot and his wife had two daughters (Gen 19:15). Laban and his wife also had two daughters, Leah and Rachel (Gen 29:16). Zelophehad and his wife had five daughters (Num 26:33). Elkanah and his wife Hannah had four sons and two daughters (1Sam 1:20, 2:21). Shimei had sixteen sons and six daughters (1Cron 4:27). The prodigal son was one of two sons (Lk 15). Noah and his wife had three sons (Gen 7:13). Mattathias Maccabees and his wife had five sons (1Mac 2:2).

As can be seen, biblical families came in many different configurations. Some were small and some large. Some had only sons and others only daughters; still others had both sons and daughters. Some were childless. Except for teaching that more is better than less, the Bible never presents us with an ideal family in terms of composition or size.

Just as with biblical families, the number of children God wants modern couples to have is going to vary from one couple to the next. However, in all cases, couples are called to be fruitful and to be open to God's will for them. They should always listen carefully to what God is saying to them. Through prayer, love, a generous heart and a prudent evaluation of their own life circumstances, they will come to know what God wills for them.

Modern pagans are generally not open to life. In fact, many have no intention of having any children.[108] Modern pagans (like their ancient counterparts) do not see children as blessings from God. Instead, many only see children in economic terms and so view them as financial liabilities. Others see children as burdens which restrict their freedom and limit their fun. If and when pagans do decide to have children, their family planning decisions are never made with reference to the plans God has for them. This pagan approach to new life is in marked contrast to Christian teaching. Sadly, when it comes to family planning and family size, this pagan approach has also greatly influenced the thinking of many of today's Christians.

Modern cultural norms and attitudes with regard to family size are not based upon Christian teaching. Quite the contrary, modern pagans

---

[108] Couples who are not open to life reject God's invitation to partner with Him in bringing new life into the world. It should be noted that without the intention to have children, there is no true marriage in God's eyes. Instead, a couple who is not open to life has entered into a man-made relationship which only partially resembles marriage as designed by God.

differ profoundly from Christians in their idea of what constitutes a normal, completed family. Pagan family size is not based upon how many children God wants to give a couple; it is not based upon God's command to be fruitful. Rather, the ideal pagan family size is based upon the replacement rate for a stable population (which, according to demographers, is 2.1 children per family).

In fact, pagans have been campaigning to reduce family size for some time now, and they have been remarkably successful. Over the past fifty years, our culture has gradually come to accept that small families consisting of only one or two children are best. Three children are now considered a large family and having four or more is simply inconceivable. Even most Christians now think two children is about right when considering the perfect family. Yet, well into the 1970s, there were still many families with three, four or even more children.

It bears repeating that pagan family size is not based upon God's command to be fruitful, but rather on what is needed for a stable population. However, Christians were not commanded to keep the population stable but to "fill the earth and subdue it (Gen 1:28)." That means Christians should think about family size using different standards than those of the pagans.

So how should Christians think about family size? In answer, consider the following analogy. In baseball, a one to nothing game is the lowest possible winning score while a high scoring game can be ten to twelve runs or even more (in very rare instances teams have scored more than twenty runs in a nine inning game). Using a range from one to ten, a low scoring game would be from one to three runs, an average score would be from four to six runs and a high scoring game would be from seven to ten runs. Anything more would be a very high scoring game. With this analogy in mind, let us consider the realistic lower and upper limits to family size.

The lower limit would be no children at all. To determine the upper limit, consider the following hypothetical couple. This couple marries when both are age 23. Both the husband and wife are healthy, and they start having children right away. By using NFP, they are able to space their babies exactly two years apart.[109] Finally, let us assume each pregnancy resulted in a live birth

---

[109] Nature being what it is, a baby needs its mother's milk. Nursing normally suppresses ovulation, and so, until a child is weaned, most women cannot conceive.

and that their last child is born when the wife is age 42.[110] Based upon these assumptions, our couple would then end up having ten children over the course of their fertile years.

Obviously, changing the assumptions will change the outcome. Couples who marry later would have less time to have children. If the same couple married when both were age 28, they would end up with seven or perhaps eight children. Some couples may become infertile at an earlier age. If a couple marries at age 23 and their last child is born when the wife is age 37, they would only have seven or eight children. If that same couple married at 28, they would have only five children. On the other hand, some couples may still be fertile into their mid-forties or even later. If they married at age 23, they might be able to have eleven or even twelve children. Some couples may have difficulty conceiving and may have only one or two children or perhaps no natural children. Others may suffer a miscarriage or even a number of miscarriages. Others might experience multiple births. Still others may find that they conceive while the wife is still nursing, and their children are born only eighteen months apart (or less).

While there are many variables in setting an upper limit, let us assume ten children as the upper limit a normal healthy couple could have over the course of their fertile years. Using the same standard for family size as we have devised for baseball, a small family would be from zero to three children, a medium size family would be from four to six children and a large family would be

---

That means children would be spaced naturally about two years apart for women who nurse.

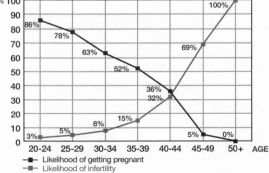

110 In the chart above, pregnancy rates are calculated over the course of one year of normal sexual activity. Beyond age 40, a woman's fertility declines dramatically.

from seven to ten children. Anything more would be a very large family.[111] Today, few would agree that a medium size family consists of between four to six children. Still, if the mean lies between the lowest and highest possible number, the math is what it is.

Our pagan culture virtually insists that couples have small families. It also urges them to wait until they are well established in their careers and financially secure before having children, and it does so because our culture is selfish and does not see children as God's blessings.

Christian couples must resist these temptations to be selfish with their gift of fertility. Also, they should not fear being open to life. Fear motivates couples to limit family size, but God never asks of us more than we can handle. It would be well for couples to remember that "perfect love casts out fear (1Jn 4:18)." Couples should trust that God will take care of them and provide for them so they can in turn care for the children He wishes to give them.

Here it might be helpful to reflect upon the experiences of some couples who have given in to the temptation to have fewer children than God had planned for them and later came to regret their decisions. One grandmother said, "I am missing grandchildren I should have had." She did not mean that her daughters did not have the children they were supposed to have, but rather that she did not have the children she was supposed to have, and so, she was missing the grandchildren her missing children would have had. Another mother said, "there is a place missing at my table." She realized that God had wanted her to have another child, but she and her husband had said no. While she later regretted their decision, by then it was too late. After his son and daughter had left home and moved out of state, a father remarked, "Having only two children was the greatest mistake I made in my life." Similar sentiments have been expressed by many who came to realize only too late that they were meant to have more children.

As children come along and one's family grows, husbands need to be supportive of their wives and to defend them, especially when they are expecting. Expectant mothers who have more than two children will often

---

[111] Note however, that this is not a scientific description of family size, nor is this approach found anywhere in Church teaching or in the scriptures. It is simply one way to look at family size based upon how many children our hypothetical couple could possibly have.

experience rude and insulting remarks and not just from random people but even from family members and fellow parishioners. "Don't you know where babies come from?" "Are you done now?" "You are using more than your fair share of the world's resources." Satan attacks at this time because he hates new life. Remember that Jesus called him "a murderer from the beginning (Jn 8:44)." Friends and others should make it a point to congratulate and support mothers (and fathers) who are open to life. So too should people at church. As part of God's family, they should be excited at the addition of a new little brother or sister in Christ.

At certain times, there will be good reasons for postponing pregnancy. Perhaps a couple is feeling overwhelmed with a baby, a two year old and a four year old. As their family grows, a couple may need time to enlarge their home or to move. A woman may experience serious health issues related to pregnancy that require delaying another pregnancy until her body heals or, in some cases, even for the rest of her fertile years. Some couples may have serious emotional or psychological problems. Others might have financial problems. Some couples may have a special needs child who requires more time from them.

In these and similar cases, postponing pregnancy is perfectly reasonable. A couple does nothing wrong with taking a break and deciding to wait for a time before having another child. Couples should take a lesson from nature. Fruit trees are pruned and cared for so that they are fruitful but also to prevent them from bearing so much fruit that their branches break.

When the time comes where a couple is again able conceive, they are called to be generous with their power to bring new life into the world. Couples should remember that children are blessings from God. While they do require work and sacrifice, that work and sacrifice nearly always pay off when the love parents have for their children is returned to them later in life. Those couples who are generous with God will find that God will be even more generous with them.

TWO RELATED ISSUES

Some have argued that in fulfilling God's command to be fruitful, it is sufficient for a couple to have children at some point during their marriage but that in between having children or when they have all the children they

153

want, they can then contracept or even be sterilized. However, that is not a morally acceptable position. If God did not want conception to be possible on a monthly basis, He would not have designed us as He did.

It is interesting that with regard to fertility, man is different from nearly all other living creatures. In nearly all animals, mating and reproduction take place on an annual basis. Many mammals only come into heat once a year. Similarly, most birds propagate only during the spring. Even the reproductive cycle for many insects is tied to the seasons of the year, and most plants also produce seeds according to an annual cycle. Human beings on the other hand are quite different.

God has designed the woman's body in such a way that each month she has the potential to conceive. That means each month, there is the potential for new life; during that time, married couples must reflect upon the power they have to bring new life into the world. Each month they must prudently consider if God is calling them to have another child. Married couples may go through this process as many as two hundred times (or more) over the course of their fertile years.

Couples must remember that they hold their fertility in trust with God, the author of life, and that they partner with Him in bringing new life into the world. That means they cannot simply view this part of themselves, something that God has built into their lives, as accidental to human nature or as something unintended by God. Being open to life means being open to the possibility of new life whenever they are intimate.

****

There are some who maintain that the reasons for postponing pregnancy must be serious (which is true), but by serious they mean extremely serious to the point of being almost non-existent. So, except in very rare instances, they believe one cannot do anything to postpone pregnancy and that couples should just let nature take its course. However, these are extreme positions.

Clearly there are times when conception is not a good thing. For example, a single woman goes against God's will if she decides to have a baby outside of marriage. So too would married couples if they decide to have a child but lack the means to care for that child. They act irresponsibly by presuming that God (or someone) will take care of them. Conception is only a good thing if it is

God's will.

God commands that couples be fruitful, but nowhere does God command that couples have as many children as they can possibly bear. If that were the case, mothers should not nurse their babies so their fertility would return faster. In fact, they could take fertility drugs to increase the possibility of multiple births. However, doing these things is clearly wrong.

Serious reasons for postponing pregnancy will differ from one couple to the next, and because people are so different, what may be serious for one couple may not be serious for another. That is why the Church has never precisely defined what it means by "serious" other than to say that it means not trivial. As with the decision to have a child, a couple's reasons for postponing pregnancy should be discerned through prayer, prudence and common sense. With a generous heart, couples should ask God to help them do His will and then act according to their conscience.

By way of analogy, couples might compare the decision to have another child to how they decide what they will give to their church or charity. Giving nothing is too little. Giving everything is too much. Between the two lies a happy medium. A couple making $100,000 a year can afford to give more than one making $30,000 a year. A couple making $100,000 a year with six children will be able to give less than a couple making a similar income but with only three children. Exactly how much each should give will be based in part on prudence and in part on their generous response to God's invitation. In the same way, for the average couple the right number of children will be somewhere between zero and ten where more is better than less.

Chapter Sixteen
INFERTILITY

Infertility is excruciatingly painful. It is a source of great frustration and can also put tremendous stress on marriages. Because Hannah had no children, "she was deeply distressed and prayed to the Lord, and wept bitterly (1Sam 1:10)." Rachel, who dearly desired children, cried out in anguish to Jacob, "Give me children or I shall die (Gen 30:1)!" When Saint Elizabeth finally conceived in her old age, she said, "Thus the Lord has done to me ... to take away my reproach among men (Lk 1:25)."

There are countless couples today who very much want to have children, but who have difficulty conceiving. While statistics vary, some indicate that as many as 10% of couples in America struggle with infertility. Some of these couples wanted children as soon as they married. However, as the months turned into years, their hopes for conceiving faded. Some resigned themselves to a life without children. Others turned to adoption as a way for them to have children of their own to love and care for.

Other couples who were contracepting before and during the early years of their marriage but who still planned on having children later, often find themselves struggling to conceive. This is not surprising for several reasons. First, more women are marrying later in life, and this is problematic. By her mid-twenties, a woman's fertility has already begun to decline, and this gradual decline rapidly accelerates as she reaches her mid-thirties. That means, a woman in her mid-30s who finally decides she is ready to have a child is already more than ten years past her peak fertile years. Those in their late 30s and early 40s are even less fertile. A woman's biological clock is relentless and cannot be turned back.

A second cause of infertility is the damage done to the reproductive system by pre-marital sex and its aftermath. Sexually transmitted diseases (which cannot be contracted by a husband and wife who were virgins when they married and who are faithful in marriage) do great damage to the reproductive system, and these diseases often go undetected until after the damage has been done. Abortion can also result in damage to the reproductive system. Sadly, modern pagans seldom mention these things as they encourage young men and women to live the pagan dream of sex without commitment or responsibility.

****

To overcome their infertility, many couples have turned to medical science. Before the advent of in vitro fertilization, the phenomenon of identical twins was the only example of asexual reproduction. In that process, the embryo divides at a very early stage and two genetically identical babies then develop. Today however, there are literally millions of individuals who were conceived with the help of fertility clinics and the various treatments they offer.[112] Nearly all of these treatments involve some form of asexual reproduction (at least for part of the process). These include,

* Artificial insemination and sperm donation for those couples where the husband is infertile or for single women who wish to have a baby.

* In vitro fertilization which brings together a sperm and egg outside of the womb. A variation is IntraCytoplasmic Sperm Injection where a technician injects a single sperm cell into an egg. The newly conceived child is then implanted into a designated womb for gestation.

* Fertility drugs used to hyper-stimulate the development of eggs in a woman's ovaries. In some cases, this is done to increase a woman's chance of conceiving. In others, this is done with the intention of "harvesting" the eggs. The eggs are then used by other women who have ovarian problems or who are past menopause but still wish to gestate a child.

* Surrogate mothers for women who cannot or do not wish to bear their own children. Surrogates are also hired by homosexual men who wish to raise a child.

---

[112] Louise Brown was born on July 25, 1978; she was the first child both conceived and born as a result of using in vitro fertilization. By October of 2010, when Dr. Robert Edwards was awarded the Nobel Prize in medicine for his work in developing this process, over 4,000,000 babies had been born using it. In vitro fertilization is now used for the conception of 3% of all babies born in developed countries (New York Times, October 5, 2010).

Eliminating life from love has serious consequences, but so too does having babies apart from spousal intercourse. While many people have no qualms about using the above methods to have children, none of them are morally acceptable for Christians, and there are good reasons for this.

When a couple engages in sexual intercourse, their union of bodies symbolizes both their oneness of heart and their openness to life. Their physical union symbolizes their total gift of one to the other. Once more, a couple's fidelity expressed in their physical union endures on in their children. Each child a husband and wife conceive is the result of their gift of self to the other; each child serves as living, breathing image of that couple's love. In that sense, children are a permanent sign of their union. That means love and life can never be separated to such a degree that either one or the other is excluded. Doing so divorces the meaning of marriage which is love from the good of marriage which is life.

A second reason why these practices are morally unacceptable is that fidelity demands each spouse become a parent only through the other. When the goal is simply to produce a child and the couple no longer comes together in body, at least one other person is introduced into marital intimacy. When conception takes place in the lab and that new child is then introduced into his or her mother's womb, a third party stands between love and life. Fidelity between husband and wife cannot be maintained when scientific technology is used to produce a child and when there is a medical or biological intervention by a technician. This is true even if the egg and sperm are obtained from the husband and wife. Conception is no longer the result of an act of love between them. Instead, it becomes a science project.

For married couples, this process becomes even more intrusive when genetic material must be obtained from outside the marriage. In that case, besides a technician, the couple must introduce yet another party into their marriage, something which clearly violates the total gift of one to the other. The introduction of genetic donors or surrogates into the marriage then becomes a kind of virtual adultery. If sexual intercourse is to be a sign of the total gift of one spouse to the other and a total acceptance of that gift, introducing a third person (or even a fourth, fifth or more) into the marital relationship cannot be allowed.

Some would argue that the use of various infertility treatments is morally acceptable when the third party is someone who sincerely cares about the couple, a sister or mother or brother or a best friend. Out of a misplaced sense of love and compassion, that relative or friend may offer to be an egg donor or a sperm donor or to gestate the child. However, even then, love and life are still separated, and the introduction of multiple persons into the marriage still occurs.

In practice, family members and friends are usually not available which means using infertility treatments creates even more ethical problems. For example, if her husband is infertile and sperm is obtained from another man who is not her husband and used for insemination, even if by mechanical means, is not the wife allowing herself to be penetrated and impregnated by another man who is not her husband? By bearing the child of another man, has she not entered into an extra-marital affair? What becomes of her marital relationship which she promised would be exclusively between herself and her husband?

Similarly, if the wife is infertile, and her husband's sperm is used to inseminate another woman, even if by mechanical means, is not the husband inseminating and impregnating another woman who is not his wife? By fathering a child with another woman, has he not entered into an extra marital affair? What becomes of his marital relationship which he promised would be exclusively between himself and his wife?

This right to become a parent only through one's spouse cannot be taken away or voluntarily surrendered any more than one could voluntarily submit to selling his or her body for sex. Neither case is moral. No one is free to do that which is immoral and still remain in God's grace. That means couples who struggle with infertility cannot allow a third party to bring their genetic material together to produce a child. Doing so (even willingly) violates the integrity of their marriage and can never be sanctioned even when having a child (which is a good thing) is the desired goal.

Finally, what of the child? Every child also has rights, a fact almost always overlooked when babies are produced in the laboratory. Every child has the right to be conceived, be carried in the womb, and be born to a father and mother he or she knows, to parents bound to each other in marriage.

When technology is responsible for new life, the newly conceived child does not result from an act of love between its parents. There is no longer a relationship between persons, between parents and children, all equal in dignity before God. Rather, the relationship is now one of producer to product. Technology now has dominion over the origin and destiny of the child. Technology presides over fertilization. The child conceived is reduced to a commodity, and this is a violation of the child's dignity. It must be remembered that children too have rights, even very tiny children.

Church opposition to these asexual means of procreation has caused frustration for couples who greatly desire to have a child. Couples who are trying to have a child find it hard to reconcile the Church's call that they be open to life with her opposition to practices that might help them conceive. Even after considering the theological arguments against separating love from life, couples struggling with infertility may still find it hard to see why love and life must be kept together. This is all the more true in that many of these practices have now been in use for decades and are widely accepted. Why love and life must be kept together may be easier to understand after considering real life consequences of separating them, some of which are discussed below.

* Artificial insemination, a process developed in the 1950s for cows and other livestock, is one means of fertility treatment. It involves inserting sperm into the woman, usually from someone other than her husband. Single women now routinely have themselves impregnated at fertility clinics. However, women can also buy sperm on the Internet, have it delivered to their door and then inseminate themselves at home, a process similar to that used for cattle. While one such mother was picking up her daughter at day-care, the teacher said to her, "She looks just like you," but the teacher then added, "Well I don't know what the father looks like." The woman replied, "None of us knows what he looks like!"[113] Children conceived and born this way, like all children, have an innate desire to know their fathers (and mothers), and some are now seeking them out through the sperm banks which their mothers frequented.[114]

* Artificial insemination has also led to another problem. Some donors have dozens (or even more) children by different women. These children whose mothers unknowingly used the same donor are actually half-siblings.

[113] "Single Women in Their 30s Create Their Own Baby Boom" by Cindy Rodriguez, Duluth News Tribune (Boston Globe), October 18, 2002.

[114] "Woman Seeks to Meet Dad – A Sperm Donor," Mesabi Daily News (AP), January 31, 2002.

This has raised fears that some of these children could unknowing meet, fall in love with and marry their own sibling.[115]

* Husbands and boyfriends who have died in traumatic accidents have had sperm (which is still alive for some hours after death) removed from their testicles. Then their wife or girlfriend was impregnated with it. In one case, a woman went to court suing for paternity benefits for a child she conceived using her dead husband's sperm.[116]

* Fertility drugs are routinely prescribed for women to hyper-stimulate their ovaries. Along with IVF, this has been responsible for the huge rise in multiple births as multiple eggs are released at the same time. In some cases women have conceived quadruplets, quintuplets and even more babies at the same time. This has led to premature births and huge medical expenses to care for these children who generally suffer from birth defects associated with premature delivery. To eliminate this problem, doctors now routinely resort to "selective reduction" which is a euphemism for abortion. Using this procedure, doctors make decisions as to which babies seem healthiest and abort the rest. This allows a woman to bear twins who will be delivered nearly full-term and healthy. However, this practice also places couples in the strange position of wanting babies but then when they do become pregnant, of having their "extra" babies killed.

* More recently, selective reduction is being chosen as an option by women who have conceived twins or triplets naturally but who only want one baby. When a woman is pregnant with fraternal twins, and one is a boy and the other a girl, the doctor will then ask, "Do you want to keep the boy or the girl?" As one individual commented after reading about this practice, "Dr. Mengele would be proud."[117]

* In vitro fertilization (IVF), first used in 1978 has become commonplace.

---

[115] "One Sperm Donor, 150 Offspring" by Jacquiline Mroz, New York Times, September 5, 2011.

[116] "Dead California Man Becomes Father" by Louinn Lota, Duluth News Tribune (AP), March 27, 1999. "Widow Sues to Legitimize Child Conceived Post-Mortem" by Ellen Goodman, Boston Globe, January 27, 1995.

[117] "The Two-Minus-One Pregnancy" by Ruth Padawer, New York Times, August 10, 2011.

Homologous IVF and embryo transfer (ET) uses gametes from a man and a woman joined in marriage. Heterologous IVF and ET uses gametes taken from at least one donor other than the spouses. The sperm is obtained through masturbation and the eggs are obtained by hyper stimulating the ovaries with fertility drugs and then extracting them from the woman. The sperm and eggs are then brought together in the lab where conception takes place. Normally, multiple embryos are produced, but eggs can also be frozen and saved for later use. Some embryos are then transferred into a designated uterus. Success rates vary depending upon many factors including the age of the mother and the number of embryonic children implanted into her. One statistic indicates that only about 23% of attempts result in a live birth. These procedures are always expensive.

* Besides always separating love from life, IVF also has other problems. It almost always involves the destruction of new life, and that is because more embryos are produced than will be needed. When a couple has the number of children they want, they are often left with "extra" embryos. The question then becomes what to do with their extra frozen embryos. Many are simply allowed to die by thawing them out. Others are used for research.[118] Some people have proposed that these "extra" embryos be adopted by women who would allow them to be implanted into their wombs in order to give these tiny babies the opportunity to grow and develop. This has been presented as a humane alternative to killing them. However, that solution, while meritorious in its desire to save lives, is not morally acceptable because the means by which implantation takes place is not morally acceptable.[119]

* Pre-implantation screening has now become common. Here, IVF takes place and the embryos are allowed to develop to the point where genetic material can be extracted from them without harming them. This material is then tested for possible defects or for sex selection. After identifying

---

[118] The 1989 legal battle between Mary Sue Davis and Junior Lewis Davis over the custody of their seven embryonic children is described by Dr. Jerome Lejune in his book, The Concentration Can, 1992. Lejune also testified at the trial.

[119] Dignitas Personae, 19.

the desired traits, boy or girl, free from a genetic disease and so on, the selected embryo is then implanted into the designated uterus and the rest of the embryos are discarded (killed).[120]

* When the wife is unable to bear a child and a couple resorts to using a surrogate mother, the most obvious problem is that a third person becomes involved in the marital relationship. In one case where the wife was infertile, her sister donated an egg which was then fertilized using the husband's sperm and IVF. A sister-in-law then gestated the child. At birth the child was presented to the couple.[121] However, the use of surrogates has also led to other problems. In some cases, surrogates have become attached to the child they are carrying and refused to give the baby up to the couple who hired them. This has resulted in court cases where couples and surrogates have battled for custody of the children.[122] In some cases, after birth couples have refused to "take delivery" because the product (baby) was defective, they were in the midst of divorce or the surrogate delivered twins and not just a single baby.[123] At the same time, the surrogate who had no intention or desire to keep the child did not want it either. She had only agreed to gestate it.

* Couples from first world counties have discovered that they can hire surrogates from third world countries for much less than it would cost them at home. Thus, a cottage industry has sprung up in certain villages in India where wealthy couples exploit poor women by hiring them to

---

[120] "More Couples Seek Embryo Screening at Fertility Clinics" by Rick Weiss, Washington Post, September 24, 2006. "Designer Babies with Defects are a Test of Ethics" by Lindsey Tanner, Associated Press, December 24, 2006. "Designer Babies," Reader's Digest, July, 2001. "Special Delivery" by Christopher Joyce, USA Weekend, May 14–16, 1999.

[121] "Surrogacy Debated, But Still the Answer for Some" by Steve Johnson and V. Dion Haynes, Chicago Tribune, January 17, 1993.

[122] One of the first of these cases involved William and Elizabeth Stern and their surrogate, Mary Beth Whitehead, who bore Baby M on March 27, 1986. A court later awarded the child to the Sterns.

[123] "Twins Rejected, Surrogate Birth Mother Sues" by John M. Glionna, Los Angeles Times, August 11, 2001.

bear their children.[124]

* Older women past menopause have also been having babies. This is accomplished by giving a woman hormones which cause the uterine lining to develop, at which point an embryo is implanted into her womb. In effect, the woman becomes a surrogate mother, but one who intends to keep the baby. Here it should be noted that there is a natural reason for menopause. Because a human baby does not mature for many years, children need parents. A woman in her 50s who has a baby would be over seventy when that child graduated from high school. Older women or couples who undergo this treatment in order to have a child practically guarantee that the child will be either orphaned by his or her teenage years or will be taking care of invalid parents. This kind of selfishness has no regard for the child.

* Homosexual men are hiring surrogates to produce children for them. Again, as with post-menopausal women, adults are deliberately depriving children of the experience and the right of having both a mother and a father. It is hard to see how this narcissistic self-indulgence at the expense of an innocent child is not simply a new form of child abuse.

* Egg brokers now advertise on college campuses for donors who meet their client's specifications. Willing donors allow their eggs to be "harvested" for a fee.[125] One ethicist commented, "There is not much difference between those ads and what goes on with prize breeding of animals." This invasive procedure requires the egg donor to take medication which may be harmful to her. It requires unnecessary surgery, and the donor will always be the biological mother of any children conceived with her eggs. In that sense, she becomes involved with another man outside of marriage.

* The long-term effects of treating the child like a commodity are seldom considered. Children have rights just like everyone else, but that has not

---

[124] "India Nurtures Business of Surrogate Motherhood" by Amelia Gentleman, New York Times, March 10, 2008.

[125] "Human Egg Donation Raises Many Ethical Questions" by Kenneth R. Weiss, Star Tribune (Los Angeles Times), July 8, 2001. "Designer Babies," Reader's Digest, July 2001.

stopped some couples and individual women from having a baby to use for tissue donation for someone else.[126] One couple whose daughter had leukemia had another baby (naturally in this case) with the hope that the child could be a tissue donor and save their daughter's life.[127] Women have also volunteered to became pregnant and then abort the baby in order to supply fetal tissue for therapeutic reasons. This has prompted discomfort and ethical concerns among some of those involved with these practices.[128]

* Other practices being proposed include ovary transplants, harvesting of ovaries or eggs from aborted female babies, artificial wombs and cloning. While not yet available for humans, cloning is only a matter of time. Dead pets have already been cloned. Making identical genetic copies of dead children cannot be far behind.

As can be seen from the above examples, separating love from life has led to numerous ethical problems. Most infertile couples simply want a baby, and they see these various means of artificial reproduction as a source of hope. However, they cannot do just anything to have a baby. Husbands and wives must also do what is moral. The transmission of human life is different from that of animals and plants. Just because something is technically possible does not make it morally permissible.[129] The end does not justify the means.

As they try to conceive, Christian couples who struggle with infertility must keep in mind three principles. They must always keep love and life together so that any children they conceive are the result of an act of love between them. They must not go outside of their marriage to have children. Finally, they must keep in mind that any treatments they seek out must respect

---

[126] "Baby Created to Save Ailing Sister" by Margaret Taus, <u>Duluth News Tribune</u> (AP), October 4, 2000.

[127] "A Healing Birth" by Lawrence Elliott, <u>Reader's Digest</u>, June 1997.

[128] "A Policy Concerning the Therapeutic Use of Human Fetal Tissue in Transplantation" by Robert M. Nelson, MD, <u>Western Journal of Medicine</u>, April 1990, pp. 447–448.

[129] <u>Donum Vitae</u>, 4.

and safeguard both the life and dignity of any child that is conceived.

IVF, artificial insemination, surrogate mothers, sperm or egg donors and similar techniques and procedures are morally unacceptable because they all violate these fundamental principles.[130] If any of these techniques is accepted in principle, then where one draws the line as to what is not permitted becomes arbitrary. In fact, there is then no logical reason why any of these techniques cannot be allowed.

****

In the past, when little was known about human procreation, couples who experienced infertility had little recourse but to accept it, or they could pray that God would miraculously intervene (both of which they can still do). However, modern medicine now offers hope to many couples struggling with infertility.

Just as in other areas of human health, identifying and treating the underlying causes of infertility is key. Dr. Thomas Hilgers, founder of the Pope Paul VI Institute, has been a pioneer in the field of women's reproductive health.[131] He has helped numerous couples overcome their infertility and conceive healthy babies, and his success rate is higher and less costly than fertility clinics. In his research, Dr. Hilgers has worked to discover and treat the underlying pathologies women experience. His research has led him to develop new diagnostic and surgical techniques to cure infertility problems in women. His research has also led to the development of NaProTECHNOLOGY, which applies the results of his research to the healing of patients suffering from problems in their reproductive systems.

Dr. Hilgers' approach has been to always treat the person with utmost respect. At the same time, he acts within ethical and moral guidelines that do not go beyond the marital relationship between husband and wife, do not

---

[130] These fundamental principles also eliminate infertility treatments for unmarried women, or the use of surrogate mothers so that male homosexual couples can have children.

[131] Pope Paul VI Institute is located at 6901 Mercy Road, Omaha, Nebraska 68106, 402-390-6600, www.popepaulvi.com. See also, www.naprotechnology.org.

endanger new life, and do not treat the child as a thing or an object but rather as a person.

This approach of the Pope Paul VI Institute is in marked contrast to that of commercial fertility clinics. Ultimately, these clinics treat those who come to them as customers to whom they offer services for a fee. They are not very interested in questions concerning the dignity or even the humanity of the human embryo. They are not very concerned with what happens to unused, unwanted or "defective" embryos. Whether these tiny babies are used for research or destroyed is also of little concern to them. They do not worry about the source of the sperm or eggs which they use. Finally, they are not interested in the marital status of those who use their services. In all of this, they ignore that most basic of all moral principles: the end does not justify the means.

****

All couples must keep in mind that having children is not a right. Rather, children are God's gifts freely given to those whom He chooses. Keeping this in mind may help those couples who are dealing with infertility maintain a proper perspective.

Unfortunately for some couples struggling with infertility, no help can be offered (at least not in a moral way). Those couples who have exhausted all legitimate medical options are encouraged to pursue adoption, to practice generous service to others and to unite themselves with the Lord's Cross.[132] By gracefully carrying their cross of infertility, they will be sanctified, and God will bless them in other ways. God's individual plans for us are unique, and He has other gifts in store for those couples whom He has not blessed with children.

---

[132] <u>Catechism of the Catholic Church</u>, Second Edition, 1997, #2379.

Chapter Seventeen

TEACHING YOUR CHILDREN ABOUT SEX

Jesus once said to the Apostles, "Let the children come to me and do not hinder them (Mk 10:14)." Our Lord's command is especially relevant when it comes to teaching children the proper understanding of sexuality. We are all either male or female from the time we are conceived, and that means we are also sexual beings from the moment of conception as well. At some point, children will need to learn about this sexual part of themselves. The question is who will teach them?

In God's plan, sex is for both love and life. With regard to the life-giving end, it goes beyond simply fathering a child or giving birth to a child. It also includes the education of children in all aspects, spiritual, moral, intellectual, physical and sexual, the whole person in other words. While parents can delegate their child's education to others in most areas, that is not true for their sexual education. Teaching children about sex and its purpose is not the job of the government, the schools nor any other organization. Rather, it is the responsibility of parents.

That said, many parents are unsure as to what should be discussed and when. Some are only too happy to leave these matters to someone else or to some institution. Others put off discussing these things or leave their children to fend for themselves and find answers to their questions from other sources.

When that happens, modern pagans are only too happy to lend a hand. They have no qualms when it comes to talking about sex. Rather, they seem to have a perverse interest in sexual conversations and not just with adults, but also with children. Pagans will take every opportunity to mislead your children and start them down a lifelong path of sorrow and heartache.

For that reason, Christian parents must do their level best to see that this does not happen. Failure to take the initiative in discussing the nature and purpose of sex with your children simply means that they will not learn about God's plan for sex. Rather, pagans will step in and fill your children with their ideas. Here is a good rule of thumb. If what you are hearing from your children at the dinner table is not what you believe, then someone else is teaching your children.

****

Because of its intimate nature, most parents will be a bit uncomfortable talking about sex with their children. This does not mean they are "hung up" or that they should leave their child's sexual education to someone else. Parents are sexually intimate behind closed doors, and their younger children do not know what goes on behind those doors, nor do they need to know. So when a child asks a sexual question and the parent answers it, the parent is, in effect, opening that door a bit. It would be unusual if any normal parent was perfectly comfortable doing so and felt no embarrassment at all.

As parents, you should not be overly concerned about undertaking your child's sexual education. After all, you already know about sex, and you also know your children best. Remember that sex is part of God's creation and is therefore good. Remember too that God meant sex to be both a physical sign of the love between a husband and wife and the source of new human life. As parents you should be prepared to discuss these topics with your children at the proper time and place and within the proper context. Remember too that teaching your children about sex requires a sense of timing. You do not need to discuss everything all at once. In fact, your child's sexual education will be an ongoing process. Before you begin, ask the Holy Spirit for guidance, and you will receive it.

As to the content, what you teach your children about sex should be based upon what they need to know. Obviously, they will need to know about their bodies and also something about the bodies of the opposite sex. Beyond the physical, they will need to know why God has made us sexual beings. They will need to know what love is and also what it means to be open to life. They will need to know that marriage is the only place for sexual intimacy. Finally, because sex is such a powerful force and our sexual appetite is difficult to control, they will need to know how to lead a virtuous and chaste life.

A large part of your child's instruction will be experiential and will result from how you live out your own lives as husband and wife. From birth, children will observe how their parents interact. They will naturally observe physical differences. Daddies have whiskers and deeper voices. Mommies hold you and feed you and sometimes have babies in their tummies. Children soon figure out that they are boys like daddy or girls like mommy.

Children will also see the love and affection parents have for each other. They will pick up on masculine and feminine roles (as opposed to jobs). As you model them in the home, children will see how the role of a mother and the role of a father are lived out. They will see how loving husbands respect and care for their wives and how loving wives support and care for their husbands. It is not necessary to teach these lessons with words. Your example alone will be enough to leave deep impressions on your children.[133]

Remember that sex is natural and comes from God and what comes from God is good. When children see their mother pregnant, nursing a baby or the baby being changed, they will learn about the differences in boys and girls in a matter of fact way. This is also the time to begin teaching them about modesty. Small children should be taught to keep their clothes on and to always cover their private parts in public and especially in the presence of members of the opposite sex.

As the children grow older, verbal instruction can begin. These can start with questions that come naturally as children learn about the world: Where do babies come from? Why do mommy and daddy kiss? Why are boys and girls different? How did the baby get in mommy's tummy?

Do not be overly concerned with these questions. Young children are not looking for adult answers. When your five year old asks, "Where do babies come from?" He or she is not asking you to explain the mechanics of sexual intercourse. You can simply say, "They are gifts from God." Or, "Daddy and Mommy loved each other so much their love spilled over and made a baby." Children will be quite happy with simple one sentence answers like these.

As children begin to grow, parents will need to explain the changes they are experiencing in their bodies. Boys will experience erections long before puberty. Girls will begin to experience menstruation and the development of breasts. At the beginning of this process, parents should explain what will happen physically. The father should take the initiative with his sons and the

---

[133] This experiential learning of male and female roles is essential in a child's development. If a parent is missing from the household for whatever reason, the custodial parent should make sure that the children have time with a trusted adult of the opposite sex. They should seek out someone who can provide the experiences they themselves cannot give.

mother with her daughters. That way, the appropriate parent can better help the child understand his or her experiences. Depending upon the child's age and maturity, this may or may not be the time to also explain why these things are happening. If the child is still too young, you might simply say, "That is just part of growing up and becoming a man (or a woman)." Then leave it at that.[134]

As the child grows older, the time will come for explaining sexual intercourse. Again, fathers should discuss this with their sons and mothers with their daughters. Teaching your child the mechanics of sex is a relatively simple task, and it should be done in a frank and clear way. Use the proper terms. You should explain that this is perfectly natural and part of God's plan. As proof, you might point out that human sexuality is addressed in the Bible in many places. Also, let your children know that if they have questions, they can come to you for answers.

After explaining the physical changes and answering the questions your child may have, parents should then discuss why God has designed us in this way. Point out that we are creatures composed of body and soul. Then explain that God designed sex for love and life and that sexual intercourse allows husbands and wives to express their heartfelt love in a physical way. Their union of bodies is meant to be a sign of their union of hearts, a union established when their marriage vows are exchanged. Here point out that this union of bodies can only express true love within the context of marriage. Outside of marriage, it is a selfish act where two people end up using each other instead of loving each other.

This is also the time to discuss conception and pregnancy. Explain that this too is part of God's plan and that God calls married couples to partner with Him in bringing new life into the world. Here teach them that children are God's blessings and that couples should be open to life and to having the children God wants to give them.

Sexual pleasure should be addressed at this time. Point out that pleasure is part of sex but not the reason for it. Rather, pleasure is to sex as taste is to eating. Here, masturbation should be discussed. Tell your child that this is an

---

[134] Since children develop at different rates (both physically and emotionally), they should not be lumped together and given information about sex at the same time. Nor should boys and girls be taught together in mixed classes. There should be an effort to preserve childhood innocence for as long as possible.

incomplete sexual act and is neither loving nor life-giving. As such it is a selfish act and a sin.

This is also the place for a discussion on intimate touching. Explain to your daughters that they should not allow boys to touch their breasts or genitals, not even if that boy is her fiancé. Those kinds of touches should be reserved for her husband. Boys should be told not to ask for these things, and to refuse them if they are offered.

Here a frank discussion of the sexual appetite is in order. You should tell your children that the sexual appetite is very powerful. It is like a fast flowing stream. As long as you stay on its banks, you will be safe, but if you enter the water, you will be swept away. Point out that "it is necessary that temptations come (Mt 18:7)." Girls will be tempted more from the desire to be loved. Boys will be tempted more from a desire for physical pleasure. Remind your children of God's words to Saint Paul, "My grace is sufficient for you, for my power is made perfect in weakness (2Cor 12:9)." Urge them to pray for the grace to be chaste and to resist temptation.

The final part of your instruction will involve teaching your child how to lead a virtuous and chaste life. Even before any verbal instructions, the virtues of modesty and chastity should be encouraged and modeled in your home. Prayer and penance should be cultivated so that your child is not swept away by the first temptation. Boys should be taught to respect and honor girls. Girls should be taught to respect and honor boys especially by dressing modestly.

Explain that virtues are good habits, and that they must be cultivated. Here point out that charity is the motivation behind every other virtue. That means love of God and neighbor is always the basis for why we do what we do. Chastity is the virtue that governs our sexual behavior. One definition of chastity is this: "The successful integration of sexuality within the person and thus the inner unity of man in his bodily and spiritual being."[135]

To live a chaste life is to affirm what is good about sex, and we live chastely out of love for others. Thus we do not have sexual intercourse outside of marriage because to do so would be to use the other person for selfish interests and that is neither loving nor good. We are modest because we do not want to be a source of temptation to others.

At this point, you can discuss practical things your child can do to live

---

[135] <u>Catechism of the Catholic Church</u>, Second Edition, 1997, #2337.

chastely. These will include prayer and fasting, not using alcohol or drugs, dressing modestly and praying together with your date.

Finally, in talking about sex, note that there is always a boundary between talking about it in a general way (as you are now doing) and talking about one's intimate relationship. For example, you can tell your child that the way mom and dad express their love is private and between them alone and not the business of anyone else, even their children. Each couple's love is special and not for public consumption. In all of this, your goal should be to help your child understand the beauty and the holiness that comes from giving oneself to another out of love.

****

Part of your job as parents is to protect your children from harm. That means having and enforcing rules. Teens need boundaries. Teens will also test those boundaries (and test your patience in the process). Nevertheless, hold your ground. Consider it a badge of honor to be called "The meanest dad/ mom in the world." It is a good sign that you are doing your job.

To avoid problems, have some common sense rules pertaining to dating and Internet use for your teens. Here are several:

* No individual dating until the age of sixteen (nor dating someone younger than sixteen). It is simply ludicrous to allow eleven or twelve year old children to have boyfriends or girlfriends. If you do, do not be surprised if you become a grandparent in the not too distant future.

* No "going steady" in high school. Such arrangements seldom end well. Teens should date a series of people and go out in groups.

* No large age differences when dating. For example, juniors can date juniors or seniors (sophomores are generally not yet sixteen and hence cannot date). Your daughters should not be dating boys who have graduated from high school or men in their twenties. Period.

* No Christian-Muslim dating or Christian-Atheist dating. The cultural and religious differences are too great and will create insurmountable issues later on if marriage should follow. This also makes sense to a lesser degree with Christian-Jewish dating or Christian-Mormon dating where

major religious differences will have to be addressed.

* Require parental approval before dating is allowed. You must meet the boyfriend or girlfriend first. Find out something about the potential date's family, religion, the extent to which they practice it, and so on.

* Know where your children are and with whom. Enlist other parents you know and trust to be part of this surveillance network. Even good teens should not be left alone with their dates. When together at your home, have an open door rule. Things can and do happen when teens are left unsupervised even for a few minutes. In fact, most teen pregnancies happen at home in the afternoon when parents are not yet home from work.

* Children (boys especially) should not have Internet access in their rooms. Period. Nor should they have unsupervised access at all. The Internet is too powerful to be used unsupervised. It has destroyed good children who became addicted to Internet porn, online gaming or become victims of sexual predators.

* Only allow your children the use of simple cell phones.

* Reserve the right to visit web-sites and to look at all messages as a condition for having Internet access and electronic devices.

Before your child begins dating, have a frank and loving talk with him or her. Explain to them that dating is ultimately about finding someone to marry. It is a time to learn about the other person, their likes and dislikes, their hopes and fears, their dreams and desires and goals, their faith and their moral stature.

Remind them to pray. Tell your sons to respect their girlfriends. Tell your daughters to demand respect from their boyfriends.

Remember that your children are growing up. You cannot treat older children in the same way you treat younger ones. "Because I said so" is generally not a good way to answer a teen's question. They also need to know why. Sometimes it also works better to put the burden on the child; "Why can't you come in at 11?" "Why should you stay out until 2?" Keep the lines of communication open. Have discussions and not lectures. However, once you have stated your position you can then say, "Those are my reasons, and that's final." If your child then tells you that you are a rotten parent and they hate you, you can then say, "I am going to do what is in your best interest even if you hate me. I have to answer to God."

Know there will always be two tensions going on at this time. One is your desire to protect your child, and the other is your child's desire to grow up and be his or her own person. Naturally, you do not want them to be hurt in the process of growing up, but your child will also need the freedom to make mistakes if he or she is going to excel. There is an old proverb that says, "A mistake is evidence somebody tried to do something," and that is not a bad thing.

In the end, parents need to realize that children have minds of their own. Once you have taught them what they need to know, at some point, they will have to make their own choices and take responsibility for their own lives. Hopefully, they will base their moral choices on the things you have taught them.

For your part, you will have the satisfaction of knowing that you have done your part and faithfully discharged the duties God entrusted to you. Blessed Mother Teresa once said, "We have been created in order to love and be loved." If your children have learned this lesson, then you have taught them well.

TWO RELATED ISSUES

Jesus said, "Whoever causes one of these little ones who believe in me to sin, it would be better for him if a great millstone were hung round his neck and he were thrown into the sea (Mk 9:42)." It is a fact that we live in a pornographic culture. It is also a fact that even with the best of intentions and with absolute vigilance, parents simply cannot prevent their children from being exposed to every single sexual image and influence spawned by our pagan culture. This is true even if you never let them out of your home. Resign yourself to the fact that your children will be exposed to things at an earlier age than you would like or that is appropriate.

To counter these influences, you will need to be proactive. This unwanted exposure to pagan practices will require explanations and guidance from you. So be on the lookout for examples of pagan practices in magazines, TV programs, billboards, displays in stores, discussions on the radio or with friends, on how people dress, on how people live and so on. Use these things to initiate discussions with your children about how Christians live differently from pagans. Remind your children that we are in the world but not of the world. When issues do come up such as cohabitation, gay marriage, public nudity, pornography and so on, be prepared to address them at an age appropriate level. Better still, address them before they come up.

For example, when a cohabiting couple moves in next door, you can point out to your younger children, say from age seven to ten, that the neighbors are not married. Then say that God expects that a man and a woman get married before they move in together.

When children are older and know about sexual intercourse, you could say more. For example, you could explain that when a man and woman cohabitate, they sin in two ways. First, by setting a bad example because of the justifiable presumption they are having sexual intercourse. Second, by having sex before marriage, they are not loving each other but only using each other. You could then say, our expectation is that you would never embarrass our family or offend God by doing such a thing.

****

Public school sex education is a widely accepted practice. However, these programs are generally harmful to your children. By and large they have been created and are controlled by pagans. Nearly all of these programs start with the assumption that sexual behavior outside of marriage is natural and normal and that young people will inevitably participate in it at some point before they marry. These classes do not affirm marriage as the only proper place for sexual intercourse.

Since pagans believe sex is only for personal pleasure, they think the only thing young people need to know about it is how to have "safe sex." Consequently, their programs focus primarily on the physical risks associated with sexual activity and on how teens can best avoid these risks and protect themselves when having sex. For the most part, the only risk they really try to prevent is pregnancy. These programs take a more indulgent attitude toward the risk of contracting STDs, and they generally only talk about "prompt treatment" after the fact.

Some programs teach children as young as grades K-2 about masturbation. They suggest teens watch erotic movies, shower together and participate in oral sex.[136] Some schools go even further and have classes which focus on the pleasure of sex, on various sexual techniques, and on the acceptance of deviant practices.[137]

If sex were only for pleasure, then these programs would be doing a great job, and these twisted ideas would make sense. As it is, they only serve to lead young people away from God and into sin.

---

[136] See for example, <u>Our Whole Lives</u> by Barbara Sprung, 1999.

[137] That approach is taken at the Friends' Central School in Philadelphia. This school's curriculum involves the discussion of sexual techniques, discussions about the sexual relationships the students have had, how birth control works and how to use it, slang words for sexual activities and so on. See, "Teaching Good Sex" by Laurie Abraham, <u>New York Times Magazine</u>, November 20, 2011.

PART FIVE

OTHER ISSUES

PART FIVE: OTHER ISSUES

There are several issues which do not fit neatly into any of the previous sections. However, they are too important to pass over without comment.

The first of these involves our sexual appetite. What is it and how do we control it? What sort of things are natural and normal and what are the things we must avoid? How does the virtue of chastity come into play when dealing with our sexual appetite?

The second involves modesty. This pertains to both what we wear and how we adorn our bodies. In one sense, these things are very personal issues because they involve how we express ourselves through what we wear and how we adorn ourselves. On the other hand, these things also involve respect for others because if how one dresses causes another to sin, then Christians should not dress in that way. So then, what is modest attire? Are the rules different for men as opposed to women, and if so, why?

The third issue concerns sex and the single person. While most of what has been said previously pertains to sex within marriage, all of us have been single for at least part of our lives. During that time, we were as we still remain, sexual beings. Consequently, it makes sense to consider how the single person should deal with his or her sexual appetite. What is moral behavior for one who is not married? What does it mean for a single person to live chastely?

The last issue is celibacy. Is there a place for those who do not feel called to marriage? Is there such a thing as celibacy for the sake of the kingdom? If so, what is the rationale behind it?

These issues will be discussed in the chapters which follow.

Chapter Eighteen
THE SEXUAL APPETITE

Because we are sexual beings, there will always be an underlying sexual dimension in our relationships with others, and that sexual dimension will color how we interact on many levels. In general, one of the first things we notice about another person is their gender, whether they are male or female.

Much of the time, other concerns will push this sexual dimension into the background. When we are in need of medical care, it seldom matters whether the doctor is male or female. When we take a class, it generally does not matter whether the instructor is male or female. When our computer needs maintenance, whether the technician is male or female is usually irrelevant.

With regard to family and friends, this sexual dimension is also less important. While every one of our relatives is either male or female, the fact that they are kith and kin is generally more important than their gender. To a lesser extent, this is also true with our friends. Finally, this is also the case with fellow believers. With regard to God's sons and daughters, Saint Paul said, "there is neither male nor female; for you are all one in Christ Jesus (Gal 3:28)."

On the other hand, there are clearly times when this sexual dimension does come into play and does make a difference. In those times, it very much affects our interactions with others. For example, it makes a difference when playing contact sports. It makes a difference when we are getting dressed or in need of physical privacy. It makes a difference when we are seeking someone to marry, and it makes a difference when we are making love to our spouse.[138] At these times, the sexual dimension not only makes a difference, but it should make a difference.

One reason why this sexual dimension makes a difference is because in these and similar instances, our sexual appetite can be aroused. Jesus once taught, "You have heard that it was said, 'You shall not commit adultery.'

---

[138] Obviously, the assumption here is that marriage is between a man and a woman. Homosexual relationships (which a number of states now include within their definition of marriage) do not involve a spousal relationship.

But I say to you that every one who looks at a woman lustfully has already committed adultery with her in his heart (Mt 5:27–28)." The same could be said for a woman. If she looks at a man lustfully, she too has committed adultery in her heart. Our Lord's remarks remind us that we all have a sexual appetite. Furthermore, this appetite can be aroused, and it can be a problem for us even if we only allow it free reign in our thoughts.

To understand our sexual appetite, we might consider how our appetite for food works. The sight of food has the potential to arouse our appetite, but not always. If we are not hungry, we are unlikely to eat something when we see food. When ill, we generally have no appetite. Even when we are hungry, we may choose not to eat. We may be in the midst of something that requires our full attention and so, we cannot stop to eat. We may be fasting in which case we choose not to eat.

On the other hand, when we are hungry, it is not hard for our appetite to be stirred by the sight or smell of food or by the sound of food cooking. When our appetite is stimulated, we begin directing our attention to food and to eating. We even experience physical reactions; we begin to salivate and so on.

Like our appetite for food, our sexual appetite has the potential to be aroused by its proper object. The sight of a woman has the potential to arouse the sexual appetite in a man but not always. The sight of a man has the potential to arouse the sexual appetite in a woman but not always. Similar to our appetite for food, we may be engaged in some activity which requires our full attention and so we cannot stop for sex.

Just like our appetite for food, we are more interested in sex at certain times. Both men and women are more easily aroused when the woman is ovulating. Men because of changes in the woman's body which they sense subconsciously, and women because of the hormonal changes in their bodies.

Men and women are also aroused in different ways and by different stimuli. Men are more easily aroused by what is sensual, by what they see or smell. That explains why a woman who is wearing revealing clothes will get more attention than one who is not. Women are more aroused by what they feel and imagine. That explains why a man who is sensitive and listens is more attractive to a woman than one who does not pay attention to her feelings. Men think short term and are more interested in the physical act. Women think long term and are more interested in the relationship.

The analogy between our appetite for food and our sexual appetite is not total because engaging in sex is not necessary for sustaining one's individual life, but food is. A person could live out his or her whole life without ever having engaged in sexual intercourse and be quite happy and healthy. On the other hand, sex is necessary for sustaining the human race. If no one had sexual intercourse, the human race would eventually die out.

To control their sexual appetites, both men and women must cultivate the virtue of chastity, and this is just as true for married people as it is for single people. Just as a temperate person will eat what is necessary to sustain life, a chaste person will live according to his or her state in life. A chaste married person will not have sexual relations with someone other than his or her spouse. Chaste married people will guard their sexual thoughts, speech and behavior and restrict their attentions to their spouse. Chaste single people will not have sexual relations with anyone and will avoid behavior that arouses them.

Intemperate people have no self-control when it comes to food. They do not cultivate the virtue of temperance. When they see or smell food, they immediately seek it out and begin to eat. These people eat more than is warranted to sustain a healthy life. They are gluttons.

In a similar way, unchaste people have no self-control when it comes to sex (where lust is to sex as gluttony is to food). When their sexual appetite is stimulated, they immediately give in to the temptation. People enslaved by lust seek only the pleasure of sex and not its loving and life-giving ends.

If we do not control our sexual appetite, it will begin to control us and can become the motivation behind all of our actions. Lust can enslave a person to the point that he or she no longer thinks rationally.

Lust can compel people to do immoral things both inside and outside of marriage, and the Bible contains numerous examples of this. Consider how the two perverted judges acted towards Susanna. When she refused to give in to their lustful demands (as had the daughters of Israel before her), they sought to murder her (Dan 13:1–64). King David was inflamed with passion for Bathsheba, and he eventually ended up murdering her husband to cover up his adultery with her (2Sam 11:2–27). Allowing himself to be overcome with lust, Amnon raped his sister Tamar (2Sam 13:1–14). In his lust, Herod Antipas divorced his wife and married his niece Herodias (who had in turn left her husband Philip). When the two were rebuked by Saint John the Baptist, Herodias became so enraged she successfully plotted to have the Baptist killed

(Mk 6:17–29). Similar things have occurred in modern times to many people who have allowed lust to enslave them.

Temptations are part of life. As Jesus said, "Temptations to sin are sure to come (Lk 17:1)," and the devil is one source for these temptations. Satan was even bold enough to tempt our Lord (Mt 4:1–11), and that is why both Saint Matthew and Saint Paul call him "the tempter (Mt 4:3, 1 Thess 3:5)." However, the devil is not the only source of temptations. As Saint James points out, "Each person is tempted when he is lured and enticed by his own desire. Then desire when it has conceived gives birth to sin; and sin when it is full-grown brings forth death (James 1:14–15)."

This is especially true with the sexual appetite. It is both powerful and unwieldy. It might be likened to gasoline where there is hardly any time between the liquid state and a gaseous explosion. As long as our sexual appetite is not stimulated, it can be controlled. However, just like gasoline, once the match is lit, there is almost always going to be a fire. That is why we should take great care to maintain self-control. We should do our best not to let our thoughts run away with us or to stimulate our sexual appetite outside of marriage.

Saint Paul speaks about sexual self-control both within and outside of marriage. He says that husbands and wives can abstain from relations by mutual agreement for a time to devote themselves to prayer, but then they should come together again, "lest Satan tempt [them] through lack of self-control (1 Cor 7:5)." Likewise he counsels the unmarried to remain single, "but if they cannot exercise self-control, they should marry. For it is better to marry than to be aflame with passion (1 Cor 7:8–9)."

This self-control with regard to our sexual appetite must be cultivated through prayer and fasting. If one asks God for the grace to be chaste, God will give it. At the same time, Christian men and women must also do their part. They should be conscious of not being occasions of sin to others; they should take care not to arouse the sexual appetite in others by how they dress, speak or behave.

Both married people and single people should keep proper respect for those who are married. Those who are married should not be alone or go out alone with a married person of the opposite sex. Married persons should not be alone or go out alone with single persons of the opposite sex either. These situations can very easily become opportunities for temptation. Besides, married persons set aside these kinds of liaisons once they exchange their vows.

Their place is with their spouse.

Likewise, single people should not be alone or go out alone with someone who is married. There is no reason for this; married people are already vowed to their spouse. Single people should also take precautions when dating so that they are not tempted beyond their strength. At work, keeping office doors open or using offices with windows should be the norm when working with members of the opposite sex. Pornography should be avoided like the plague.

Our sexual appetite is part of God's creation and, as such, is a good thing. God created the sexual appetite to help bring couples together for love and for life within marriage. In that sense, the sexual appetite has a very important part to play in sustaining the human race. At the same time, Christians must practice the virtue of chastity according to their state in life. With the help of God's grace, self-control is possible and people can and do live chastely. Doing so will also give us joy knowing we are living as God would have us live.

Chapter Nineteen
MODESTY

Modesty has to do with the degree to which we cover our bodies, in other words, with what we wear. By extension, it also has to do with how we speak about our bodies. All Christians have an obligation to dress modestly, but as we shall see, this obligation falls more to women than to men. That said, modesty is a difficult subject in our culture because what we wear and how we choose to adorn ourselves is considered a personal decision. That means any objective standards with regard to how we dress are generally seen as a violation of our personal freedoms and of our right to self-expression. Our independent "No one can tell me what to do" American attitude, makes any discussion about modesty immediately suspect. Nevertheless, most would agree that one cannot go around stark naked in public and therefore implicitly admit there must be at least some limits to our personal self-expression.

Because the body is the object or goal of the sexual appetite, the sight of a naked body will usually stimulate the sexual appetite (a fact which hardly needs mentioning). There is an innate understanding, a natural sense, that those parts of our body that stimulate the sexual appetite should be covered. Saint Paul spoke of this when he said, "our unpresentable parts are treated with greater modesty, which our more presentable parts do not require (1Cor 12:23–24)." That is one reason why a modest person will conceal his or her body from others.

When naked, our bodies are fully exposed, and nothing remains hidden. To see us naked is to see us as we truly are with all of our flaws and imperfections, and when this happens, it makes us uncomfortable. Symbolically, we are revealed to others through our bodies. After Adam had sinned, he hid from God and when God called out to him and asked "Where are you?" Adam responded, "I heard the sound of Thee in the garden, and I was afraid because I was naked; and I hid myself (Gen 3:9–10)." Adam was guilty before God who saw his soul in all its nakedness and with all its guilt. This experience caused Adam humiliation and shame (a shame which of course was self-inflicted).

To strip someone of their clothing and to expose them against their will is to shame them. Doing so always causes great distress and humiliation. That was the intention of the soldiers who stripped Jesus of His garments (Jn 19:23–24). This was also true for Noah who inadvertently became drunk and was lying naked. That is why his two older sons covered his nakedness so that he would not be shamed (Gen 9:20–27). Today, without a proper sense of modesty, many underdressed people are also without a proper sense of shame.

While men and women are equal in dignity before the Lord, they are different in nearly every other way. For example, on the level of size and strength, the sexes are clearly unequal. Men are almost always bigger and stronger than women. Most men could easily overpower most women. Saint Peter refers to this fact when he counsels husbands "live considerately with your wives, bestowing honor on the woman as the weaker sex (1 Pet 3:7)."

Understanding this inequity with regard to physical size and strength is helpful for understanding another reason for modesty and that is the inequity with regard to our sexual appetite. It is no secret that men and women respond to sexual stimuli differently. Men are very visual, and so, when a woman dresses in a revealing way, she can easily stimulate a man's sexual appetite. A chaste man will then be left fighting temptations and struggling to control himself and his imagination. When a woman reveals her body, most men will very quickly move from seeing her as a person to seeing her as a sexual object. Generally, the reverse is not the case. Men who are underdressed do not garner the same response from women as underdressed women do from men. Often a woman's reaction is more one of disgust than lust.

With regard to sexual power, it is the woman who is stronger and the man who is weaker. That is why modesty is more of an obligation for women than for men. This also explains why Saint Peter advises that wives be modest. He says let yours not be "the outward adorning with braiding of hair, decoration of gold, and wearing of fine clothing (1 Pet 3:3)." Then, when husbands see your "reverent and chaste behavior" some will be won over to Christ (1 Pet 3:1).

It might be helpful for women to consider the following analogy. Just as a man can overpower a woman physically but should not out of respect for her, so too a woman can overpower a man sexually but should not out of respect for him. A man who does not use his strength to threaten but to protect and defend will inspire trust in the woman he loves. In a similar way, a woman who does not use her sexual powers to tempt or manipulate allows her beloved to be at ease around her and love her for who she is.

This explains another reason for concealing the body from public view: to avoid being used and not loved. It is a fact that the more we reveal of our bodies, the more attention we get, but also, the less we are seen as persons to be loved and more as objects to be used. Someone who is underdressed or naked attracts the attention of others but not for who they are as a person nor for their accomplishments. Rather, they attract attention because they have become an object of sexual interest. A stripper may be very witty and intelligent, but her mental abilities will be lost on those who come to see her body. A man who exposes himself may be a great musician, but his musical skills will be lost on those who see him. Men or women who draw attention to their sexuality and make it the central focus of their relationships will always be seen more as objects than as persons. Deep down, most people find this experience unpleasant, and that is true even for those who deliberately expose themselves.

Modern pagans care little about modesty. Instead, they have created a pornographic culture where sexual imagery abounds. They enjoy revealing their bodies. They take pleasure in "showing their stuff." Super Bowl ads for Victoria's Secret products and Dallas Cowboys cheerleaders in skimpy outfits hardly raise an eyebrow. Speedos on the beach and bikinis have long since entered the mainstream. Starlets at the Oscars or Emmys wearing gowns with plunging necklines or slit entirely up the leg are expected. Nudity in movies and on cable TV is standard fare.

While older feminists object to Hollywood's use of women as sex objects, they also object to any limitations on what a woman can wear. These feminists believe that a woman should be able to dress however she likes. If what she is wearing turns a man's head, that is his problem. In their minds, a woman has no obligation to him whatsoever.

While our pagan culture has virtually eliminated any standards for acceptable attire, it has also placed women in a strange position. On the one hand, women are told they must demand respect for their intelligence and accomplishments but on the other, they are told they will not be noticed unless they appear sexy. This notion is reinforced by the widespread use of pornography which twists our understanding of feminine beauty and human sexuality.

All of these things have conspired to transform women's fashions. Our pagan culture has so over-exposed the female body that most young women no longer have any proper sense of modesty. Shorts and cut offs far above the knee, bare midriffs and low-cut tops are common attire for teen girls. Few women would think twice about wearing strapless evening gowns (or even wedding dresses) that reveal ample cleavage. Someone once quipped, "gownless evening straps," is a better and more accurate name for these dresses. It is ironic that women who have more to cover up than men generally end up wearing less than men. Women's tops are sleeveless whereas men's shirts have sleeves. Women's shorts are mid-thigh or higher whereas men's usually extend to the knee. Men's shirts cover their chest and back whereas women's do not and so on.

Pagan fashions have distorted what is considered modest attire and reveal far more than what was formerly acceptable. Even many Christians now take their cue from modern society and simply wear what pagans wear without shame. However, modern pagan fashions are not modest. They are designed to stimulate the sexual appetite and consequently are inappropriate for anyone, let alone for Christians.

No Christian should ever deliberately be the cause of temptation or sin in another. We are our brother's keepers. That includes with regard to how we dress and adorn ourselves. We should take care not to arouse the sexual appetite in others. No Christian should ever be seen as a sex object. Instead, we should be seen by others as the sons and daughters of God that we are.

Christian women are daughters of God and temples of the Holy Spirit. They should never defile that temple nor cause its defilement in another. Women who dress immodestly and who are overexposed defile that temple, and they also demean themselves by presenting their bodies as objects and as things to be used. In so doing, they make it very difficult for Christian men who are sincerely trying to be virtuous to treat them with respect and dignity.

Many women, and especially younger women, do not realize the powerful sexual messages they are sending when they are overexposed. This ignorance was illustrated by several Christian women who were discussing whether a bride's strapless wedding dress was modest.

One said, "Modesty has always been more than just a dress." Another commented, "I saw her dress reveal her femininity and womanliness in what seemed to me to be all the right contexts. I think within the right contexts along with discernment and insight from others it is completely possible for a woman to choose a strapless dress and still be modest. More than anything, I think modestly is in the heart not the neckline."[139]

It is telling that these comments were made by Christian women. What is clear is not only how far our culture has shifted regarding what we consider modest but also, and even more importantly, that women do not think like men. While these women truly saw themselves as being modest, most men would not agree. Instead, most men would be aroused by how much skin was showing. If asked, they would also say that underdressed women make them "uncomfortable."

Modesty is not about how a woman feels about herself or about how she sees herself. It is not a subjective thing. Rather, modesty is mainly about how much skin is showing. This fact may require some women to rethink how they view what is and what is not modest.

So what is modesty? How should one dress? Where does one draw the line? In answer, any standard for what is acceptable should begin with our natural sense that those parts of the body which can stimulate the sexual appetite should not be exposed (except to one's spouse). Also, as with all virtues, modest attire will lie between the two extremes, in this case, between being totally covered from head to foot and being totally naked.

When applying these principles, here is a good rule of thumb. Stand in front of a mirror and then bend over; then straighten up and stretch. If something is showing at the top, in the middle or at the bottom, then what you are wearing is not modest. Remember, what you can see in the mirror is also what can be seen by everyone else. A second rule goes with the first. If you are in doubt, ask yourself what is the loving thing to do? Will I be tempting someone by what I wear? Is there enough material to cover me as I move about? If I turn, bend over or sit will things slip and show? If you follow these rules, you can be sure that what you are wearing will be modest.

These rules also mean that some clothing which is considered socially acceptable by almost everyone is in fact immodest. To be specific, that would include bikinis, most other swimsuits, strapless gowns (especially at weddings), most outfits worn at proms, shorts that go more than a few inches above the knee, exposed cleavage and bare midriffs, halter tops, skin tight clothes and so on. These kinds of outfits should not be found in a Christian woman's closet.

---

[139] See <u>Family Foundations</u>, March 2012, p 24.

Most women enjoy attention from the opposite sex, and this is not wrong in itself. A woman likes compliments, and a man appreciates a woman who has taken the care to make herself attractive for him. The question is really how should she go about doing this?

Overexposing her body is not the right way. That is not a loving act but a selfish one. Seeing too much of her body will arouse the man's sexual appetite and only reminds him of the pleasures of sex and of sexual intercourse. It will not inspire love, and it will not cause him to appreciate her other qualities as a person or as a daughter of God. One can see this by noting that any woman could get a lot of attention by simply walking through the mall wearing nothing but heels. But is that the kind of attention she wants?

Concerning men, when it comes to modesty, not all lies with the woman. In their clothing, actions, behavior and speech, men should also be modest and chaste. Men also have responsibilities in how they dress. They are sons of God and temples of the Holy Spirit. Consequently, they too should never defile that temple nor cause its defilement in another.

Furthermore, it is the man's responsibility to practice self-control. Men cannot demand that women wear burkas or cover themselves from head to toe (as do Muslim men). To do so suggests that every temptation or sexual sin is the woman's fault and that men bear no responsibility whatsoever. Obviously, that is not true. Men must develop and practice the virtue of chastity. Men must learn sexual restraint and self-control. When a woman is dressed modestly, a man is obligated to treat her with the dignity and respect she deserves. If she is doing her part, it is only right that he does his, and even if she is not, he must still behave virtuously.

With regard to their children, parents should set standards for them early on. Sons should be taught to respect women as the weaker sex. Daughters should be taught to dress modestly so as to not tempt men. Parents should not give in to societal pressures with regard to how their daughters dress. "Because everyone is doing it," is no excuse for immodesty. Neither is complaining that modest clothes are too hard to find. To follow Christ is to be different.

With regard to speech, everyone is obligated to be modest. Comments that are suggestive or that draw attention to our bodies for the purpose of arousing sexual interest are immoral. Seductive speech and dirty jokes are an abuse of the gift of speech and are also sinful.

In our pagan culture, Christians must make a conscious effort to cultivate modesty, and not just in dress but also in speech, thought and action. Modesty is an important virtue. It helps us to see others as persons, and as the sons and daughters of God they are.

TWO RELATED ISSUES

Nursing your baby is quite natural, and a woman's breasts were designed for exactly that purpose. The Bible mentions nursing mothers in several places. When Pharaoh's daughter found the infant Moses, she said to his mother, "Take this child away, and nurse him for me (Ex 2:9)." Hannah nursed her son Samuel (1 Sam 1:23). When Jesus was teaching, "a woman in the crowd raised her voice and said to Him, 'Blessed is the womb that bore you, and the breasts that you sucked (Lk 11:27)!'" In Christian art, there are medieval paintings and statues of the Blessed Mother which show our Lady with her breast exposed as she nurses our Blessed Lord.

Breast feeding is a natural and normal thing, and mothers should be eager to cooperate with God's plan for them and their infant as they supply the natural nourishment their infant needs. Nursing also helps mothers bond with their babies. As was mentioned earlier, breastfeeding is a natural way of regulating births. For these reasons, mothers should resist the pressure not to nurse at all (as for example, when they are working outside of the home) or to quit nursing after only a few months.

Because a mother must be ready to stop what she is doing to care for her child, nursing is clearly a form of love and self-sacrifice. A mother cannot say to her infant, wait until I am done with whatever I am doing; I will feed you when I am ready and not when you are hungry. Rather, it is she who must interrupt what she is doing to care for her child, but her sacrifice in doing so helps her to grow in love.

Along with nursing, there is the issue of modesty. There are some who see no problem here. They advocate a kind of militant breastfeeding. They deliberately go into public places and feed their babies. They argue that nursing is natural and so men should simply deal with what is their problem and not hers. In some cultures, nursing mothers can feed their babies in public, and no one pays the least attention. However that is not true in our society where a woman's breasts have become highly sexualized. That means nursing mothers must take into account the feelings of men. The sight of a woman's breast is not just of interest to curious teenage boys but to adult men as well.

Consider that many parts of our body have more than one purpose. The mouth is used to both eat and to form words; the foot is used to stand or it can be used to kick a ball; fingers are used to hold and grasp things and to feel and sense things. So too with the breasts; they also have more than one purpose. A woman's breasts are used to feed her child, but they also differentiate her from men and so, they naturally stimulate the sexual appetite in men.

For that reason, nursing mothers need to be aware not only of their child's needs for nourishment but also of their responsibility to help their brothers in Christ remain chaste and pure. Nursing mothers should feel free to nurse when their baby needs to eat, even in public as for example at Mass, services, a Bible study or in restaurants and so on. However, when nursing in public, they should make an effort to be discrete. During those times, they should use a nursing blanket to cover themselves or, if that is not possible, position themselves in a way that they are out of view or else retire to a place where they can nurse their baby in private.

At home, mothers obviously have more freedom. When their spouse, their other children or other women friends are present, a mother need not be as concerned about her breast being exposed. On the other hand, if she is having company over, she should adopt a more discrete approach.

For their part, men should give nursing mothers respect and when in public avert their eyes and allow her the privacy she needs until she is finished and has covered herself before resuming closer conversations.

****

Many have questions about the morality of tattoos and piercings. These things are not simply a question of taste or the freedom to do what we want with our own bodies. In the Book of Leviticus we read, "You shall not make any cuttings in your flesh on account of the dead or tattoo any marks upon you: I am the Lord (Lev 19:28)." This prohibition emphasizes in part the respect we should have for our bodies as temples of the Holy Spirit. Because the body is a temple of the Holy Spirit, we are not free to disfigure or deface it. To a certain degree, both tattoos and piercings do just that.

For some cultures, tattoos and piercings, like clothing, are forms of adornment. This was true even in Biblical times. When God compares Israel to a young woman whom He had clothed and adorned He said, "I decked you with ornaments, and put bracelets on your arms, and a chain on your neck. And I put a ring on your nose, and earrings in your ears, and a beautiful crown upon your head (Ez 16:11–12)." From this, it is clear that these things are not intrinsically wrong when respect for the body is preserved. If done, the body must not be mutilated or disfigured, and proper modesty must also be maintained.

Piercing the genitals, breasts, or nipples is never acceptable. Doing so requires exposing oneself to someone not a doctor or a spouse and that is immodest. Piercing the tongue can damage nerves, cause infection and chip the teeth. No dentist would recommend it.

Tattoos in private areas also require exposing oneself to someone not a doctor or a spouse. They too are unacceptable. Themes for some tattoos which are immodest, immoral, racist or satanic are also unacceptable. Some tattoos because of their placement (such as the face) are a cause of revulsion for those who see them.

From a practical standpoint, persons considering tattoos should remember that they cannot be removed except at great cost, great pain and great effort (and often not completely). They would be prudent to think about it for a year, and then after a year, to wait another five before doing something they will probably come to regret when they are older. Along these lines, one parent suggested to his children that if they liked art, they should buy a picture and hang it on the wall. Then, if they got tired of it, they could always take it down and put up something else, and that is something you cannot do with a tattoo.

Chapter Twenty
SEX AND THE SINGLE PERSON

During a meeting with young people at the 1980 World Youth Day in Paris, Pope John Paul II was asked, "In questions of a sexual nature, the Church has a rather intransigent attitude. Why? Are you not afraid, Holy Father, that young people will move further and further away from the Church?"

In reply, Pope John Paul said, "If you think of this question deeply, going right to the heart of the problem, I assure you that you will realize only one thing, which is that in this domain the only demands made by the Church are those bound up with true, that is, responsible, conjugal love. She demands what the dignity of the person and the basic social order require. I do not deny that they are demands. But that is the essential point, that man fulfills himself only to the extent that he knows how to impose demands on himself. In the opposite case, 'he [goes] away sorrowful (Mk 10:22)' ... Permissiveness does not make men happy. The consumer society does not make men happy. It never has done [so]."[140]

Behind this question is the assumption that virtually everyone today is sexually active whether married or not. This belief that sexual activity has little if anything to do with marriage is reinforced in popular TV programs, movies and music. It is modeled by Hollywood celebrities and by others whose lifestyles almost never include lifelong marriage. It is also taught in most high school sex education programs which stress having "safe sex" rather than waiting until marriage.

However, as Pope John Paul observed, divorcing sex from marriage does not lead to either love or happiness. Rather, true love requires that we always respect the dignity of the other person. In fact, true love demands that we never use the other person for our own pleasure. As we have seen, God has designed sex for both love and life, and uncommitted sex is neither love-giving nor life-giving.

---

[140] This question was asked at the Parc de Princes in Paris, June 1, 1980. <u>Be Not Afraid</u> by Andre Frossard and Pope John Paul II, Saint Martin's Press, 1984, p. 111.

Chastity is a virtue. By it we are able to moderate and control our desire for sexual pleasure, and to submit those desires to right reason.[141] All Christians are called to practice this virtue, and the particular challenge for Christian singles is to live chastely according to their state in life. Accepting that challenge means taking a different approach to life than that of the pagans. It will mean living differently from most people they know, including friends and possibly even family members. While difficult, the demands of living a Christian single life are not impossible. Quite the contrary, Christian singles should know that those who serve God will be given all the graces they need to live as He calls them to live.

Most people will be called by God to the married life. Those who are should prepare themselves for marriage, and they should do so long before they ever meet the one they will marry. Before all else, they should resolve to save themselves for marriage. Their virginity is something that they can only give once and to only one person, and that makes their virginity precious.

We treat special things with greater care and respect. Family heirlooms are placed where they will not be damaged and are only handled with great care. No one drinks a fifty year old scotch at an outdoor barbeque; it is saved for special occasions. Legal documents are not stored with old magazines and newspapers; they are kept in a safe place where they will not be lost. We save special things.

So too with our virginity. We save ourselves for the one we will marry. Only virgins, whether men or women, can give themselves entirely to the ones they love. In that sense, those who are preparing for marriage know they have saved themselves not just for marriage in general, but for that special person whom they will someday marry.[142]

This idea is also expressed in Scripture. Speaking of Israel and its people, the Prophet Isaiah declares, "as a young man marries a virgin so shall your sons marry you. And as the bridegroom rejoices over the bride, so shall your God

---

[141] Summa Theologica, II–II, Q 151, Articles 1–4, by Saint Thomas Aquinas. Catechism of the Catholic Church, Second Edition, 1997, #2337–2359.

[142] In a second marriage where a previous spouse has died, these same emotions are less strong and perhaps even absent. Nevertheless, in a second marriage, both know that they were in a sacred union blessed by God. It was not some uncommitted relationship.

rejoice over you (Is 62:5)." In this passage, Israel is compared to a virgin bride who has not given herself to another, and God is compared to the bridegroom who rejoices over the pure gift He is given. In a similar passage from the Book of Revelation, Saint John compares the beauty of the heavenly Jerusalem to "a bride adorned for her husband (Rev 21:2)."

Pagans fail to appreciate any of this. Instead of saving themselves for marriage, they lead promiscuous lives or have random sexual liaisons before becoming engaged and marrying. When people who have "slept around" do meet someone they wish to marry, they often have trouble seeing how sex symbolizes a union of hearts or even how it is a sign of a serious commitment. Furthermore, they can only offer part of themselves to the other. That is because each time they had sex before marriage, they gave away part of themselves. Consequently, their spousal gift can be neither complete nor intact. It is similar to a box of chocolates that has already been sampled and picked over, and who would want to give that kind of gift to his or her future spouse? Furthermore, who would want to receive that kind of gift?[143]

Having sex before marriage will also leave a person with powerful images and memories. Normally these diminish over time, but that does not mean they will go away entirely. Even years later, they can still lurk about in the recesses of the mind. In times of stress they can resurface, intruding into the marriage and raising unwanted comparisons between one's spouse and former sexual partners. Pornographic images viewed on the Internet or elsewhere will also do this.

In our formerly Christian society, norms were observed to help people lead chaste lives. Women (and men) dressed modestly, and movies were censored. Airwaves were monitored for obscenities, and dances were chaperoned. Today, that is not the case. Now topics that stimulate the sexual appetite are continuously before us, presenting almost constant temptations.

To resist these temptations, Christian singles must learn to be proactive. The sexual appetite is a powerful thing, and it can only be controlled with

---

[143] Christ came to save sinners and calls us all to holiness. For those who have lost their virginity, whether they are Christians who have sinned through weakness or they are those new to Christ, all is not lost. Those who have been sexually active before marriage can repent and resolve to live chastely from that point onward. Some refer to this as "secondary virginity" where one says, "From now on, I am going to save myself for my future spouse."

effort and constant vigilance. Living chastely will require deliberate and well thought out steps. It will also require God's grace. There will always be temptations and sometimes very strong ones, but this is true for everyone and not just for single people. That is why Jesus taught us to pray "lead us not into temptation, but deliver us from evil (Mt 6:13)."

Some temptations will come from the world. We live in a pagan society and so, we need to remember that how people dress, talk, and behave as well as what they watch and listen to is generally not Christian and does not reflect a Christian way of life. Christian singles must be prudent and wary of how these stimuli can shape them.

Some temptations are part of the human condition and the result of original sin. Baptism and God's grace heal these injuries to our human nature, but not entirely. That means one should be prepared for these temptations and not be surprised when they occur. Human weakness is a reality. Remember that at one point, even Saint Paul cried out, "For I do not do the good I want, but the evil I do not want is what I do (Rom 7:19)." Prayer and penance will be the first line of defense.

Temptations will also come from the pagans themselves. Generally, they do not care at all about the sentiments of those who desire to lead Christian lives and have resolved to remain virgins until they marry. In fact, many pagans find the righteous man a burden who disturbs their consciences. There are even some who would consider it a challenge to seduce those trying to lead chaste lives (Wis 2:12–20).

Christian singles should seek out friends who share their beliefs. Associating with those who do not share your beliefs will wear you down. As Saint Paul said, "Bad company ruins good morals (1Cor 15:33)." Without friends who share your faith, it will be nearly impossible to keep your resolution to live chastely.

Finally, pray each day that God will help you lead a chaste life. Meditate on God's word. Pray to your guardian angel for help and ask God's saints to watch over you. Doing these things will give you the strength to live as God expects and demands.

TWO RELATED ISSUES

Engaged couples or those who are dating seriously must still live chastely.

As their love for each other grows, there will be a natural desire to express their affection in physical ways. At the same time, as single people, they do not have the right to the sexual pleasures that come with marriage. They cannot have sexual intercourse, nor can they engage in intimate touching.

The question then arises: When do actions or behaviors cross the line and become sinful? To put it another way, how far can unmarried couples go? Asking these questions is quite similar to asking when night becomes day. Everyone knows the difference between night and day, but exactly when one becomes the other is a much harder question to answer. So when do thoughts or physical affections move from expressions of love to ones of lust? The answer can be found in another question, "What is the loving thing to do?" If one desires what is best for the other, that person will avoid any actions or behavior that could lead them to sin.

Common sense comes into play here as well. If you know you will be tempted by stopping in at your girlfriend's apartment after a date, kiss her goodnight at the door. If you experience strong temptations when the two of you are alone, instead of going to a private place, go for a walk in a public place such as a city park. Then you can talk and enjoy each other's company for as long as you like but are, in a sense, "chaperoned" by the other people who are also using the park. If you know a certain outfit is too "hot" for your boyfriend, then do not wear it (and in fact, get rid of it). Help him to see you as a person and a daughter of God.

Long distance relationships present another problem. Engaged couples or those who are dating seriously but live in different cities or states need to have appropriate overnight plans for when they visit. Those visiting should not be sleeping overnight at the other's apartment or home, nor should they be staying late into the night. Acceptable sleeping options would include staying with their fiancé's parents or siblings, staying with mutual friends or staying in a hotel.

Since no two people are alike, each person will be stimulated a bit differently from the next. Nevertheless, it is clear that close physical contact, day-dreaming or obsessing about the other person, unsupervised or extended time alone, and immodest clothing are going to create problems. So too will passionate kisses, embraces, and intimate touching. These things will only increase and not lessen temptations and the natural attractions that are always present.

Finally, long, drawn-out engagements, or dating for years only leads to temptations. It should not take five years for someone to figure out that they want to marry. When two people love each other and have decided they want to marry, they should do so. They do not need to have their college completed, all of their bills paid or own a new home before they marry. Finally, if a couple finds it becoming too difficult to resist temptations, they should get married. As Saint Paul said, "It is better to marry than to be aflame with passion (1 Cor 7:9)."

****

All good parents want to protect their children from harm, and this is all the more true when they begin dating. Long before this happens, parents should have a plan. They should establish ground rules for dating early on. As was mentioned earlier, these should include: No dating until sixteen. No unsupervised time alone. Modest clothing. A requirement that potential dates be introduced to parents prior to the actual date. Open door rules. Church attendance.

Studies have shown that children tend to live up to their parents' expectations. For that reason, parents should restate them from time to time. Parents should also cultivate open communication in the form of discussions and not lecturing. Remind your children that the purpose of dating is not just to go out, but to find someone with whom they can spend the rest of their lives.

By doing these things, parents can help their children remain chaste while dating. However, at some point parents must allow their children the freedom to put into practice the things they have been taught. They must accept that as their children mature, the responsibility for making good decisions and living a moral life will become that of the child and not of the parents.

Chapter Twenty-One

VOWED CELIBACY FOR THE KINGDOM OF GOD

Jesus once said there are some "who have made themselves eunuchs for the sake of the kingdom of heaven (Mt 19:12)." Here our Lord was referring to the fact that God calls some people to the single life and not to marriage.

Without the obligations and duties that come with marriage, these individuals are free to serve God and His Church in ways that are not possible for married people. Single people can pray more, and they can be of greater service in their parishes and congregations. When natural disasters occur, they can go to help those who are suffering. They can devote their lives to the betterment of man's lot here on earth. They can care for aged parents or for sick family members. In all of these ways and more, they can help to build up God's kingdom here on earth.

Sometimes, this call to the single life is within the context of vowed celibacy for the kingdom, a concept pagans find absurd. Life without sex is incomprehensible to them. Even many devout Christians find it hard to imagine a life which intentionally excludes marriage and sexual intimacy. Yet in heaven, there will be neither sexual intimacy nor marriage.

Once, in an effort to discredit Jesus, the Sadducees had proposed the hypothetical case of a woman who had seven husbands one after the other. After each had died in turn, the woman herself finally died. The Sadducees then posed this question: "Whose wife would she be in heaven?" Jesus answered that, "In the resurrection they neither marry nor are given in marriage (Mt 22:30)." Our Lord's answer revealed that marriage is an earthly institution; it exists in time and not in eternity. Hence, marriage vows require the parties to promise fidelity only until they are parted by death.

In God's plan, marriage is for both love and life, and sexual intimacy within marriage is designed to facilitate both love and life. Yet, we also know that deep, personal love can exist apart from marriage and sexual intimacy. There can be profound love between parents and children, between grandparents and grandchildren, between the flock and its shepherd, and even between husband and wife when intimacy is no longer possible or where it is

205

voluntarily set aside for a time (1Cor 7:5).

The Scriptures tell us that Heaven will be populated with a great multitude "from every nation, from all tribes and peoples and tongues (Rev 7:9)." These are the saints who were all begotten on earth but who now dwell in heaven. They "have washed their robes and made them white in the blood of the Lamb (Rev 7:14)." Because new human life will neither be created nor begotten in heaven, sexual intimacy will not be needed there.

In heaven, our greatest joy will be in seeing God. Any thoughts of physical pleasure will pale in comparison to the spiritual delights of seeing God face to face. For now this is hard to understand because "we see in a mirror dimly (1Cor 13:12)," but in heaven we shall understand fully because we shall see God face to face. In heaven, we will also know our loved ones (as well as the saints and angels), and our love for them will be similar to our love for God. It will no longer be encumbered by the effects of original sin. Consequently, sexual intimacy will no longer be needed to facilitate or enhance the love we will share as brothers and sisters in Christ.

Vowed celibacy for the kingdom as practiced by Catholic priests and nuns, by Orthodox monks, nuns and bishops, and by some Anglicans is often explained in terms of practical necessity. Work done in the Lord's vineyard leaves little or no time for family activities. A married priest would be a disservice both to his wife and to the Church. While this explanation is true as far as it goes, there is a more profound reason for celibacy. It is the desire to give oneself entirely to God and while yet here on earth, to seek a bit of the divine intimacy experienced by those already in heaven.

Everyone, whether married or single, is called to this divine intimacy, but to gain it, we must love God above all things, above even our spouse and our children. Recall that Jesus said, "If any one comes to me and does not hate his own father and mother and children and brothers and sisters, yes, and even his own life, he cannot be my disciple (Lk 14:27)." Obviously, the meaning here is not literal, but symbolic. Jesus did not mean that we must hate our family, but rather that love of God must come above all else, including one's own family.

Our Lord's words remind us that while marriage is a good and holy thing, the married person's heart is divided (1Cor 7:33). As Saint Paul points out, a husband is desirous of pleasing his wife, and a wife is desirous of pleasing her husband. The need to please his wife distracts the married man from giving his full attention to his relationship with God. So too the wife as she seeks to please her husband.

However, "the unmarried man is anxious about the affairs of the Lord, how to please the Lord (1Cor 7:32)." His heart is not divided. One who is celibate for the kingdom gives his whole life to God. The celibate has more time for prayer and study. He can ponder the Scriptures at length and read from the works of the great theologians and from the Fathers of the Church. Because he does not have to provide and care for a family, he can give all of himself for the building of the kingdom of God.

Here it should be made clear that the celibate does not view marriage as somehow deficient. Marriage is a good thing as are all the things God has created. In saying no to marriage, the celibate is also saying yes to something better, to a higher calling that requires greater sacrifice but also offers greater joy and happiness.

Often, our earthly friendships and being around others causes us to forget that there is still an emptiness in us that only God can truly fill. As he addressed God, Saint Augustine once wrote, "Our heart is restless until it rests in you."[144] Without a spouse and family, a celibate is more aware of this emptiness. It is true that there is a loneliness because of the absence of a spouse and family. Yet, the celibate is also more aware of the real cause for this loneliness. He is also aware of its remedy which is a deeper relationship with God.

Celibacy is not and never has been foreign to Christianity. From Saint Paul down to the present age, there have always been those who embrace it for the sake of the kingdom and for their own sanctification. Some do so in the context of religious orders such as the Dominicans or Franciscans or Carthusians. There they lead a communal life, and together with their spiritual family, they work and pray for the sake of the Kingdom. Celibate priests[145] do not lead a communal life but instead serve God's people as parish priests and in other ways. As they seek a deeper union with God, hermits, both men and women, devote their lives to intense prayer for themselves and for God's people.

While the celibate does not experience marital intimacy and even more importantly, the lifelong friendship that comes with a happy marriage, there

---

[144] Confessions by Saint Augustine, Book I, Chapter I (1).

[145] Those in the Eastern Churches generally do marry and are not celibate.

are other consolations. There is the joy of tending to God's flock and of offering God's consolations to His flock. In the Catholic and the Orthodox Churches, there is the joy of celebrating the Holy Sacrifice of the Mass and the Divine Liturgy. Describing the kind of life priests are called to live, a French priest once wrote,

> To live in the midst of the world with no desire for its pleasure;
> To be a member of every family, yet belong to none;
> To share all sufferings, all joys;
> To penetrate all secrets;
> To heal all wounds;
> To go daily from men to God;
> To offer Him their homage and petition;
> To return from God to men to bring them His pardon and His hope;
> To have a heart of steel for chastity, and a heart of fire for charity;
> To teach and instruct;
> To bless and be blessed forever;
> What a wonderful life! And it is yours, O priest of Jesus Christ![146]

The celibate life is something all young people should consider as they prayerfully reflect upon the life God is calling them to lead.

---

[146] Fr. Jean-Baptiste Henri-Dominique Lacordaire, OP, (1801–1861).

PART SIX

SOME WAYS IN WHICH
SEX IS MISUSED

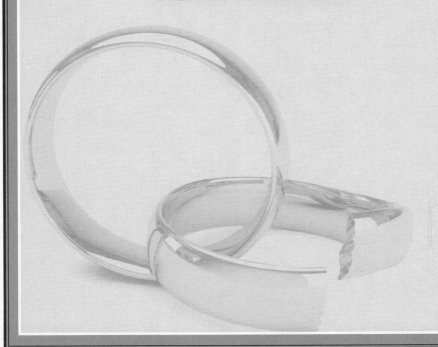

PART SIX: SOME WAYS IN WHICH SEX IS MISUSED

In our world today, few people have heard about God's plan for sex. Consequently, they end up misusing sex, not so much out of malice, but simply out of ignorance. Unfortunately, some of the ways in which they misuse sex are quite serious. For their part, modern pagans not only regard these acts against God's plan for sex as permissible but even good. For that reason we need to examine six issues in particular.

The first concerns sterilization. What is it and why it is wrong? What should couples (or individuals) who have been sterilized do?

The second concerns cohabitation and premarital sex. Why is this never a good thing? How does it differ from marriage, and why is it never a good preparation for marriage?

The third concerns divorce. What exactly does Christ teach about divorce? How are His teachings being followed today? What are some of the things Christians can do to help those who are struggling in their marriages?

The fourth concerns homosexuality and homosexual sex. What is meant by the term homosexuality? What are its known causes? How can Christians support and assist those who struggle with same sex attractions?

The fifth concerns pornography and obscenity. What are the effects of these things on individuals and on our society? How can one avoid falling into the habit of viewing pornography? What can those who are addicted to it do to overcome their addictions?

The sixth concerns abortion. What is meant by the term abortion? How does life begin and why must it be respected from conception onward? Where can those experiencing problem pregnancies or the aftermath of an abortion go for help?

These six issues will be discussed in the chapters which follow.

Some Ways in Which Sex is Misused

Chapter Twenty-Two

STERILIZATION

Sterilization is the most widely used form of birth control in the United States, and this is not a recent development. Statistics for the year 2000 revealed that approximately 21% of men between 35 and 39 years of age had been sterilized.[147] About the same time, by age 35, about 65% of women with at least one child had also been sterilized.[148] Combined, these figures mean that in the year 2000, of those between the ages of 35 and 39, about four in ten had been sterilized. These figures are even more significant when one considers that to render a couple infertile, only one partner needs to be sterilized. These statistics point to the fact that by their mid to late 30s, the vast majority of couples have been rendered infertile by sterilization.

Sterilization's purpose is to prevent conception on a permanent basis. The Church defines direct sterilization as "Any sterilization which ... has the sole immediate effect of rendering the generative faculty incapable of procreation."[149] In the woman, this surgical procedure involves cutting the fallopian tubes through which the egg travels. In the man, it involves cutting the vasa deferentia, the tubes through which the sperm travels.

In contrast to direct sterilization, indirect sterilization results from a surgical procedure or treatment intended to cure some illness. While the end result is the same (conception is no longer possible), the two differ in that direct sterilization is intended to prevent conception on a permanent basis whereas indirect sterilization is the unintended result of some other medical procedure (a hysterectomy for example).

---

[147] "End of the Line," <u>Saint Paul Pioneer Press</u>, September 27, 2000.

[148] "Sterilization and Its Reversal in Women" by Lorna L. Cvetkovich, M.D., <u>Ethics and Medics</u>, November 2002, Volume 27, Number 11.

[149] Sacred Congregation for the Doctrine of the Faith reply on Sterilization in Catholic Hospitals "Quaecumque sterilizatio" March 14, 1975 (AAS LXVIII 1976, 738–740, no. 1).

From a Christian standpoint, anything which deliberately thwarts the life-giving end of marriage, either for a time or permanently, is never morally acceptable.[150] Since direct sterilization falls into this category, it is never morally acceptable. In fact, undergoing direct sterilization is also unacceptable for another reason. It is a deliberate and unnecessary form of mutilation,[151] something which always violates the fifth commandment.

Many couples (and individuals) who have made the choice to be sterilized have come to regret their decision. Some have described this regret as a feeling or sense of "not being whole." Reflecting on their decisions later in life, others have expressed a sense of missing children they were meant to have. As these couples have grown in faith, they have come to recognize that with their fertility impaired, their gift to each other as husbands and wives is no longer complete.

Sin always damages our relationship with others, and both contraception and sterilization are sins. Often, the effects of sin remain for some time and even permanently in some cases. Drug abuse can result in the loss of one's job, deceit in the loss of friendship, adultery in the breakup of a marriage and so on. Fortunately for us, God is rich in mercy (Eph 2:4), and those who sincerely repent of their sins and resolve to sin no more will be forgiven.[152]

However, sometimes the process of forgiveness requires additional steps besides repentance and a resolve to sin no more. Justice demands that we restore things as closely as possible to the condition or state in which they existed before the sin was committed.[153] While we can never restore everything to its original state or condition, many effects of our sins can be overcome. An apology can restore a hurt relationship. Telling the truth can restore a good name, and restitution can restore material goods.

The demands of justice are most obvious in cases of theft or vandalism.

---

[150] See chapters 11 and 13.

[151] Strictly defined, mutilation is the severing of part of the body from the body itself.

[152] Catholics have the further obligation of confessing their sins in the Sacrament of Penance and Reconciliation.

[153] For more on restitution see <u>Summa Theologica</u>, II–II, Q 62, by Saint Thomas Aquinas.

214

In those cases, restitution is required as a condition for receiving God's mercy. A car thief cannot simply apologize to the victim, be forgiven and then drive away with the victim's car. Stolen property must be returned. When restitution is possible, even if it is arduous or will take a long time, the demands of justice must still be satisfied, and the Scriptures affirm this.

In the Old Testament, God spoke to the Israelites through Moses and said, "When a man or woman commits any of the sins that men commit by breaking faith with the Lord, and that person is guilty, he shall confess his sin which he has committed; and he shall make full restitution for his wrong (Num 5:7)." God also instructed, "If a man steals an ox or a sheep, and kills or sells it, he shall pay five oxen for an ox, and four sheep for a sheep (Ex 21:37/22:1)." Enforcing this law, King David would have required the rich man who had taken the poor man's ewe lamb to restore it fourfold (2Sam 12:6).

Jesus taught that, "if you are offering your gift at that altar, and there remember that your brother has something against you, leave your gift there before the altar and go; first be reconciled to your brother, and then come and offer your gift (Mt 5:23–24)." Our Lord warned that those who fail to reconcile with their accusers will be thrown into prison and "will never get out till [they] have paid the last penny (Mt 5:26)." A similar idea is expressed in the parable of the unforgiving servant. After refusing to deal mercifully with his fellow servant, the king had him imprisoned until he had paid back all his debts (Mt 18:23–35). You cannot be reconciled to God without also being reconciled to your fellow man.

While artificial birth control eliminates the possibility of new life on a temporary basis, sterilization does so permanently. When a couple's fertility is impaired, things are no longer as God intended, and both the love-giving and life-giving ends of marriage are affected. The life-giving in that new life is no longer possible and the love-giving in that the sterilized spouse can no longer give himself or herself completely to the other.

By renouncing their fertility, couples "break faith with the Lord (Num 5:7)" and remove from their marriage something God intended they care for and treat with respect. In that sense, what they have done might be likened to vandalism where some good thing is damaged or destroyed by the vandal.

For those married couples who have been using some form of artificial birth control, the resolution to sin no more must include reintegrating into their married lives a proper respect for their gift of fertility. Clearly that means

215

ending the use of artificial birth control so that conception is once again possible and the life-giving end of marriage is restored. However, in the case of sterilization, the restoration of one's fertility is not so easy.

In the not too distant past, reversals were simply not possible. Later, even when surgery had advanced to the point that reversals were possible, success rates were still very low. Today, with the advent of micro surgery, that is no longer the case. Now, reversals are not only possible but depending upon the type of sterilization procedure used, the female success rate can be as high as 90% in achieving open tubes and somewhat less in achieving pregnancy.[154] The rate in men varies more depending upon several factors including how much time has elapsed since the sterilization surgery was performed.

When reversals first became possible, moral theologians continued to argue that there was no obligation for those who had been sterilized to seek a reversal. They took this position for several reasons. These included the fact that some sterilization procedures were so extensive that a reversal would not be possible, and that even if it were possible, a successful outcome could not be guaranteed. They also argued that every surgery has potential risks to which one need not submit, and that the costs for the surgery may present a financial burden beyond the individual's means.

It seems clear now that advances in medicine have changed the state of things. What was once impossible is now possible. The fact that reversals are now not only possible but routine and fairly successful raises new questions. Is it enough to simply ask pardon for the sin of sterilization to be forgiven, or is there a moral obligation to do more? Can those who have been sterilized simply continue through the rest of their fertile years without making any effort to have their fertility restored? Is there now an obligation to seek a reversal as part of the process of forgiveness? In certain cases, it would seem that the answer to this last question is yes.

Now that reversals are possible, just like with other forms of contraception, sterilized couples must take reasonable steps to fix the problem and restore the integrity of their marriages. The obligation to seek a reversal might be likened to the obligation to make restitution. Just as with theft, one has an obligation to restore what was taken, so too with sterilization, one must make a reasonable

---

[154] "Sterilization and Its Reversal in Women" by Lorna L. Cvetkovich, M.D., <u>Ethics and Medics</u>, November 2002, Volume 27, Number 11.

effort to repair the damage. Bearing these things in mind, let us consider how this principle might be applied in real life situations.

Married couples in the midst of their child bearing years where conception is normally possible would be obligated to seek a reversal. Past objections to this position now seem weak. As in the past, it is still true that success is not guaranteed, but success rates are now much higher than before. In the face of permanent infertility, making an attempt to repair the damage, even if that attempt fails, seems far better than doing nothing at all.

It is also true that the cost is not negligible.[155] However, couples in a position to buy something extra or unnecessary (such as a new car, a vacation to Hawaii or a larger house) are also in a position to have a reversal. Couples should sacrifice these material comforts in favor of restoring the life-giving part of their marriage. The material things can wait.

A potentially more serious objection is the risk of surgery, and all surgery has its risks. These should be reviewed with one's physician. In those cases where there is truly a danger to health or life, there would be no obligation to seek a reversal.

Married couples where the wife is beyond her child-bearing years and no longer able to conceive (when she is past menopause) would have no obligation to seek a reversal. Nature has already taken the life-giving end of marriage away, and a reversal would do nothing to change that. Also, in cases where fertility would not or could not be restored (as when the sterilization procedure so damaged the sexual organs that they could not be repaired), there would be no point and no obligation to seek a reversal. Finally, those who do not have the financial means or the access to a qualified physician are not obligated to seek a reversal.

In other cases, the obligation to seek a reversal decreases as the chances of success drop or the degree of difficulty increases. Married couples where the wife is nearing the end of her child-bearing years and where conception would normally be rare would fall into this category. Similarly, as the risks associated

---

[155] In most cases, reversals are considered elective surgery and are not covered by insurance. In 2012, a brief Internet survey revealed that doctors specializing in female reversals were charging between $4,000 and $7,000 with additional hospital costs of between $1,500 and $2,000. Doctors specializing in male reversals were charging between $1,500 and $2,500 with no hospitalization required.

with surgery increase, the obligation would decrease accordingly. Finally, as the financial burden increases, the obligation to seek a reversal will decrease.

Single men or woman present different considerations. Those who intend to marry should follow the guidelines for married couples. Thus, if the woman is in the midst of her child-bearing years, she would have an obligation to seek a reversal. If a sterilized man is marrying a woman still in her child bearing years, he would have an obligation to seek a reversal. On the other hand, if the woman was nearing the end of her child-bearing years, her obligation to seek a reversal would decrease. So too would the man if his fiancée was nearing the end of her child bearing years.

If the woman is beyond her child-bearing years, she would have no obligation to seek a reversal. A man who is marrying a woman beyond her child bearing years would also have no obligation to seek a reversal. Finally, a single person who has been sterilized but who believes he or she is called to the single life and has no plans of marrying would have no obligation or reason to seek a reversal.

In less clear cases, couples should still seriously consider a reversal and pray for guidance to know God's will. As they do so, they may find the issue of reversal surgery continues to come up. If so, it is very likely that God is inviting them to a greater healing in their marriage and to restore what He always intended would be there. All things being equal, the obligation to set things right outweighs doing nothing at all.

After sincere prayer, if a couple has discerned that pursuing a reversal is not God's will, some other form of restitution should still be made. Adopting a child, supporting organizations that care for or educate poor children, becoming foster parents and so on are all ways of making restitution.

****

Many couples who have answered God's call to have reversal surgery have found greater peace and have grown closer to each other. They have also grown closer to God. With their fertility restored, they can once again give themselves totally to each other. In many cases, their decision has also brought them greater joy as God has blessed them with additional children and enriched them with larger families.

Those seeking reversal surgery should find a doctor who specialize in this procedure. Doctors who perform this surgery on a regular basis and those who specialize in it have higher success rates than those who do not. Many of these doctors advertise on the Internet and have videos on how the procedure is done and what to expect. To find them, do a Google search and look under "sterilization reversal." The Website "One More Soul" onemoresoul.com is also an excellent source for more information about reversals.

Chapter Twenty-Three
COHABITATION AND PREMARITAL SEX

Living together before marriage has become a very common practice and is now widely accepted by both pagans and Christians alike, especially among the young. According to census data and other statistics, the number of cohabiting couples has grown from 439,000 in 1960 to 7,529,000 in 2010.[156] In raw numbers, this represents a seventeen-fold increase over that fifty year period. Percentage-wise it represents an eleven-fold increase.[157] While some of these cohabiting couples see living together as a prelude to marriage, for many others, cohabitation is viewed as an alternative to marriage, an institution they no longer consider relevant.[158]

In the not too distant past, cohabitation was called "shacking up" or "living in sin." These derogatory expressions were a mark of society's disapproval. However, societal taboos against cohabitation have now largely disappeared. There is no longer any public scandal associated with living together outside of marriage as was the case forty or fifty years ago, nor do most cohabiting couples feel any sense of shame about their living arrangements. Among those living together without marriage, one can now find many prominent people including politicians, corporate executives, movie stars, entertainers,

---

[156] "The State of Our Unions, Marriage in America, 2011," National Marriage Project University of Virginia, table on p. 77.

[157] Percentage-wise, cohabiting couples represented 1.04% of all couples married and cohabiting in 1960 versus 11.2% in 2010. However, cohabiting couples are concentrated among the young. In its 2011 report, "The State of our Unions," the National Marriage Project statistics indicate that about one in four unmarried women ages 25 to 39 are currently living with a partner and that 60% of first marriages are now preceded by cohabitation (see page 75).

[158] "Barely Half of U.S. Adults Are Married — A Record Low," by D'Vera Cohn, Jeffrey Passel, Wendy Wang and Gretchen Livingston, Pew Social and Demographic Trends, December 14, 2011. This same report notes that in 1960, 72% of adults 18 and over were married whereas in 2010, just 51% were married.

physicians, educators and major league sports figures. Along with the rich and famous, there are millions of ordinary people from every walk of life, ethnicity, race, and demographic group who are also cohabiting.

In spite of the dramatic societal shifts in attitude and practice, faithful Christians cannot join with pagans in giving approval to this practice. Christians must remember that Church teaching has not and will not change with regard to sexual relations outside of marriage. Adultery, fornication and sodomy remain serious sins.

Just to be clear, adultery refers to sexual relations between two people where at least one is married to someone else, fornication refers to sexual relations between two people neither of whom are married, and sodomy refers to sexual relations between two people of the same sex. Sexual sins can also be committed in one's thoughts as is the case when one gives in to lust.[159]

Before the coming of Christ, the Israelites were prohibited from having sexual relations outside of marriage (Deut 22:13–30). In most cases their sexual sins were to be punished by death. Thus, when the woman caught in adultery was brought before Jesus, the Scribes and the Pharisees said to our Lord, "Moses commanded us to stone such [as her] (Jn 8:5)." For His part, Jesus did not condemn the woman, nor did He exonerate her. Instead, He instructed her, "go and sin no more (Jn 8:11)."

Jesus also addressed sexual sin on another occasion. While traveling through Samaria, our Lord had stopped to rest at a certain well. At the time, a woman had come to draw water, and Jesus asked her for a drink. In the ensuing conversation, Jesus spoke of living water that would quench all thirst and bestow eternal life. Intrigued, the woman then asked for this water. In reply, Jesus said, "Go call your husband." She was then forced to admit that she had no husband and that she had lived with five men previous to the one she was living with at the time. Her sinful life was an obstacle which prevented her from receiving living water (see Jn 4:5–18).

Sexual sins are addressed frequently by Saint Paul; he warns often of how they lead to damnation. In Galatians he writes, "Now the works of the flesh are plain: fornication, impurity, licentiousness, idolatry … I warn you, as I warned

---

[159] In teaching about the sixth commandment, Jesus said, "You have heard it said, 'You shall not commit adultery.' But I say to you that every one who looks at a woman lustfully has already committed adultery with her in his heart (Mt 5:27–28)."

you before, that those who do such things shall not inherit the kingdom of God (Gal 5:19–21)."

In First Corinthians he writes, "Do you not know that the unrighteous will not inherit the kingdom of God? Do not be deceived; neither the immoral, nor idolaters, no adulterers, nor sexual perverts, not thieves, not the greedy, nor drunkards, nor revilers, nor robbers will inherit the kingdom of God (1Cor 6:9–10)."

In Ephesians he writes, "But fornication and all impurity or covetousness must not even be named among you, as is fitting among saints (Eph 5:3)." "Be sure of this, that no fornicator or impure man ... has any inheritance in the kingdom of Christ and of God (Eph 5:5)."

In Colossians he writes, "Put to death therefore what is earthly in you; fornication, impurity, passion, evil desire, and covetousness, which is idolatry. On account of these the wrath of God is coming (Col 3:5–6)."

Elsewhere in the New Testament it states, "Let marriage be held in honor among all, and let the marriage bed be undefiled; for God will judge the immoral and adulterous (Heb 13:4)," and "But for the cowardly, the faithless, the polluted, as for murderers, fornicators, sorcerers, idolaters, and all liars, their lot shall be in the lake that burns with fire and sulphur, which is the second death (Rev 21:8)."

Cohabitation amplifies these sexual sins by adding to them the sin of scandal. With cohabitation comes the reasonable assumption that a couple is not just sharing a place to live, but that they are sharing a bed too, that they are having sexual relations.[160] Cohabitation sets a bad example by making public what was a secret sin; it flaunts Christ's teaching that the only place for sexual intimacy is within marriage, and it also weakens marriage by treating a sinful lifestyle as though it were an acceptable alternative to marriage.

Besides the harmful spiritual consequences associated with having sex

---

[160] While there are certainly a few cohabiting couples who are not having sex, they are the exception and not the rule. Consequently, it is not rash judgment to assume that cohabiting couples are sexually active. In fact, those very few cohabiting couples who are not sexually active have an obligation to eliminate any scandal that might ensue from their living arrangements. They must do so by telling friends, family, coworkers and neighbors that they are not sleeping together and that they have serious reasons for what they are doing. These reasons might include dire poverty, caring for one or the other who is sick and so on.

before (or outside of) marriage, there are also detrimental natural consequences, and this should come as no surprise. Breaking God's commandments always harms us and usually harms others as well. For example, the harm from sins like assault, drunkenness or rage is clear and becomes apparent almost immediately. While the harm from sexual sins may take longer to appear, it is no less real. The harmful effects of sexual sins include a habit of using and not loving the other, poor communication, unplanned pregnancies, sexually transmitted diseases, and increased rates of divorce.[161]

As was discussed previously, it is only within marriage that a man and woman can give themselves completely to each other. The inspiration for their gift of self comes from a love which gradually grows and matures during courtship. Over time, the two become one in heart, and their heartfelt union is ultimately expressed publically with their exchange of vows. Afterwards, when they consummate their marriage and the two become one flesh, their physical union becomes the outward sign of their union of hearts and of their love for one another.

Within marriage, this physical union between husband and wife serves to unite the couple and help them grow in love. Not only does this make sense on an intuitive level, it is also confirmed by science. During intercourse there is a biochemical reaction in the human body causing various chemicals called neuropeptides to be released. These chemicals promote bonding and make the individual more receptive to his or her spouse.[162]

Outside of marriage, sexual intercourse still bonds and unites; it still does what God designed sex to do. However, the intense feelings that come with intimacy can conceal significant differences in thoughts, goals, personalities and other dimensions of life. In addition, the absence of commitment creates a kind of emotional tension where one is both attracted and repelled by one's partner at the same time. This is sometimes referred to as "premature sexual bonding" where there is a union of bodies but not a union of hearts.

---

[161] There is some dispute over whether living together prior to marriage can be linked to increased rates of divorce. However, if those couples who move in after they have decided to marry are separated from the rest of couples who are cohabiting and who later decide to marry, divorce rates are clearly higher.

[162] "And the Two Shall Become One" by Dianne S. Vadney, <u>Ethics and Medics,</u> April 2005, Volume 30, Number 4.

Premature sexual bonding can be the cause of suspicion and mistrust in a relationship. Because both parties have given and received each other physically, there is a sense of possession (that the other is mine) similar to how husbands and wives feel towards each other. However, without any commitment, there can also be fear or anxiety that one's partner will leave the relationship or will not be "faithful" to the other. This feeling is all the more ironic in that no promise of fidelity has been made.

Having sex before marriage also gets in the way of communication. Instead of learning how to talk things out when there are problems, the couple has sex. Differences are covered up by intercourse but remain to be dealt with at a later time. If marriage does follow cohabitation, this sort of behavior usually continues until the differences can no longer be avoided and must be addressed. At that point the couple may find that their differences present insurmountable obstacles to the success of their marriage. Too late do they learn that they are incompatible. The result is divorce, something cohabitation was supposed to have prevented.

Fear of pregnancy is yet another problem with sex before marriage, and this is especially true for the woman. On the one hand, she may feel pressured to have sex because she fears that if she does not, her boyfriend will leave her for someone else. On the other hand, she also fears becoming pregnant along with all of the responsibilities that go with being a parent.

If pregnancy results, couples who may have had no intention of getting married (let alone raising a child) must now deal with the situation. Some choose to marry "for the sake of the child" but find that they are incompatible and struggle in their marriages. Others turn to abortion. Still others end up separating with the woman usually left alone to raise the child.

One more problem with cohabitation is this. Couples deprive themselves of the joy and excitement of becoming one for the first time on their wedding day. Having sex before marriage is like opening your Christmas presents in November. It eliminates the anticipation, excitement and joy in giving the gift of self to the other and of receiving that gift in return for the first time. There is now nothing to look forward to. This fact may explain why many cohabiting couples feel the need to have such elaborate weddings. They have already moved in together and have become one flesh, but they still feel a need to celebrate something. Their elaborate weddings and receptions satisfy that need in some fashion.

It is a fact that most cohabiting couples have trouble explaining the difference between living together and being married. This is partly because they have separated sex from babies and partly because intimacy gives the illusion of commitment. Only after they have had the nature of a committed marital relationship explained to them, do they begin to see how living together without any commitment is not marriage. Cohabitation is really more like having a roommate than a spouse. You share expenses and chores with a roommate, but not your life or your bed. Sadly, many cohabiting couples learn this only too late.

****

The time before marriage is meant to be a time for a man and woman to get to know each other. Courtship should be a time for talking things over and for learning how to show affection apart from sexual intercourse. It is a time for them to see if they are compatible and to learn how to work out their problems and disagreements. In a chaste courtship, couples are able to see more clearly. Along with the things that unite, the things which divide are also revealed and, when significant, may be reasons why certain courtships do not lead to marriage.

That said, there is a common belief among modern pagans that living together is a good preparation for marriage. For that reason, some people deliberately plan to cohabit as one step on the road to a possible future marriage. The idea is that you get to see the other as they really are, up close and with all of their good and bad habits. You get to know what it is like to live with that person and to find out if in fact you are compatible with them. At first glance this idea makes some sense, but as was pointed out, that is not really the case.

Other couples who end up living together did not begin with that intention. Cohabitation was simply the end result of a series of steps which began with dating, followed by being sexually intimate, and then staying overnight occasionally, then frequently, until it just seemed logical to move in and share expenses and a common bed.

Young Christians should never underestimate the power of our sexual appetite. They should begin dating having resolved to be chaste and refrain from intimacy until marriage, and they should have a clear plan for how they are going to keep their resolutions.[163] Doing so will ensure that cohabitation never becomes an issue for them. It will also assist them later when they are married in avoiding temptations to infidelity. The self-discipline they practiced before marriage will carry over into their lives as a married couple.

Parents can help their children by establishing clear expectations for them, one being that they live chastely and not cohabit before marriage. They can also assist their children, especially when they are engaged and the temptation to cohabit is stronger or the financial demands greater. Paying for the last few months' rent at the apartment or providing a place to stay during final preparations before their child's wedding are ways parents can help their children resist the temptation to cohabit.

Parents can also provide negative reinforcement by not assisting children who choose to live in sin. They should not help furnish their homes or apartments or allow their child and his or her partner to sleep in the same bed when they are home for visits. Parents should make clear their disappointment by not making a big deal out of any future wedding.

Cohabiting couples without children who are planning to marry should separate and live apart before they marry, ideally for at least six months. That will allow them time to focus on their relationship without the distraction of intimacy. It will also allow them to reconcile with God and live in His grace. Finally, it will give them something to look forward to as they prepare for their wedding and truly give themselves to each other for the first time.

Cohabiting couples with children are in a more difficult position. Their children need them. However, they can still sleep separately and live chastely until they marry. At the same time, they still have the obligation to eliminate scandal as much as possible by informing family, friends, neighbors and coworkers what they are doing and why.

Obviously, cohabiting couples who do not plan to marry should separate immediately. Living in sin is spiritually detrimental to both and is not worth damnation in exchange for any kind of earthly benefits it may afford.

---

[163] See Chapter 20 "Sex and the Single Person."

Some Ways in Which Sex is Misused

Chapter Twenty-Four

DIVORCE

As was the case in ancient times, divorce has once again become common. Statistics indicate that nearly 50% of all marriages in America will end in divorce.[164] Because divorce is so common, many people have come to accept it as something inevitable, as something beyond their control. The attitude seems to be, "People change. Things happen." Consequently, these people approach marriage with a kind of fatalism. Some marriages last while others fail, and there is very little, if anything, one can do about it. It is just the luck of the draw. It is the way life is.

While some people may joke about their failed marriages, most people find nothing funny about divorce. It is normally a deeply distressing experience, one often associated with feelings of regret and sadness. The pain connected with divorce points to the fact that divorce involves more than just blind chance or the luck of the draw. Getting divorced is not like getting cancer or losing one's job.

Contrary to the pagan point of view, divorce does not "just happen." It is almost always rooted in sin. Selfishness, indifference to the other's needs, unwillingness to compromise, the use of pornography and infidelity all quench love. Persistent selfishness will destroy a marriage. The subsequent feelings of pain, regret and sorrow following divorce come from a recognition that things could have been different had different choices been made. Because choice is involved, it means there is almost always a moral component to divorce, a fact made clear by our Lord's response to the Pharisees when they questioned Him about the subject.

The Pharisees had asked Jesus, "Is it lawful for a man to divorce his wife?" Our Lord responded by posing a question of His own. He asked, "What did Moses command you?" When the Pharisees replied, "Moses allowed a man to

---

[164] "Confronting the More Entrenched Foe: The Disaster of No-Fault Divorce and Its Legacy of Cohabitation" by Michael J. McManus, The Family in America, Spring 2012.

write a certificate of divorce ... (Mk 10:2–4);" Jesus acknowledged that was so. However, He then went on to say that Moses only permitted divorce because of the people's "hardness of heart." It was because they were unloving and uncaring that Moses had allowed them to divorce their wives.

After this exchange, Jesus then took the conversation in an unexpected direction. Our Lord first quoted from the Book of Genesis. He said, "From the beginning of creation, 'God made them male and female.' For this reason, a man shall leave his father and mother and be joined to his wife, and the two shall become one flesh. So they are no longer two but one flesh (Mk 10:6–8)." Jesus then added, "What therefore God has joined together, let not man put asunder (Mk 10:9)." With these words, Jesus not only renewed marriage but also raised it to a new level.

For the Jews, Christ's teaching on marriage was revolutionary. In their day, divorce had become so common and so accepted that even the apostles were surprised by this "new" teaching. Had they heard right? Did Jesus really mean what He said? In fact, the apostles were so troubled by our Lord's teaching that as soon as they were alone with Him, they again asked about the matter. Jesus not only affirmed His teaching but then added, "Whoever divorces his wife and marries another, commits adultery against her; and if she divorces her husband and marries another, she commits adultery (Mk 10:11–12)." His words prompted one man to say, "If such is the case of a man with his wife, it is not expedient to marry (Mt 19:10)."

When modern pagans hear about Christ's teaching on marriage, they react in much the same way as did the Israelites: with astonishment. Modern pagans do not regard marriage as something established by God, as something having certain unchanging properties and characteristics. Rather, they consider marriage to be a man-made institution that can be shaped and modified to suit the times.[165] Consequently, they simply cannot accept the fact that they might actually be held to their vows. Sadly, not a few modern Christians and

---

[165] See "Marriage is Broken. Here's How to Fix It." by Amanda Hess, Slate, November 6, 2012. Suggestions include: making the marriage a five year renewable contract; expanding parental rights to include others besides the birth parents; eliminating the "titles" husband and wife; making marriage "love-neutral" and picking a "point-person" to whom one would be legally united be that a spouse, parent, friend, and so on; eliminating the idea of monogamous marriage as unrealistic and replacing it with an open relationship where one can have multiple sexual liaisons.

Christian denominations also share this view.

However, the Lord was both clear and unambiguous in His teaching on marriage, something affirmed by both Scripture and Tradition. In essence, Jesus taught that divorce involves breaking a solemn vow to one's spouse, a vow made publically before God and His people. Divorce violates the covenant of marriage, and as such, constitutes a grave sin. This teaching is still in force, and it is something neither man nor the Church can change; both lack the authority to do so.[166]

So, why does God forbid divorce? Why was our Lord so inflexible on this subject? The answer is that marriage is larger than any individual couple. Marriage is meant for the common good of society. Thus before considering what is good for an individual couple, society must determine what is good for everyone, and what is good for everyone is that there are stable marriages and loving homes. Divorce harms both.

God created marriage for both love and life. He also intended that marriage be a holy thing. As Saint Paul proclaims, the unity between a man and woman in marriage is a sign of the unity that exists between Christ and His Church (Eph 5:32). Married couples are called to be signs of this union. That explains why Saint Paul calls marriage "A great mystery." Even more, the human family, the husband, wife and children are also a reflection of the Holy Trinity. Using this imagery, it should be as hard for us to imagine a married couple divorcing as it would be to imagine Christ divorcing His Church.

To help couples live as images and signs of the union between Christ and His Church, and so that children can grow up in stable homes, God has included unity and indissolubility as essential properties of marriage. Love cannot mature and deepen without these properties, nor could children be properly raised without them. In addition, between baptized persons, our Lord has raised marriage to the level of a Sacrament. Through this Sacrament, God gives married couples special graces and assistance to perfect their love and to strengthen their unity. The Sacrament of Matrimony helps to sanctify them on their way to eternal life.

Our pagan culture appreciates none of this, and so it makes divorce very

---

[166] Shortly before His Ascension, Jesus instructed the Apostles to go to all the nations "teaching them to observe all that [He] had commanded them (Mt 28:20)." Nowhere does He give them authority to alter or change His teachings.

easy, and this has led to the kind of society we have now. It is a society where commitment is not valued. It is a society where the needs of children are set aside for the needs of adults. It is a society where children are seen as burdens and not gifts. It is a society where infidelity has become easy and where people fear making long-term commitments. All of these things explain why God said, "I hate divorce (Mal 2:16)." God forbids divorce because divorce harms society and hurts people.

It would be right to say that Christ's teachings on divorce and remarriage are among the most difficult of all His teachings, and it is not hard to see why. Not only does it prohibit divorce, but in those cases where a civil divorce has been obtained, remarriage is still not an option. Were they to remarry in a civil (or even a religious ceremony in those Christian denominations which allow divorce), that marriage would be invalid. As far as God is concerned, the couple is still married and their vows are still in force. A divorced person who remarries before his or her spouse dies would be going against the clear teachings of Jesus and would be guilty of adultery.

****

While it is true that divorce is usually a sin, it is also true that those who divorce hardly ever share equally in the guilt of that sin. In fact, one spouse may be completely innocent (as is the case with desertion). Marriage requires that two people cooperate for the good of the whole, but when one spouse refuses to do so, it can leave the other in an impossible situation. The one may have done everything possible to save the marriage, but if the other was unwilling to do at least something, there can be no success.

There are also some troubled marriages in which a legal separation or even a civil divorce may not only be an option but a necessity. These include marriages where there is physical abuse, drug abuse or recurring infidelity. Staying in these marriages could very well endanger the mental or physical health (or even the life) of the innocent party. There may also be times when a spouse has a duty to leave the marriage because the children are in danger from an abusive spouse. If the situation is irreversible, the innocent party has no obligation to remain in the same house with a dangerous or abusive spouse.

When these marriages end, the innocent party may feel a sense of guilt. They may also feel responsible or that they could have done more to save the marriage. Even more, they may feel estranged from God. Those who have experienced divorce need to know that God has not abandoned them; they are still very dear to Jesus. They also need to know that they were not responsible for the actions of their spouse. They are only responsible for their own actions.

At the same time, those who are divorced have a very heavy cross to bear. They are still called to witness to the indissolubility of marriage, perhaps in a more profound way than even those couples who remain married. That is because even if their spouse remarries, they must still bear witness to the holiness and permanence of the marriage bond by living as single persons. This will be possible only by the grace of God and with the regular use of the Sacraments.

Those who are divorced must keep close to Jesus. They should pray often. They should offer up their sorrows and unite themselves to the Lord's sufferings. They must also avoid relationships where they will be tempted. Friendships with people of the opposite sex are possible, but always with the understanding that these friendships must not be intimate, nor can they lead to marriage. Catholics should go to daily Mass when possible and also go to confession regularly.[167] Those who were at fault in the divorce but who have repented should follow these practices as well.

Catholics who have divorced might also see if there are grounds for an annulment. An annulment is a declaration by the Church that no valid marriage took place, that something was lacking in the consent or the ability to give consent of either one or both spouses when they married. If there are grounds and an annulment is granted, that person would then be free to marry again.

****

Today there is hardly a family that has not been affected by divorce. Yet virtually nothing is being done to stem the tide of sorrow and unhappiness that results from it. Were society dealing with a disease or natural disaster that caused as much suffering, there would be a national outcry and a universal call to action. Yet, that is not the case with divorce.

---

[167] Catholics who are divorced and who have not remarried are still in good standing with the Church. They are not barred from going to Holy Communion.

Most of us are reluctant to intervene when we learn of someone who is struggling in his or her marriage. We may think it is none of our business. We may not know what to say, or we may be fearful of the reaction if we do say something. Yet silence is the wrong approach. By doing nothing, we abandon the people we care about the most, our children, our family members and our friends, people who desperately need our help and encouragement.

Divorce does more to destroy peace in the home and in society than virtually anything else, and that is why Christians have a special obligation to fight against it. All Christians are called to be peacemakers (Mt 5:9). All marriages have their ups and downs, and we need to help couples when they are down. We all have a certain influence over the people in our lives. Often all it takes is for someone that a troubled spouse trusts, a co-worker, friend or relative to encourage them to work harder at his or her marriage, and these kinds of interventions can and do help. When successful, they save marriages and lives are changed for generations.

With any intervention, there is always a risk. The person may get angry or might tell you to mind your own business. However, most people are grateful, and even those who do get angry usually get over it. Most of the time, their anger is not directed so much at you as it is an expression of their own frustration and helplessness. They do not know what to do or where to turn for help. So get involved and help them. Later on, they will often thank you.

When you learn of people who are having marital problems, you should immediately begin praying for them, and you should also pray for words of wisdom that you might say to them. You may be the one God calls to help them on the road to reconciliation. Perhaps you can offer advice based on your own life experiences. If you are not sure what to say or how to help, you can still encourage them to get counseling, and you can assure them of your prayers.

Avoid taking sides. Parents and siblings naturally tend to side with their family member, but the family member may be the very one who needs a talking to. Remember that there are always two sides to every story. Also remember, that there is usually enough blame to go around on both sides. So instead of siding with one or the other, side with the marriage. Help them both work things through.

Finally, encourage husbands and wives to pray together. Remind them that God wants their marriage to succeed. After all, it is He who has joined them together. Couples who pray together and who ask for God's help will receive it (Mt 7:7).

Modern pagans think that life-long marriage is impossible. They believe that divorce, while not a good thing, must always be available as an option, but that is not what Jesus taught. In the face of these pagan attitudes, Christians must stand as witnesses to all of the Lord's teachings, even the difficult ones that pertain to marriage. We must all do what we can to strengthen marriage, and not just for society's sake, but for the good of the Church as well. With God's help and a desire to do something, we can make things better.

Chapter Twenty-Five
HOMOSEXUALITY AND HOMOSEXUAL ACTS

Being sexually attracted to members of the opposite sex is the natural state or condition of the human person. This is called heterosexuality. While this is the natural state, there have always been some people who are sexually attracted to members of the same sex. This is called homosexuality. There are also people who are sexually attracted to members of both sexes. This state or condition is called bisexuality.

Homosexual acts refer to a wide variety of sexual practices between persons of the same sex. For men, these include anal intercourse and oral-genital contact. For women, these include oral-genital contact, or penetration with fingers, toes, or sex toys. Some of these practices are unhealthy. They can and do cause physical harm, and they can also spread disease. Finally, they are also unnatural in that the sexual organs and other parts of the body were not designed to be used for homosexual acts.

In most western countries, people have become increasingly tolerant of homosexual acts. What was until quite recently viewed by nearly everyone as perverse and even outlawed in the criminal code is now regarded by many, especially among the young, as simply an alternative life-style.[168] They see homosexual acts as just one among many legitimate forms of sexual expression. Even more people believe that when it comes to sexual matters, consenting adults ought to be free to do as they please.

Several countries have gone beyond the mere tolerance or acceptance of homosexuality. For example, Canada and Sweden have used legal sanctions to punish those who write or speak out publically against homosexuality. Other countries, while not willing to limit free speech or religious freedom (as yet), have changed their laws so as to include homosexual unions within the

---

[168] "Two-Thirds of Democrats Now Support Gay Marriage," The Pew Forum on Religion and Public Life, Pew Research Center, July 31, 2012. This survey includes commentary along with detailed tables of American opinion on Gay Marriage and Adoption.

definition of marriage.[169]

This widespread but still recent acceptance of homosexuality is the direct result of a decades long campaign to change societal attitudes.[170] That campaign has employed newspaper editorials, TV programs, films, books, commentaries, talk shows, school curricula, and support from prominent politicians and Hollywood personalities.

In the 1980s and 1990s, the campaign to include homosexual relationships within the definition of marriage began gaining momentum. Particularly troubling to supporters of marriage was the 1993 ruling by the Supreme Court of Hawaii that the state needed a compelling interest to prohibit same sex marriage. These developments prompted marriage supporters to seek federal legislation that would define marriage as between one man and one woman. Their successful campaign resulted in the Defense of Marriage Act (DOMA). It was passed by large majorities in both houses of Congress and signed into law on September 21, 1996 by President Clinton.

However, even as DOMA was being passed, support for it was eroding. Fifteen years after its passage, attitudes about homosexuality had changed significantly, so much so, that the Obama administration felt safe in criticizing the law. On February 23, 2011, Attorney General Eric Holder announced that the administration believed section 3 of DOMA (the part of the law which defines marriage as the legal union between one man and one woman) to be unconstitutional. For that reason, he said the administration would no longer be defending that part of the law against legal challenges.

On September 20, 2011, the administration went a step further in its efforts to eliminate what remained of the social stigma associated with homosexuality. On that day, it ended the military policy commonly called "Don't ask, don't tell." That policy had prohibited discrimination against homosexual service

---

[169] In 2000, the Netherlands became the first country to include homosexual unions within the definition of marriage. By the end of 2012, eleven countries (Argentina, Belgium, Canada, Denmark, Iceland, Netherlands, Norway, Portugal, Spain, South Africa, and Sweden) and several sub national jurisdictions (parts of Brazil, Mexico and the United States) were included in this group.

[170] One place to find detailed tactics for this campaign is in the book, After the Ball—How America Will Conquer its Fear and Hatred of Gays in the 90's by Marshall Kirk and Hunter Madsen, 1989.

personnel as long as they did not reveal their sexual orientation, but it also retained the ban on openly homosexual persons from serving in the military. With the policy no longer in place, active homosexuals could for the first time serve in the military. After ending the policy, the administration also required all military personnel to undergo sensitivity training in order to break down their opposition to homosexuality.

On June 26, 2013, in a five to four decision, the Supreme Court struck down that part of DOMA which defined marriage as between one man and one woman. The Court declared that DOMA violated the equal protection clause guaranteed under the Constitution's Fifth Amendment. Writing for the majority, Justice Kennedy said that DOMA "places same sex couples in an unstable position of being in a second tier marriage." He also said that by its recognition of homosexual marriage, the State [of New York] had acknowledged that the intimate behavior of homosexual couples was "worthy of dignity in the community equal with all other marriages."

Society's rapidly changing views with regard to homosexuality have left many people confused and with numerous questions. Some are basic. What is homosexuality? What causes it? Is it natural? Others have to do with morality and faith. Can two men or two women really get married? As a Christian, how should I respond to someone who is a homosexual? Others come from those who struggle with same sex attraction. If I am homosexual, can I still follow Christ? Can I still be a member of the Church? These questions will be addressed below.

****

While many today regard homosexuality as normal (including many psychiatrists),[171] that viewpoint is not logical. In reality, same sex attraction is neither natural nor normal; things are not as they should be. To demonstrate this one need only point out that the bodies of two men or of two women are

---

[171] In 1973, the American Psychiatric Association (APA) board of trustees voted to drop homosexuality as a mental disorder and preferred instead to regard the condition as "a normal variation of sexual expression." This decision of the board was confirmed by a referendum among the membership by a vote roughly six to four in favor. Because homosexuality is now regarded as something normal by the APA, most professionals no longer attempt to cure it.

not complementary. To put it bluntly, the parts do not fit. There is simply no way for a homosexual person to satisfy his or her sexual appetite in the normal physical order, that is, through normal sexual intercourse. Instead, homosexual persons must engage in unnatural sexual behavior to satisfy their sexual urges. All that is possible for them is erotic activity which is neither love-giving nor life-giving. Simply put, homosexuality is a disorder.[172]

Homosexuality is not a new thing. It was practiced openly in ancient Greece and Rome. It is also mentioned in the Bible (Gen 19:1–19, 1 Kings 14:24, 15:12 and 2 Kings 23:7) and in other ancient writings. What is new is the demand that it be accepted as something natural. What is also new is the view that homosexual relationships are equivalent to marriage (as Justice Kennedy argued when striking down DOMA).

Accurate figures on the number of homosexuals in the general population are hard to come by, due in large part to the highly politicized nature of the subject. However, the 10% figure claimed by the homosexual lobby is clearly inflated. It had its origins in a 1948 study by Alfred Kinsey.[173] However, Kinsey's subjects were not a representative sample of the American male population. Rather, sex offenders, prison inmates and ex-cons were over represented in his subject population. Good statistics indicate that somewhere between 2% and 4% of the male population experiences same-sex attraction. In the female population, the number is about a percentage point lower. These figures are much smaller than the 10% claimed by the gay rights activists.

In most cases, homosexuality is not chosen. However, there are some individuals who do choose to engage in homosexual activities, and this is true especially when members of the opposite sex are not available.[174] On the other hand, some maintain that personal choice has absolutely no role to play in sexual orientation. Starting from this position, they have attempted to show homosexuality is inborn or genetic. At this point, the results from good

---

[172] When our natural instinct is self-preservation, the willingness of homosexuals to engage in extremely compulsive, highly reckless, and self-destructive behaviors is further evidence homosexuality is unnatural and a disorder.

[173] Sexual Behavior in the Human Male by Alfred Kinsey et al., 1948.

[174] This happens in settings where only one sex is present such as in prisons or camps.

research on this matter are inconclusive.[175] Researchers have yet to find any clear and definite genetic cause.

In those cases where homosexuality is clearly not chosen (the vast majority), there appear to be multiple causes, some environmental, and some perhaps beginning even in utero. Causal factors linked to homosexuality include sadness and loneliness caused by childhood rejection and ridicule by peers. This rejection and ridicule can be related to poor athletic abilities. It can also be related to a weak masculine identity due to absent or poor fathers. Other factors linked to homosexuality include fear and mistrust resulting from traumatic experiences in youth with an unloving father or overbearing mother, addictive disorders, narcissism or selfishness, attempts to flee responsibility, sexual trauma in childhood, and anger resulting from not having the kind of body one would have liked, or of having a body their peers ridiculed.[176] That said, in many cases, there is simply no clear or certain explanation.

Psychologists point out that psychosexuality is a postnatal development. Because our core gender identity as male or female is based upon our bodies, and because we are male or female in every cell of our body, we cannot choose or change our gender. We are irrevocably male or female.[177]

However, it is also true that the sexual identity may or may not match the core sexual identity. In other words, an individual who is male may not accept or relate to the masculine identity that goes with his being male. Similarly, an individual who is female may not accept or relate to the feminine identity that goes with her being female.[178] Taking this one step further, in the homosexual person, there is "an incomplete or arrested psychosexual development" where

---

[175] See "Key Aspects of Homosexuality" by Jeffery Keefe, O.F.M., in The Truth About Homosexuality, 1996, pp. 44–51.

[176] "The Origins and Healing of Homosexual Attractions and Behaviors" by Richard Fitzgibbons, M.D., in The Truth About Homosexuality, 1996, pp. 307–324.

[177] Sex change operations and hormones can alter physical characteristics and behavior, but were one to examine any cell of the body, it would still retain the genetic gender of the person, a gender established at conception.

[178] See "Key Aspects of Homosexuality" by Jeffery Keefe, O.F.M., in The Truth About Homosexuality, 1996, pp. 34–35.

the person never moves from a homo-psychosexual stage of development to become heterosexually oriented.[179]

With regard to the intensity of same sex attraction, there is no uniform state or condition. Some individuals may have mild feelings towards persons of the same sex whereas others may have intense feelings. For some, these feelings may change over time and with greater maturity. They may even go away entirely. For others, these feelings may be life-long and irreversible.

That feelings may go away entirely belies the assertion by gay rights activists that change is neither desirable nor even possible. Some homosexual persons can and have been converted to heterosexuality. Others, with the help of God's grace, resist the temptations to engage in homosexual acts and some have even gone on to live in committed heterosexual marriages.[180] On the other hand, some Christian groups believe change is always or nearly always possible, but that is not true either. In reality, because homosexuality is such a deep-seated problem, change is usually very difficult and for many simply not possible.

Fr. John Harvey, the late founder of Courage, insisted that any real change requires three things: Psychological counseling, a solid spiritual life which includes a spiritual director (who is allowed to work with the psychologist), and finally, participation in a group which provides peer support and accountability.[181]

From a Christian standpoint, those who struggle with same sex attraction must not act on these attractions, and the Scriptures are quite clear on this matter. The Cities of Sodom and Gomorrah were destroyed by God because the outcry against them was so great and their sin so grave (Gen 18:20). Their very grave sin involved homosexual acts (Gen 19:5).[182] Saint Jude says that

---

[179] "The Origins and Healings of Homosexual Attractions and Behaviors" by Richard Fitzgibbons, M.D., in The Truth About Homosexuality, 1996, pp. 346–350.

[180] Melinda Selmys is one example. In her book, Sexual Authenticity — An Intimate Reflection on Homosexuality and Catholicism, 2009, she describes her journey from a lesbian relationship to a monogamous heterosexual marriage and family.

[181] The Truth About Homosexuality by Fr. John Harvey, 1996, p. 114.

[182] The word sodomy, the name for homosexual sex, comes from the City of Sodom.

the punishment of eternal fire received by Sodom and Gomorrah for their sin of "unnatural lust" should serve as an example for those who are unbelievers (Jude 7).

In the Old Testament, homosexual acts are specifically forbidden. It states, "you shall not lie with a male as with a woman; it is an abomination (Lev 18:22)." "If a man lies with a male as with a woman, both of them have committed an abomination; they shall be put to death, their blood is upon them (Lev 20:13)." Homosexual acts are also condemned in the New Testament. In First Corinthians Saint Paul declares, "Do you not know that the unrighteous will not inherit the kingdom of God? Do not be deceived; neither the immoral, nor idolaters, nor adulterers, nor sexual perverts,[183] nor thieves, nor the greedy, nor drunkards, nor revilers, nor robbers will inherit the kingdom of God (1 Cor 6:9–10)." In First Timothy he declares, "the law is good ... the law is not laid down for the just but for the lawless and disobedient, for the ungodly and sinners, for the unholy and profane, for murderers of fathers and murderers of mothers, for manslayers, immoral persons, sodomites,[184] kidnapers, liars, perjurers and whatever else is contrary to sound doctrine (1Tim 1:8, 9–10)."

In his letter to the Romans, Saint Paul says that one cause of homosexuality and its consequences is the rejection of truth. He states, "The wrath of God is revealed from heaven against all ungodliness and wickedness of men who by their wickedness suppress the truth ... Therefore God gave them up in the lusts of their hearts to impurity, to the dishonoring of their bodies among themselves, because they exchanged the truth about God for a lie and worshiped and served the creature rather than the Creator ... For this reason God gave them up to dishonorable passions. Their women exchanged natural relations for unnatural, and the men likewise gave up natural relations with women and were consumed with passion for one another, men committing shameless acts with men and receiving in their own persons the due penalty for their error (Rm 1:18–27)."

These scriptural teachings that homosexual acts are immoral and are

---

[183] The Greek word ἀρσενοκοίτης (arsenokoites) means a male partner in homosexual intercourse (see 88.280 in Louw and Nida). Another translation is "a man who lies with a man."

[184] The Greek word here is the same one that is used in 1Cor 6:9.

serious sins have been consistently taught by the Church from the time of Christ to the present day.[185] They have been and will remain part of the unchanging moral law. They are also consistent with the rest of the Church's teachings on sex in that they reject intimate sexual acts outside of marriage, and this teaching is as true for the heterosexual as for the homosexual.

****

There is a great deal of difference between those who struggle with a same sex attraction and those who act out on it, and this distinction is very important. The former are carrying their cross and living as God wills. The latter have embraced the gay agenda and are living in sin.

To put it another way, a homosexual orientation is one thing; homosexual behavior is quite another. There are many who experience same sex attraction but never act on it. Instead, just like other single people, they resist the temptation to become sexually active with others and remain celibate. For the Christian, this distinction is key.

This distinction also explains why some use different language to describe themselves depending upon whether or not they are sexually active. The terms "gay" or "lesbian" are generally used by those who are involved in same sex relationships or those who have embraced that lifestyle. These terms are not generally used by those who experience same sex attractions but who are also committed to living a chaste life.

Just like heterosexuals, homosexual persons are precious in God's eyes. They too are created in God's image and likeness, and being created in God's image and likeness, they too possess a dignity and worth no different than that of heterosexual persons. Christian homosexuals should remember that through baptism they have become part of God's family and been made His adopted sons and daughters. To define themselves only by their sexual attraction is to limit themselves and to see themselves as someone far less than who they really are.

---

[185] See "Letter to the Bishops of the Catholic Church on the Pastoral Care of Homosexual Persons," Congregation for the Doctrine of the Faith, October 1, 1986; <u>Catechism of the Catholic Church</u>, Second Edition, 1997, #2357–2359; "Consideration Regarding Proposals to Give Legal Recognition to Unions Between Homosexual Persons," Congregation for the Doctrine of the Faith, March 28, 2003.

Christian homosexuals must remember that Christ calls everyone to holiness. In fact, everyone, whether heterosexual or homosexual, is called with the help of God's grace to self-mastery and to live chastely according to his or her state in life. While those who experience same sex attractions have a heavy cross to bear, they can be certain that God will give them the grace and the courage to live a chaste and virtuous life.[186]

****

Most of us know of someone who is homosexual. Perhaps they are a relative, a friend or a son or daughter. They may be someone who is very close to us, someone we love a great deal. Many of those we know who struggle with same sex attraction find it very painful. Their struggles are made all the more painful by the hurtful remarks and comments of others. There is a natural desire to protect them from this pain. Modern pagans would do this by affirming them in their sexual desires.

However, Christians have an obligation to respond differently than do the pagans. Their response must always be based upon the Christian principles of love and truth. That means there can be no place for disrespect or maltreatment of homosexual persons. As was noted, they have the same dignity as everyone else whom God has made. Realizing the difficult life they have to live, all Christians should give them support and encouragement. Christians should look upon those who struggle with same sex attractions with kindness and compassion, but at the same time, they should not pretend that everything is in order.

Along with love, Christians must also respond with truth (something sorely lacking in the pagan's approach to homosexuality). Christians should speak the truth in love (Eph 4:15). They must be clear that the existence of a strong sexual desire is no argument for the rightness of satisfying that desire.

---

[186] Courage, a support group for Catholic homosexuals, is one organization where homosexuals can find support and encouragement. It is based upon the Alcoholics Anonymous model. This approach has worked for those homosexual persons who desire to lead chaste lives. Its website is couragerc.net. The National Association for Research and Therapy of Homosexuality (NARTH) also offers support, resources and help for individuals who wish to overcome unwanted same-sex attractions. Its website is narth.com.

If that was true, then one could justify adultery, incest, bestiality, polyamory, pedophilia and other disordered sexual practices. Christians cannot tolerate, accept, embrace or justify homosexual acts or any other intimate behavior between homosexuals. The most loving and compassionate response for those who struggle with same sex attractions is to encourage them to live chaste lives.

For their part, modern pagans (and also many who have a mistaken sense of compassion) are usually prepared to denounce anyone who would say that homosexuality is a disorder. They call those who disagree with them homophobes or bigots, and they accuse anyone who does not accept homosexual behavior of being prejudiced. Gay rights activists refuse any rational discussion on this subject. They would say gay rights are a matter of justice and that those who disagree with this position are hateful. Yet, nothing could be farther from the truth. Acknowledging that something is amiss is not hateful, but rather, it is the first step towards living in peace with oneself and with others. Christians have an obligation to help those struggling with same sex attractions to take that step.

****

In God's plan, marriage was meant to be both life-giving and love-giving. Sexual intimacy is meant to be a sign of that love and also the means by which new human life comes about. Hence, its only proper expression is within the context of marriage and married love. That is why sexual activity outside of marriage can never be justified. It will always lack either the life-giving dimension or the love-giving dimension or both.

Some argue that homosexual relationships can be very loving, and this is true in a certain sense. However, to love someone is to desire what is good for them, and our greatest good is to see God. Serious sin will prevent us from seeing God, and homosexual acts are serious sins. That means a homosexual relationship can never be a truly loving relationship. It can never be truly loving because the sexual sins committed in that relationship will separate those committing them from ever seeing God who is their greatest good.

Some would argue that children raised by homosexual couples do not differ in any significant way from children raised by married couples. However, that is not the case. There are significantly higher rates of unemployment, involvement in criminal behavior, suicidal thoughts, and a greater likelihood of having been sexually abused among those children who were raised by homosexual couples.[187]

Intuitively, everyone knows that children need both a father and a mother. A child's father and mother play essential roles in helping their child grow up to reach his or her fullest potential. When a parent is missing, those life experiences that are also missing can never be replaced. We seldom reflect on how our parents have contributed to who we are, but if we imagine what our lives would have been like growing up without our father or without our mother, these contributions come into immediate focus.

For these reasons, it is clear that homosexual couples who adopt or who bring a child into the world do not have the child's best interests at heart. Instead, they have chosen to deny that child the right to know who its parents are and to have both a father and a mother. For adults to deliberately bring children into the world all the while intending to deprive them of a father or a mother is not only selfish and self-serving but in reality a form of child abuse.

Occasionally, someone raised by a homosexual couple will announce that everything was just fine with his or her upbringing, and that it was no different from that of children raised by a father and a mother. That is like someone from Hawaii saying that life without snow is great and they never missed it. How would they know if they have never experienced it? Not growing up with both a father and a mother, children of homosexual couples are in no position to judge which upbringing is better.

Besides the problems children encounter, there is another issue with homosexual couples "having" children. Homosexual relationships are utterly sterile. It is not possible for a homosexual couple to have children except by using immoral means (sperm donors, artificial insemination, surrogate mothers and so on).

Modern pagans do not believe that marriage is the only proper place for intimacy; they also reject that sex is meant by God to be both life-giving and love-giving. On the other hand, Christians believe that sex within marriage is a good thing, but that sexual activity outside of marriage, whether heterosexual

---

[187] See "How different are the adult children of parents who have same sex relationships? Findings from the New Family Structures Study" by Mark Regnerus, Social Science Research, July 2012, pp. 752–770.

or homosexual, whether cohabitation or one night stands, can never be compared to marriage.

****

In conclusion, no one has the right to engage in sinful behavior; sin is not a "civil rights issue." That means Christians are perfectly within their rights to disapprove of sinful behavior whether it be lying, thievery, or sodomy. Consequently, opposing efforts to promote or legalize homosexual life-styles does not make one a bigot any more than opposing adultery makes one a bigot. Indeed, it is the efforts to force others (students, teachers, health care workers, military personnel, and so on) to approve of, support, or promote this sort of behavior that are unjust. While it is an unpopular position to maintain that homosexuality is a disorder and that homosexual acts are sinful, it is one to which Christians must continue to hold because it is the truth. In the face of criticism, Christians should remember that just as Jesus came to bear witness to the truth (Jn 18:37), so must they and all who consider themselves His disciples.

Chapter Twenty-Six
PORNOGRAPHY AND OBSCENITY

In the time of Christ, pornography didn't exist in print form, nor were there any movies, photographs, or digital images as there are today. Yet pornography did exist. There were paintings, statues and mosaics that depicted sexual scenes and imagery. One example still visible today is at Pompeii, a Roman city that was buried by volcanic ash during the eruption of Mount Vesuvius in 79 A.D. There, archeologists uncovered a brothel, and on its walls can be found pornographic paintings typical of the time.

Today, as was the case in ancient pagan societies, pornography is once again commonplace. In fact, in our modern pagan society, it can be found nearly everywhere. It is on cable TV. Hotel chains provide it for their guests. It can be found in magazines and in other forms of print media, and most of all, it is all over the Internet.

Statistics as to the prevalence and use of pornography vary widely depending upon how the terms are defined and the studies formulated. That said, one study indicated that 13% of all web searches were for erotic content. The same study noted that about 4% of the million most visited Internet sites were sex related.[188] Nearly all studies agree that a majority of American men view pornography at least once a month and that as many as one in five regularly view pornography at work.

With easy Internet access, children are often exposed to pornography at early ages. One study found that 72.8% of participants (93.2% of boys, 62.1% of girls) had seen online pornography by age eighteen.[189] According to another study of teens ages ten to seventeen, 9.6% have been involved with sexting, the practice of sending or receiving sexually explicit messages or pictures to their

---

[188] "How Much of the Internet is Actually for Porn" by Julie Ruvolo, <u>Forbes</u>, September 7, 2011.

[189] "The Nature and Dynamics of Internet Pornography Exposure for Youth" by Chiara Sabina, Ph.D., Janis Wolak, J.D., and David Finkelhor, Ph.D., <u>Cyber Psychology & Behavior</u>, Volume 11, Number 6, 2008.

friends via the Internet, their smart phones or other electronic devices.[190] It should be noted that this study represents the low end of results; other studies have reported much higher percentages of sexting among teens.

Men from all walks of life, rich and poor, powerful and humble, religious and non-religious use pornography. However, as pornography has increasingly become a part of mainstream culture, viewing it is no longer a largely male occupation. Now, one out of three viewers is female. In fact, producers of pornography see women as a largely untapped market and have been developing products aimed specifically at them.

From a strictly business standpoint, pornography is a multi-billion dollar concern. How profitable it will be in the future remains to be seen. It used to be that every time someone went online to view pornography or download images, someone else got paid, but that is no longer the case. Now, a tremendous amount of porn is available for free on the Internet.

Our pagan culture has come to regard pornography as legitimate entertainment. A study published in 2008 showed that 49% of women and 67% of men aged eighteen to twenty-six considered pornography "an acceptable way to express one's sexuality" compared to only 37% of their fathers and 20% of their mothers.[191] With the mainstreaming of pornography, one might say we now have a "pornified" culture.

****

Technically, pornography falls under the larger category of obscenity which includes any obscene speech, actions or writings. On the other hand, pornography involves only the visual arts, that is, film, painting or sculptures.

In the United States, pornography is regulated under the legal standards that govern obscenity, and the courts have ruled that obscenity is not protected

---

[190] "Prevalence and Characteristics of Youth Sexting: A National Study" by Kimberly J. Mitchell, Ph.D., David Finkelhor, Ph.D., Lisa M. Jones, Ph.D., and Janis Wolak, J.D., Pediatrics, Volume 129, Number 1, January 2012.

[191] "Generation XXX: Pornography Acceptance and Use Among Emerging Adults" by Jason S. Carroll, Laura M. Padilla Walker, Larry J. Nelson, Chad D. Olson, Carolyn McNamara Barry, and Stephanie D. Madsen, Journal of Adolescent Research, January 2008, Volume 23, Number 1, pp. 6 30.

Pornography and Obscenity

by the First Amendment. That means what is obscene can be prohibited but what is not must be allowed. The problem lies in defining exactly what obscenity is, a question the courts have struggled to answer. At the present time, an exact definition of what is obscene continues to be mired in a debate over the difference between soft and hard core porn and what is legitimate artistic expression.

These court rulings have left civil authorities with hardly any legal recourse to stop pornography. When attempts are made to limit pornography or strip clubs, the producers and owners have used these rulings to their advantage. They call what they are doing "art" and claim they are simply exercising their constitutionally guaranteed right to free expression. The result has been that those who fight against pornography have virtually given up banning all but the most violent and demeaning aspects of it. About the only thing currently prohibited is using children.

Legal experts can debate the nuances of the various rulings by the Supreme Court on what constitutes protected speech and what is obscene material. However, the average person needs no legal expert to define what is obscene from what is not. They are more likely to be of the same mind as was Supreme Court Justice Potter Stewart who once wrote, "I know it when I see it."[192]

Christians are in a better position than lawyers. For them, arriving at a definition of pornography is relatively easy. It does not require making torturous legal distinctions, nor does it mean distinguishing between soft and hard core porn. To define pornography, Christians need not consider the artistic merits of the work and then balance these with the right to free expression. Rather, for Christians, whatever is designed and intended to stimulate the sexual appetite is pornographic. More specifically, pornography is exposing the human body, particularly the breasts and genitals, as objects of sexual interest.

Obviously, there are legitimate reasons for exposing one's body. For example, when someone visits a doctor, that person may need to disrobe so that the doctor can examine them. There can also be legitimate reasons for art that depicts the naked body. An example is Michelangelo's Sistine Chapel. There, the artist sought to depict creation as it was when God first made Adam.

---

[192] Justice Stewart's concurring opinion in Jacobellis v. Ohio, 378 US 184.

At that time, Adam and Eve were naked and were not ashamed (Gen 2:25).[193]

While some may argue that producing pornography has certain artistic dimensions to it, producing pornography will always be an immoral act because it has an immoral end or purpose, the stimulation of the sexual appetite. It is also immoral because it requires those who expose themselves to engage in immoral actions either by themselves or with others. Finally, pornography is and will always be an occasion of sin and a cause of temptation for those who are exposed to it. Those who use it also sin. Obviously, no Christian (nor anyone else for that matter) should be the cause for sin in another.

****

Modern pagans do not deny the effects of pornography and obscenity. They freely admit that these things stimulate the sexual appetite. In fact, that is precisely why they watch them. At the same time, pagans claim that pornography and obscenity have no real consequences. They assert that viewing pornography is a harmless private activity with no serious consequences. They say that those who are portrayed are willing participants. They also maintain that no one is compelled to watch pornography and that those who do so use it of their own free will.

Yet the harm from pornography is well known. In the late 1800s, Anthony Comstock, a New England Protestant, saw the connection between pornography, contraception, abortion and moral degeneracy. Comstock noted that obscene words and pictures were tied to birth control and promiscuity. He said pornography inflamed the passions and led its users from one vice to another, from pornography to illicit sex to the need for birth control and finally to the need for abortion to deal with the results of these illicit unions when birth control failed. Comstock was instrumental in the passage of a Federal law which made it illegal to send any "obscene, lewd, or lascivious" materials through the mail.[194]

---

[193] Because the sexual appetite is so easily aroused, in those times when there are legitimate reasons for artists to depict the naked body, great care should be taken to do so in a way that does not stimulate the sexual appetite.

[194] An Act for the Suppression of Trade in, and Circulation of, obscene literature and Articles of immoral use. Approved by the 42nd Congress on March 3, 1873.

Vladimir Lenin, the Communist theorist and first ruler of Soviet Russia, had no need for religion. He had been an atheist from his teens. Yet he ordered that "pornography and religious books shall not be released for free sale, and shall be turned over to the Paper Industry Board as wastepaper."[195] To this day, Communist China continues to enforce its 1949 law which bans pornography. In theory, anyone who produces, distributes, or purchases lewd magazines, books, or videos can be penalized.[196] At the same time the Marxists banned pornography at home, they were being accused of introducing it into western societies as part of their Cold War strategy to break down western civilization.[197]

****

Pornography does indeed harm. People who regularly use pornography live in a fantasy world, a world where worth is determined only by physical appearance and not by virtue, love or self-sacrifice. Men are presented with unrealistic images of women and of feminine beauty. In the real world, 99.9% of women do not look like the models depicted in pornographic materials. As proof consider that many of these women have had their bodies surgically altered with breast implants and other procedures.

Pornography presents an unrealistic view of relationships and persistent viewing of it reinforces those views. In this imaginary world, men are presented with imaginary partners who are always available and instantly satisfied. There is no need for them to relate to real women. Porn excites its users. They can seek out whatever sexual fantasies they like, including various forms of sexual violence. Going beyond pornography, some companies have now produced android sex robots and are presently working on more advanced models. Orders are already flowing in. One prediction is that these robots will make prostitution obsolete by 2050.[198]

---

[195] Collected Works by Vladimir Lenin, Volume 42, p. 343.

[196] "They Know It When They See It" by Christopher Beam, Slate, June 24, 2009.

[197] Cleon Skousen, The Naked Communist, goal #25.

[198] "Robots, Men and Sex Tourism" by Ian Yoeman and Michelle Mars, Futures, Volume 44, Issue 4, May 2012, pp. 365–371.

True sexual intimacy with one's spouse requires a respect for the other person and attention to his or her needs. In real relationships, bad behavior is thwarted through unpleasant consequences related to that behavior. With pornography and android sex, there are no consequences which means bad behavior not only goes unpunished but is reinforced.

Studies have found that viewing pornography leads to any number of bad behaviors. These include: an increased callousness toward women, the trivialization of rape, a distorted perception about sexuality, increased appetites for more deviant and bizarre types of pornography,[199] the devaluation of monogamy, a decreased satisfaction with the sexual performance, affection, and physical appearance of one's partner, doubts about the value of marriage, a decreased desire to have children and a view that non monogamous relationships are normal and natural behavior.[200]

All of this explains why pornography is so damaging to marriages. It undermines trust and intimacy between spouses and causes heartbreak among wives. Pornography creates unrealistic expectations that no normal woman could satisfy (or should even attempt to satisfy). Users become deceptive, and self-centered. The hunt for sexual novelty destroys the chance for romance. Many husbands actually lose interest in their wives and simply use pornography and masturbation to satisfy themselves.

Just as pornography for men presents unrealistic images of women, so too that which is designed for women presents unrealistic images of men. Pornography aimed at women differs from men's pornography in that it is less visual and geared towards a more relational level. This kind of pornography can be found in daytime soap operas and romance novels. It is also found in chat rooms on the Internet which allow women to enter into fantasy relationships.

In it, men are portrayed as creatures who anticipate a woman's every need, as excellent listeners and as creatures with profound empathy. In reality, men are not like that, and the average male will never be like that. Women who

---

[199] There are also many subcategories of pornography. Some are aimed at homosexuals and lesbians, others at masochism, violence, child pornography and numerous other perversions.

[200] "Pornography's Effects on Interpersonal Relationships" by Ana J. Bridges, 2006. Video Presentation at the Witherspoon Institute www.socialcostsofpornography.com.

use pornography become dissatisfied with their husbands when they do not behave like the men on TV or in the stories they read.

Children and teens that become ensnared in pornography can have their lives altered for years to come and in some cases, the resulting harm is life-long. Scientific studies have shown that those who consistently use pornography end up expressing increasingly antisocial behaviors. With pornography rapidly gaining acceptance among today's youth, it is likely that the world will become a more callous place as these attitudes become more prevalent.

Pornography also harms those who produce it. The actors and actresses are not necessarily willing participants. Many were coerced into the porn industry at young ages. Some come from impoverished third world countries or from Eastern Europe. Others have been forced into the sex trade. Many suffer from severe depression, nightmares, flashbacks, suicidal tendencies, drug addiction and sexually transmitted diseases. They are degraded and abused. Many become involved in prostitution and many are also raped repeatedly.[201]

****

Our pornographic culture has already shaped us in many subtle and not so subtle ways. Most significant perhaps is that it has moved the boundaries of acceptable speech and dress and also the boundaries of how men and women behave towards one another both privately and in public. What was once considered obscene is now considered normal. What was once considered immodest is now worn without a second thought.

Men have become used to seeing women undressed and naked on the Internet, and these "perfect" women set the standards for male expectations. They leave men with the impression that this is how a woman is supposed to look and behave all of the time, and that she must be always available, always beautiful. Men who regularly view pornography look at women but do not interact with them. This has made it more difficult for them when they do interact with real women to treat them with respect and dignity and not undress them in their thoughts or compare them to the women they have seen on screen.

Women are affected too. Female porn stars now set the standards for

---

[201] See, <u>Truth Behind the Fantasy of Porn: The Greatest Illusion on Earth</u> by Shelley Lubben, 2010. See also the Pink Cross Foundation website.

feminine beauty and behavior. Women feel pressured to measure up to the bodies and sexual performances of the women their men watch online. Thus, they expose more of themselves in what they wear and in how much they reveal. They also submit to surgical procedures, breast implants, tummy tucks, liposuction, collagen treatments and so on to achieve the perfect look.

Pornography has twisted our culture's understanding of sex and of what we find acceptable. Porn creates deception and distrust in the most intimate of relationships between husbands and wives. In our formerly Christian culture, modesty was valued and lived out. In our modern pagan culture, it is ridiculed and mocked. Here is what one writer had to say about pornography,

> "How sad it is. How sad everything about it is. How weary and dreary. How draining and unfruitful. How simply embarrassing. How deflating and abasing. How melancholy and grim. How sad the users and purchasers are, and how ashamed of themselves for using and purchasing and hiding what they have used and purchased; how sad the purveyors are, and how ashamed of themselves for manufacturing a product that has no substance, and how weary they are, deep in their hearts, of the tinny shrill language they use to defend their actions, for they know full well that their actions have nothing to do with free speech, with courage against the tyranny of censorship, with salty rebellion against those who would imprison speech as a crucial step to the murder of dissent. They know that they prey on sadness for money, prey on the sad women and men who perform the empty rituals, the sad men and women who run the cameras and produce the package and market the brittle shells of acts that are, when not sad, funny and powerful and glorious and moving and extraordinary, acts ancient beyond our calculation, acts without which there would be no human beings at all, acts that are holy, acts that are finally a form of dance, of speech, of prayer."[202]

Original sin has left our natures disordered. After their sin, Adam and Eve realized they were naked and covered themselves (Gen 3:7). It was only after their sin that they also had a need to cover themselves. When King David inadvertently saw Bathsheba as she bathed, he became aroused and took her

---

[202] <u>Grace Notes</u> by Brian Doyle, 2011, p. 77.

and had intercourse with her (2Sam 11:2–4). We are all aware of this reaction to the naked body and of how the sight of it stimulates the sexual appetite.

For that reason, Christians must be proactive and uncompromising in dealing with pornography. However, before taking a public stand, Christians must begin by taking a stand at home with themselves and with their families. A frank look at your TV and movie-going habits would be a good first step. What we watch does influence our behavior. There is a common saying, "Garbage in, garbage out." Much of television programming and most movies today are garbage. As such, they are unacceptable for Christians trying to live chaste lives.

Many Christians have not thought enough about this, but in reality, they should have a certain caution about the things they watch. Christians might ask themselves, how does this influence me? Is what I am watching pleasing to God? For example, do I watch movies with sex scenes in them and then tell my friends, "It was pretty good; there were only a couple of 'bad parts.'" Do I watch daytime soaps? Do I watch late-night TV and then laugh at the sex jokes?

Here is a good rule of thumb to guide your viewing habits. If the Blessed Virgin Mary or our Lord Jesus Christ were to come into your home while you were watching TV, would you be embarrassed at what you were watching? If the answer is yes, then do not watch that program.

A second step is taking great care with regard to Internet use. The problem with Internet pornography is that it is too easy to access. Serious consideration should be given to some kind of Internet filtering on your home computer. Also, put your home computer in a public place. Teens should not have computers in their rooms. Do not give younger children or teens smart phones. Dumb phones will work just fine. We do not allow children to drink, drive, get married, hold jobs or serve in the military until they have reached a certain level of maturity. We require gun safety training before they can go hunting. So why would parents allow their immature children to have a smart phone with access to everything on the Internet?

Pornography is very addictive and will quickly distort any normal idea of sexuality. Like other things which stimulate the pleasure centers of the brain, pornography must become more and more graphic to produce the same "high." Consistent use of pornography leads to a need for more and more stimulation which often leads to viewing pornography that depicts women in demeaning or degrading positions or on the receiving end of abusive or violent acts. For these reasons, Christians must be very wary of porn.

Addiction to pornography spiritually neutralizes Christian men and leaves them moral midgets. It cripples a man's ability to protect himself and his family from the attacks of the evil one. Viewing pornography leads to lust and inflames sexual desires. The sin of masturbation is the usual end result of viewing pornography. However, so too are other criminal actions. Rape and murder are often linked to the use of pornography, something that was true of the serial killers Gary Bishop, Ted Bundy and Jeffrey Dahmer.

Many men, including many Christian men, have become deeply addicted to pornography. Men often rationalize their behavior and say "everyone is doing it." They are unwilling to admit they have a problem even as they go back again and again like gluttons, gorging on food and drink. Some women will make excuses for their men and say, "Of course my guy is doing this, doesn't everyone," or "It's better than having an affair."

As with any addiction, most people need help to break it. Admitting you have a problem is the first step in dealing with it. The next step is getting rid of any porn you have. After that is accessibility. Block your access or make accessing it as difficult as possible. Put your computer in a common space. Then make yourself accountable to someone; give your spouse full access to your computer so that she can review your use. There are also good sources for help through churches and Christian organizations. Use them. Last of all pray and fast. Ask for God's help.

Jesus said, "Every one who does evil hates the light, and does not come to the light, lest his deeds should be exposed. But he who does what is true comes to the light that it may be clearly seen that his deeds have been wrought in God (Jn 3:21–22)." With regard to your Internet use, keep it in the light.

Before you go online, always say a prayer for purity. Here is one: "Almighty and eternal God, who created us in Thy image and bade us to seek after all that is good, true and beautiful, especially in the divine person of Thy only-begotten Son, our Lord Jesus Christ, grant we beseech Thee that, through the intercession of Saint Isidore,[203] bishop and doctor, during our journeys through the Internet we will direct our hands and eyes only to that which is pleasing to Thee and treat with charity and patience all those souls whom we encounter. Through Christ our Lord. Amen."

---

[203] Patron Saint of the Internet. Prayer composed by Fr. John Zuhlsdorf.

Chapter Twenty-Seven

ABORTION

Abortion is the destruction of human life in the womb. It is performed during a woman's pregnancy at some point after she has conceived[204] but before she has given birth naturally. To kill the child in utero (in the womb), abortionists use various methods. These include surgery, chemicals and drugs.

In the ancient pagan world, abortions were common. However, with the rise of Christianity, abortion was driven to the margins of society. Sadly, in the modern pagan world, abortion has once again become commonplace. In fact, abortion is now one of the most common surgical procedures in the United States.[205] Since its legalization in 1973, millions upon millions of legal abortions have been performed in this country. By 2008, that number had reached 50 million.[206] The inescapable conclusion from these statistics is that by the end of her reproductive years, at least one in three American women will have had an abortion.[207]

As common as surgical abortion is, new human life is destroyed far more often by the use of drugs or devices which act to prevent implantation. The newly conceived child dies not at the hands of an abortionist but because it cannot implant in the womb. These drugs and devices are misnamed in that they do not prevent conception because conception has already taken place.

---

[204] For the distinction between conception and implantation, see note 96.

[205] "Changes in Abortion Rates Between 2000 and 2008 and Lifetime Incidence of Abortion" by Rachel K. Jones, Ph.D. and Megan L. Kavanaugh, Dr. Ph., Obstetrics & Gynecology, June 2011, Volume 117, Issue 6, pp. 1358–1366.

[206] "Facts on Induced Abortion in the United States, August 2011," Guttmacher Institute, www.guttmacher.org/pubs/fb_induced_abortion.html.

[207] Ibid. "Each year, two percent of women aged 15–44 have an abortion. Half have had at least one previous abortion. At current rates, one in 10 women will have an abortion by age 20, one in four by age 30 and three in 10 by age 45."

When they act after conception, these drugs and devices (primarily hormonal contraceptives, RU486 (Mifeprex) and the IUD) must be classified as abortifacients and not contraceptives.

From a moral standpoint, all the various forms of abortion, whether surgical or chemical, whether they act before or after implantation are no different. They all destroy innocent human life. They differ only in that they are used at different stages of the baby's development.

The Old Testament reveals a deep respect for life in the womb. For example, in Jeremiah God declares, "Before I formed you in the womb I knew you, and before you were born I consecrated you (Jer 1:5)." Israel's great King David prays, "For Thou didst form my inward parts, Thou didst knit me together in my mother's womb (Ps 139:13–14)." Also, in Isaiah God states, "Thus says the Lord, your Redeemer, who formed you from the womb: I am the LORD, who made all things ... (Is 44:24)." These passages affirm that life begins in the womb and that even before conception we were all in the mind of God. From the Scriptures, we can see that abortion is never morally acceptable for anyone, Christian or not. It always violates the fifth commandment, "You shall not kill (Ex 20:13)."

From the time of the Apostles, Christianity opposed the pagan practice of abortion. The Didache, among the earliest surviving Christian writings, has been dated to the early second century.[208] It states, "thou shalt not procure abortion, nor commit infanticide ..."[209] Into the late Twentieth Century, all Christian denominations continuously and without interruption upheld this teaching.[210] Only in recent decades have various Protestant denominations ceased speaking out against abortion or, in some cases, even declared it to be a woman's right.

In their efforts to justify abortion, some have argued that the Church has changed its position on abortion. They point out that medieval theologians

---

[208] According to Kirsopp Lake, translator of <u>Apostolic Fathers I</u>, Loeb Classical Library, the Didache dates to "probably early second century, or possibly earlier (p. 307)."

[209] <u>Didache</u>, Chapter II, 2.

[210] See paragraphs 6 and 7, "Declaration on Procured Abortion" by the Sacred Congregation for the Doctrine of the Faith, November 18, 1974.

taught that ensoulment (that time when a soul was created) did not take place at conception. These theologians, following the teachings of Aristotle, believed that ensoulment took place forty days after conception for a male child and eighty days for a female child. Abortion proponents argue that this position would have allowed for abortion.

In defense of the medieval theologians, their belief on ensoulment was based on faulty science and not unorthodox teachings. That said, their position on ensoulment does nothing to support abortion. In fact, the medieval theologians believed exactly what the Church has always believed, that once life begins, it must be protected without exception. Furthermore, they would never have allowed abortions before the time of ensoulment. That would have been considered a form of contraception and therefore also a sin.

From a biological perspective, modern science has made it possible for us to observe cells in a way the ancients could not. Science distinguishes the various cell types of the human body based on two criteria, different composition and different behavior. It has discovered that when the sperm and egg cells come together to form a new cell (having within it different composition and different behavior from its parent cells),[211] the process takes less than a second![212] When life begins is now quite clear.

Even though we now know when life begins from a biological perspective, the Church has still to make a definitive pronouncement on when ensoulment takes place. That is a philosophical and not a scientific question. However, what the Church does say is that no matter when ensoulment occurs, the presumption must always be in favor of life.[213] There is a moral obligation to protect even the process of how life begins from conception onwards.

Some argue that abortion should be illegal in most cases, but that it should still be allowed in difficult cases such as rape, incest or some deformity in the child or to save the life of the mother. However, even in these difficult cases,

---

[211] The technical term for this cell is "zygote" or one-cell embryo. It is the first cell of the new human being.

[212] "When Does Human Life Begin? – A Scientific Perspective" by Maureen L. Condic, Ph. D., 2008.

[213] See Declaration on Procured Abortion, Sacred Congregation for the Doctrine of the Faith, November 18, 1974, #13 and particularly note #19.

one must recall that a new life has begun and that the child is also precious in God's eyes. Killing the child is therefore not an option. It is also a fact that women who have experienced the trauma of rape are not helped by adding to it the additional trauma of an abortion.[214]

****

Besides abortion, the destruction of innocent human life now routinely occurs in medical research and in various fertility clinics. Embryos are first conceived outside of the womb in laboratories. Then they are experimented upon, or frozen for future use. While not an abortion, this killing is similar in its total disregard for the rights of the newly conceived child and in its indifference to innocent human life.

Proponents argue that this research is necessary for the betterment of the human race. They believe what they are doing is good and that embryos are only potential human beings. They also point out that embryos cannot feel or think, and that they are not self-aware. Because of this, they are often bemused at objections from the Church and others over their work.

Yet, as science has demonstrated,[215] life begins at conception. Self-awareness is not the measure of a person. One could hardly say that newborns are self-aware. Neither is size or maturity the measure of a person, nor is a productive life, nor the quality of that life. Human beings are precious because they are fearfully and wonderfully made (Ps 139:14), because they are made in God's image (Gen 1:26) and because they were redeemed by the blood of Christ (Col 1:14; Rom 5:9).

To destroy innocent human life for any reason is to violate God's law, to demean that person and treat him or her as an object, and to maintain that might makes right, that because I am stronger than others, I can do what I want. The end does not justify the means. It never has.

****

---

[214] Joan Kemp "Abortion: The Second Rape" <u>SisterLife</u> (now <u>The American Feminist</u>), Winter 1990.

[215] See Condic, op. cit.

At one point, God asks "Can a woman forget her sucking child, that she should have no compassion on the son of her womb (Is 49:15)?" God's question reminds us of the great love mothers have for their children. Rare is the mother who can disown her child and walk away from the fruit of her womb. It is always cause for astonishment when a woman does this. It is always the exception not the rule.

This is no less true for women who have had abortions. Many suffer greatly for their decision. Nearly all say they would never have had an abortion had they felt they had support from the father or their family. Most felt they had no choice. It is very true that abortion leaves behind one dead and one wounded. The child dies, but the mother (and often the father too) are wounded.

In his encyclical, *Donum Vitae*, Pope John Paul II called on Catholics and on all people of good will to be unconditionally pro-life.[216] To that end, countless pro-life organizations have been established in this country and elsewhere to help mothers experiencing an unintended pregnancy and to inform them about alternatives to aborting their children.

In addition, there is help available for those who are hurting after an abortion. Organizations such as Rachel's Vineyard and Silent No More do wonderful work. They help women deal with the shame and guilt of having an abortion in compassionate and non-judgmental ways.

There are many reasons why a woman might feel strong pressure to have an abortion. However, there would be no pressure at all if love and life were kept together within the context of marriage, that place which God designed for them.

---

[216] Evangelium Vitae, March 25, 1995, #28.

CONCLUSION

Saint John tells us that God is love (1Jn 4:8), and God loves us with an infinite love. In fact, His love is so great that without the Holy Spirit's help, we could not even conceive of it (1Cor 2:9–10). By creating us in His image and likeness, God made it possible for us to partake of His divine nature (2Pet 1:4). Being able to partake of His divine nature also made it possible for us to appreciate and respond to His love.

More remarkable than His abiding love is that God looks upon us not as slaves or servants, but as His friends. Our Lord Himself said, "No longer do I call you servants for the servant does not know what his master is doing; but I have called you friends (Jn 15:15)." Even more than friends, God looks upon us as His dear children. By adoption we have become part of God's family, brothers and sisters of the Lord, beloved sons and daughters of the Father (Gal 4:5). Reflecting on this, Saint John joyfully exclaimed, "See what love the Father has given us, that we should be called children of God; and so we are (1Jn 3:1)."

Most remarkable of all is that even when we sin, God continues to love us. Our Lord's cross is the ultimate proof of His deep and abiding love. His suffering and death on the cross has saved us and reconciled us to God (Rm 5:10). Truly, our Lord's death confirms those words of Saint John, "God so loved the world that He gave His only Son, that whoever believes in Him should not perish but have eternal life (Jn 3:16)."

One more thing is this. God has always intended that we share in His love. He desires that we live with Him and that we see Him face to face (1Cor 13:12). To that end, He has offered a dwelling place to those who believe. As Jesus said to His apostles, "Believe in God, believe also in me. In my Father's house are many rooms; if it were not so, would I have told you that I go to prepare a place for you (Jn 14:1–2)?" Saint Paul also spoke of this place saying, "We have a building from God, a house not made with hands, eternal in the heavens (2Cor 5:1)." This dwelling place, this house of God is, of course, heaven.

Conclusion

For those who love God, there can be no greater joy than to live in His house, to dwell with Him in heaven, and to see Him face to face. However, getting to heaven requires a number of things. It requires a living faith, a faith that is infused with both love of God and love of neighbor. Getting to heaven also requires obedience to God's commandments, and we know this from Jesus' own words.

On one occasion, a rich young man came up to Jesus and asked, "Teacher, what good deed must I do to have eternal life (Mt 19:16)?" To that man Jesus said, "If you would enter life, keep the commandments (Mt 19:17)." At another time, a lawyer approached Jesus and asked, "Teacher, what shall I do to inherit eternal life (Lk 10:25)?" Jesus said, "You shall love the Lord your God with all your heart, and with all your soul, and with all your strength, and with all your mind; and your neighbor as yourself (Lk 10:27)."

In the commandments, God has given us rules for living well. The commandments help us to love God and neighbor. They remind us of our obligation to worship. They keep us from living selfish and self-centered lives. By following them, we avoid resentments. They assist us in showing mercy and compassion. They even help us love our enemies and do good to those who persecute us. Obedience to God's commandments is necessary for salvation. Obedience to God's commandments is also evidence of our love for Him. As Jesus said, "If you love me, you will keep my Commandments (Jn 14:15)."

Included among God's commandments are those which pertain to our sexual behavior, and these commandments also help us to love. They teach us how to live chastely according to our state in life. They teach us how to respect the dignity of others and to never use others for our own gratification. They also teach us to respect our fertility and to respect life from conception onward. Obedience to these commandments is also necessary for salvation.

****

God loves us, and He desires that we return His love, but no one's love can be forced or compelled. For love to be love, it must be freely given. That is why God will never force His way into our hearts. Instead, as the Scriptures tell us, He stands at the door and knocks (Rev 3:20). He loves us, but the choice to return His love is ours and ours alone.

If we choose to respond to God's love with love, our love will be expressed in two ways. As creatures composed of body and soul, our response will have both a spiritual and a physical dimension to it. In the spiritual dimension, our response to God's love will take the form of prayer. It will be an interior act, a spiritual conversation where heart speaks to heart.

In the physical dimension, our response to God's love will be expressed in external or bodily ways. With our lips and voice we will raise up songs of praise (Ps 47:6). Through our posture, we will bow down in worship and kneel before the Lord our maker (Ps 95:6). When at last we dwell in the house of the Lord, we will see Him face to face and will gaze upon the loveliness of the Lord with our own eyes (Ps 27:4, Job 19:27).

God's love for us and our response to that love must also be the model for our human relationships. We are brothers and sisters in Christ, siblings in the Lord. That means our relationships with others must also be founded in love, and Saint John reminds us of this. In his first letter he writes, "Beloved, if God so loved us, we also ought to love one another (1Jn 4:11)."

Similar to our love for God, our heartfelt love for others will be expressed in physical ways. These will include spoken words, songs, smiles, touches, embraces, spending time with those we love, the giving of gifts and so on.

Love between husbands and wives is a special case and is unique among all other expressions of love. Through sexual intercourse, husband and wife become one. In this most intimate of physical acts, married couples express their covenantal unity. Their union of bodies both symbolizes and expresses their union of hearts. In fact, sexual intercourse is a union so complete that it produces children who are living, breathing signs of the couple's unity and love for each other.

In God's plan, sexual intercourse is reserved for married couples; it is not meant for single persons. In fact, sexual intercourse makes sense only within marriage precisely because it symbolizes the union of hearts. Persons who are not married or who are not married to each other are not one; they are not united. Were they to have sex, their act would be a false sign. It would not be love but rather, a selfish act where each person uses the other. As such, it would be a violation of God's commandments and a serious sin.

****

Like everyone else, pagans want to be loved, but pagans have a twisted and distorted idea of love. For them, love is centered not on what is good for the other, but on what is good for them. One who truly loves seeks the good of the other, the good of the one who is loved. Pagans fail in this regard; they do not seek the good of the other. Their rejection of true love has left them in bondage. Their selfishness has left them slaves to their sins and their passions. Furthermore, their refusal to obey the commandments keeps them apart from God who is love. Like everyone else, pagans also want to be happy. However, unless they repent, pagans will never have lasting happiness because lasting happiness apart from God is impossible.

Among the many ways pagans have turned away from love, hardly any is more striking than their utter and complete rejection of God's plan for sex. They have not kept love and life together within marriage as God intends. They see nothing wrong with cohabitation, homosexual marriage or random sex. They are not open to life except on their own terms, and they are quite willing to destroy life in the womb when it suits them. In these and many other ways, modern pagans simply reject God's plan for sex.

It is a fact that our culture's sexual morality comes from these new pagans. It is also true that their ideas about sex are so pervasive that God's plan for sex is almost unknown. Even many sincere Christians know next to nothing about it. Consequently, when it comes to sexual matters, God's people often live in ways nearly identical to their pagan neighbors. Yet to live out God's plan and to embrace Christian sex is to live in a way that is radically different from the modern pagans.

****

Before the coming of Jesus Christ, sin had enslaved the world. Our Lord came into the world to free us from that slavery (Gal 5:1). To live in the freedom of Christ is a glorious thing. It is to rejoice in the living God. It is to experience peace which the world cannot give and does not have. It is to be liberated from bondage and be freed from despair. It is to be in love, and to know true love. These ideas are what inspired the first Christians to leave everything behind and to follow Jesus.

It is interesting that the Greek word κρίσις (krysis) means a decision, a turning point, or a separation. The first Christians encountered that turning point the very moment they accepted Jesus Christ. They had reached a crisis.

From that point on, they could no longer live as they had before, and so, they separated from the pagan world.

In our times, we too have reached a crisis. We can no more live like pagans than could our ancestors in the faith. We are faced with the very same choice which they faced: To live in the freedom of Christ or live as slaves to our sins and our passions. Our Christian ancestors chose freedom. They embraced all of the teachings of Jesus Christ, and we must do the same.

In addition, it is up to us not just to live out but to proclaim the teachings of Jesus just as the first Christians did. They shared their faith with their pagan neighbors, and in so doing, they converted the world. We must follow their lead. It is up to Christians who know Jesus to bring His light to the world, and Saint Peter urges us on. He declares, "you are a chosen race, a royal priesthood, a holy nation, God's own people, that you may declare the wonderful deeds of Him who called you out of darkness into His marvelous light (1Pet 2:9)." As Western society continues to unravel, we Christians must provide a witness by our lives and actions to these things or else the wonderful deeds of God will remain hidden and unknown.

Bringing Christ's light to the world is all the more urgent when it comes to God's plan for sex. His plan was designed to help us grow in love, and His plan was meant for everyone. However, because original sin has deeply wounded our human nature, living out God's plan will require His help. Satan's temptation "[to] be like God, knowing good and evil (Gen 3:5)" is still attractive. The temptation to set the terms for how to live our lives without reference to our Creator has always been man's downfall. Yet, man must submit his will to the will of God or lose eternal life. To submit to the will of God means man must live in love and for love.

Jesus came to show us the way to the Father. He came to show us the way to God who is love. He came into the world to bear witness to the truth (Jn 18:37), and He has told us that the truth will make us free (Jn 8:32). In this book, you have been presented with the truth about God's plan for sex. Knowing that truth, you now have the freedom and obligation to live in true love as God's beloved sons and daughters. My hope is that you who love God will come to experience His love even more deeply by embracing Christian sex in a pagan world.

ACKNOWLEDGMENTS

I would like to thank Mary Ann Kuharski, Kathy Blaczyk, Marshall Fightlin, Mike and Shannon Lisic, Elizabeth Hope, Joel Burch, Jon Skansgaard, Rev. Timothy Deutsch, Rev. James Stromberg and John Skalko all of whom read my manuscript and made constructive comments and criticisms. I would also like to thank Rev. Roy Lepak for his helpful comments, Jack Minor of Affordable Christian Editing for his work in editing the book, Dale Alquist of the American Chesterton Society for help in finding the quote from G.K. Chesterton and Cathy Behrens for the cover design and layout of the book. Everyone mentioned helped to sharpen the focus of this book, and for that I am very grateful.

****

ABOUT THE AUTHOR

Father Joseph A. Sirba is a life-long resident of Minnesota. He was ordained a Catholic priest for the Diocese of Duluth in 1987. Since ordination, he has served parishes in Duluth, on the Iron Range and in Cass County. He is currently pastor of Saint Patrick's in Hinckley and Saint Luke's in Sandstone. Fr. Sirba earned his M.A. in theology from Saint John's Seminary in Boston. Before entering the seminary, he contemplated going into politics and also studied electrical engineering. Besides theology, he has maintained an ongoing interest in history and science, especially in the area of bioethics.

INDICES

INDEX OF SUBJECTS

INDEX OF SCRIPTURAL REFERENCES

To order additional copies of
this book, contact:

 Leaflet Missal Company

By phone: 1-800-328-9582
                1-651-487-2818

Online: www.leafletonline.com

In store: 976 W. Minnehaha Avenue
             Saint Paul, MN 55104
             Open Monday–Saturday, 9–5